ONE
EKKLESIA

THE VISION AND PRACTICE
OF GOD'S ETERNAL PURPOSE

HENRY HON

Foreword by Doug Krieger
Northern California – USA

Copyright © 2018 by Henry Hon.

Revised, November 2018

ONE Ekklesia by Henry Hon

Published in the United States of America.

ISBN-13: 978-1-7325563-0-0

All rights reserved solely by the author. The author guarantees all contents are original and do not infringe upon the legal rights of any other person or work. No part of this book may be reproduced in any form without the permission of the author. The views expressed in this book are not necessarily those of the publisher.

Unless otherwise indicated, Scripture quotations taken from the New King James Version [NKJV]

TABLE OF CONTENTS

Table of Figures vii
Dedication xi
Foreword xiii
Preface xix
Acknowledgement xxi

1. **Introduction to One Ekklesia** 3
   Salvation through the Faith of Jesus Christ 3
   Defining Church and Ekklesia (Assembly) 4

2. **The Lord's Ekklesia Is ONEderful** 11
   What about God's Purpose and Will? 13
   The Prophecy of Caiaphas, the High Priest 14
   Becoming ONE Is the Building Up of the Ekklesia 16
   The Three Gifts for the One Body 18
   ONEness Experienced and Expressed 19
   Unity Is Not Uniformity 22
   Zion Is the Place of ONEness 23
   The Restoration of the Kingdom of David 25
   God's Eternal Purpose Fulfilled in ONE 27

3. **God's Eternal Purpose: Ekklesia (Sec. A)** 29
   God's Two-Step – The Full Revelation 29
   The Death and Resurrection of Jesus – why? 30
   Household, the Family of God – The Father's Increase 32
   The Bride of Christ – The Son's Counterpart in Love 34
   Christ's Tangible Body – He is NOT a Disembodied Spirit 37

4. **God's Eternal Purpose: Ekklesia (Sec. B)** 41
   ONE New Man – Expresses God - Crushes His Enemy 41
   The Kingdom of God 47
   New Jerusalem – Describes the Union of God & Man 53

5. **Defining the Lord's Ekklesia** 59
   Constituents of the Ekklesia are all Believers 60
   Reality of Ekklesia Is in Fellowship of the Holy Spirit 64
   The Fellowship of the Holy Spirit 65
   When did this Fellowship Begin? 67
   How to Enter into Fellowship? 71
   Where and When Should Fellowship Happen? 74
   Start Sharing and Receiving! 78
   Building Christian Community 80

6. **What Does Ekklesia Look Like?** 83
   The Meaning of Ekklesia 84
   Difference between "Secular" and Lord's Ekklesia? 87
   Churches Versus Ekklesia 89
   Churches Are Homogeneous – Ekklesia Is Diverse 92
   Bread and Cup – Blessing or Judgment? 94
   The Gifts of the Spirit Operating in the One Body 97
   Hosting the Lord's Ekklesia 99
   Blessings and Challenges of Being a Host 103

7. **Paradigm Shift: "Church" to Ekklesia** 109
   New Testament Ministers Building Up One Ekklesia 109
   Today's Ministers Building Their Own Ministries 115

8. **Greeting – Vital for Spreading Ekklesia** 119
   Solving the Most Divisive Problem: Jews and Gentiles 119
   Romans Is the Gospel to Bring Divided People into ONE 122
   Commonality between divided people 124
   Greetings Is the Essential Conclusion 126
   Crushing Satan Is a Fitting Finale 130
   Greeting Exposes Selfish Ministers 132
   Greeting Is the Way to Expand Fellowship 135
   Building Up One Body 138

9. **From Factions to Oneness** 141
   Ekklesia Starts with factions, but Arrives at Oneness 141
   Examine Yourself So Not to Bring Judgment 144

Many Diverse Members, but One Body 147
Love Is Essential in the Lord's Assembly 151
The Manifestation of Oneness answers the Lord's Prayer 154
God Is Moving in the Insignificant 157

10. What about Pastors and Ministers? 161
Special Gifts for the Equipping of the Saints 162
Equipping Every Believer to Have a Ministry 164
"Five-fold Ministry" Results in Building Up One Body 166
Leaving "Church" As Is 169
Questions and Answers 170

11. Satanic Tactics 185
Categorizing the Brethren Day and Night 185
Satan's Strategy: Cause Division 187
No Separation on Racial, Cultural, Political, Socio-Econ. 192
Deceitful Teachings Damage the Assembly 193
Differences between "Doctrine" and "Doctrine" 197
Division Is a Result of Idolatry 203

12. God's Moving to Fulfill His Purpose 207
A Short History of the "Church" 207
Great Awakenings and Revivals 212
Restoration (Recovery) Movements 214
Where We Are Today? 216
Learning from the Past 218
A Renewed Vision to Build the Assembly 220

13. Three Gifts Resulting in ONE 223
The First Gift – Eternal life; The Father's Name 224
The Second Gift – Truth 227
Who (or What) Is the Definition of Truth? 229
What Is Not Truth? 230
The Third Gift – Jesus' Glory 233
Glory Empowering Believers to Be Servants 237
Glory for Ministers to Team-Up 239

14. Practical Assembly Life (Sec. A) 243
    The Assembly Is Practical and Enjoyable…Now 243
    All Believers in Each Locality Are the "Assembly" 247
    Each Member Functions for the Building up of the Body 249
    A Description of Assembly in the Homes 251
    Genuine Local Assembly = Universal Assembly 254
    Assembly Is the Christ with Many Members 255
    A Genuine Assembly Receives All Believers 257
    An Assembly Is Part of One Fellowship 261
    One Fellowship Extends to All Assemblies and Believers 264

15. Practical Assembly Life (Sec. B) 267
    Two or Three Gathered Is Not Assembly 267
    Ministers Wrongly Competing with the Assembly 269
    John the Baptist, Competing with Jesus 273
    A Ministry Is Different from a Local Assembly 274
    Ministers Are for the Assembly 275
    Mutual Support among Ministers 277
    Leadership in a Ministry vs. Leadership in an Assembly 279
    Ready to Serve and Be Nothing 282
    Believers Excluded from an Assembly: 284
    This Assembly Really Works — A Testimony 288

Bibliography 291
Bible Versions Used 293
Scripture Index 297
About the Author 299
Another Book by the Author 301
Reviews on One Ekklesia 303

Table of Figures

Figure 1 - One Ekklesia, One Fellowship 113
Figure 2 - Corinth's Ministry Preferences... 115
Figure 3 - Traditional Churches and House Churches 117
Figure 4 - Greeting All the Saints in Rome... 137
Figure 5 - One Fellowship and One Ekklesia 139
Figure 6 - Overcoming Factions in the Assembly 144
Figure 7 - Believers Reaching Out to Fellowship.................................... 147
Figure 8 - One Fellowship, One Ekklesia 154

I do not pray for these alone, but also for those who will believe in Me through their word; that they all may be one, as You, Father, are in Me, and I in You; that they also may be one in Us, that the world may believe that You sent Me.

– John 17:20–21

Dedication

I am dedicating this book to One Body Life whose mission is to advance the message of God's eternal purpose: The followers of Jesus manifested as ONE through the building up of the Lord's *ekklesia*. Making this message practical and high-lighting the three gifts of Life, Truth and His Glory, given to each believer in John 17, to accomplish this purpose.

This includes preaching the gospel of Jesus Christ as the good news, encouraging believers to focus on their enjoyment of the Lord Jesus, while gathering believers of diverse back-grounds and ministries as His One Body — the expression of the *ekklesia* from house to house.

One Body Life has no intention to federate or organize home assemblies, but simply to connect believers together in one fellowship in Jesus Christ.

All proceeds from the sales of this book will be used for the sole purpose of this mission. For tax purposes, One Body Life is a 501-c-3 not-for-profit organization approved by the IRS. For more information about One Body Life, please go to:

www.onebody.life

I will also continue to commit myself to my family, whom I love: my wife, my four children and their spouses, and my grandchildren (six at present). I sincerely pray and hope they will continue to love and serve the Lord for the rest of their lives even when I am away in body. I want them to remember how they were raised to enjoy and serve the Lord in our home through the years and continue this pattern in their homes and in the homes of their friends.

Foreword

by
Doug Krieger

What could be more important than Jesus' prayer in John 17 — just prior to His capture, trials, scourging, denials by His disciples, rejection, and ultimate crucifixion? *"That they all may be ONE"* as the Son shares in that Oneness with the Father — *that they all may be one in us — that the world may believe the Father sent the Son.*

You are about to enter the "Fellowship of the Triune God" and why that fellowship enjoyed by the Father, Son and Holy Spirit is the very fellowship we, as *"all the children of God,"* have entered since our new birth when we accepted Christ as Savior and Lord.

Henry Hon's incredible discoveries in *ONE EKKLESIA* range from the very essence of the Trinity to why the Father's Eternal Life, Truth of His Word, and the Glory expressed in Service — all have been given to His people enabling them to be the very Body of Christ, the expression of God's Life, Truth, and Glory upon the earth.

ONE EKKLESIA must be considered a major work on ecclesiology — the doctrine of the Church. Hon's ability to separate ministry from assembly (aka, ekklesia) is a sheer work of theological genius. We are either building up our own ministries — as spiritually significant as they may be — or we are building up the saints with our ministries; equipping them with the tools to "do the work of the ministry" and thereby building up the Body of Christ by enriching the assembly. All ministries indirectly build up His One Body. If God's people are equipped to do the work of the ministry themselves, then the gifted brethren — be they apostles, prophets, evangelists, pastors, or teachers have fulfilled their calling . . . but how infrequently do we see such enablement?

Could it be evangelists are training other evangelists? Pastors and teachers are equipping other brethren to do the very work of the ministry, thereby "working themselves out of a job?" Imagine, prophets (and there are such gifted ones in the Body of Christ today) equipping God's people to become prophets themselves? Forbid, apostolic church planting is but the task of a chosen few!

It may surprise you here in America the number of pastors quitting the pastorate per year is far fewer than you may think — somewhere around 1% according to a groundbreaking 2016 LifeWay Research survey of 1,500 pastors of evangelical and historically black churches by Mark Dance (250 per month).

The missing statistic is this: What's the percentage of pastors/teachers equipping the saints to become pastors and teachers, evangelists, prophets and apostles? There is a peculiar sentiment that only the Head of the Body supplies these gifted individuals; therefore, training and/or equipping regular troops in the field "to do what we do" is up to Him, not up to those involved in four-fold/five-fold ministries. Not so! Yes, He "gave some" but those "some" are in turn called to duplicate themselves! He'll keep giving, if we keep equipping.

So, what is all this equipping about? *"For the edifying of the Body of Christ, till we all come to the unity of the faith and of the knowledge of the Son of God, to a perfect man, to the measure of the stature of the fullness of Christ"* (Eph. 4:12-13). Furthermore, when this takes place *"we should no longer be children tossed to and fro and carried about with every wind of doctrine . . . but holding the reality in love, may grow up in all things into Him who is the head — even Christ"* (Eph. 4:14-15).

What Hon repeatedly challenges members of His One Body has everything to do with becoming mature believers who "keep the main thing, the main thing" — and that has everything to do with the *"unity of the faith"* AND *"the knowledge of the Son of God."* Outside of that are a myriad of well thought-out doctrines — most of which are fascinating to behold; but which simultaneously, given the *"cunning craftiness of deceitful plotting"* (Eph. 4:14b), do NOT edify God's ultimate intention in building up *"a perfect man, to the measure of the stature of the fullness of Christ"* (Eph. 4:13).

Hon is not talking about some organizational, human-manufactured New World Order religious system wrought by ecumenical compromise and engineered by those "in name only" Christians. No, no, no — the UNITY OF THE FAITH is embedded in the experiential knowledge of the Son of God . . . it's all about Jesus Christ, knowing Him, His Person, His Work. Without entering the fellowship which the Son has with the Father, through the indwelling Spirit of the Living God — there is no unity among

God's people. Unity of the Faith comes through our enjoyment of God's Life, through the Son whose grace and truth enables us to manifest His presence to the world around us whereby when they see His glory among us ... they will believe!

The operative question in many of our minds when we contemplate "church growth" centers on skill sets relative to dynamic programs designed to meet the present need of congregants — everything from recovery groups to women's ministry; from youth-related programs to senior care. The more specificity in ministry, the thought is, the greater we'll grow the congregation. That's NOT what Henry Hon presents in his text. Hon would RESET TO ONE — bring us back to the dynamic "house to house" Church Life that rocked the Roman Empire to its core.

You're about to discover in *ONE EKKLESIA* the commonality of diverse members of the Body of Christ — diverse in culture, race, socio-economic groupings, education, male and female — but all functioning as One Body no matter what differences be there. Furthermore, according to Henry, Romans 12-16 and 1 Corinthians 11-14, plainly tell us it's time to break free from our religious boxes and meet, greet (as a command, not a suggestion) other brethren not found in our own "comfort zone."

Hard to imagine an assembly of believers gathering just around the Lord Jesus without any preconceived sermons or, frankly, some organizers leading us — good grief, think about it — we all bring our portion of the Lord's experience in our lives and testify about it! *"We can all prophesy — testify — one by one that all may be encouraged, all edified."* No, this is not a free-for-all — it's all done decently and in order as the Household of Faith, the Family of God.

What Hon distinguishes is this: Ministers and ministries, are orchestrated by the gifted minister — but that's not how an "assembly-style gathering" goes down! That's different — really different. Nor is it moving from a mega-church setting to a small home group setting under the auspices of that mega-Church's ministerial staff . . . no, it's under the direct headship of the Head of the Body — it is the replica of the "General Assembly" of the saints.

Don't think that Henry Hon's model of the Assembly hasn't undergone major altercations over the past 50 years — through much trial and error what is disclosed in *ONE EKKLESIA* has been severely scrutinized to come into maturity. He's not deprecating ministries — he's not putting down pastors, evangelists, etc. – he's refocusing their ministry's goals and aspirations in making ministers more effective servants of the Lord, while releasing their flocks to find greener pastures, greater growth, and participation as the Body of Christ.

I am gratified to have participated in the editing of this work. In so doing, the *Vision of the One Body* and the proliferation of the assembly model has come to life as never before in my thinking and practice. This is not the kind of read you gingerly skip through at several settings – it's a tough exercise to move through these pages, absorbing the truths embedded therein. Notwithstanding, the gems from the Word of God dug out by Henry Hon concerning the answer to our Lord's prayer in John 17 are not somewhere off into some distant Millennium but for here and now.

How ostentatious for us to think we should remind the Lord it's time to answer His prayer that *"they all may be one"* – well, it is time, it's here, it's now.

"Teaming Up for the Faith of the Gospel"

> Just be sure you live as God's people in a way that honors the Good News of Christ. Then if I come and visit you or if I am away from you, I will hear good things about you. I will know that you stand together with the same purpose and that you ***work together like a team*** to help others believe the Good News.
>
> (Phil. 1:27 ERV)

The Greek word for "striving together" as found in the KJV is Strong's G#4866 which is used very infrequently in the New Testament (Phil. 1:17 and 4:3 – *"Help those who **struggled** along with me"*). Its meaning is more than just contending together or coming together in a casual manner; or, for that matter, simply struggling together [*"sunathleō"* "soon-ath-leh'-o"]. It has in view a real struggle as in a wrestling match akin to that of a "tag team" – yes, a "teaming up" against a common opponent.

What Paul had in spirit and in soul (mind) seems apparent – those who minister the gospel should minister as a team – should "team up" for the faith of the gospel . . . for what is in view here is not simply the *ekklesia*, the assembly, but serving the Lord together as diverse ministries set upon to do the work of the ministry for the building up of His One Body.

When we "team up" against our opponents as in a "tag team" in a wrestling match, it is mandatory we *"stand fast in one spirit and one soul [mind]"*– otherwise, without a tag team — we will not defeat our opponents. Teaming up for the faith of the gospel as His One New Man, One Body of Messiah, is more than demanding — it mandates for us to be one in spirit, one — even in soul!

Our opponents will oppose this tag team — no doubt — but *"not terrified in anything by those who oppose"* (Phil. 1:28) . . . *"which to them truly is a proof of perdition* [aka "destruction'] *but to you of salvation, and this from God* (Phil. 1:28b). The "perdition" [Strong's G#684] is the same word used for the "son of perdition" in John 17:12 concerning Judas Iscariot, as well as the "son of perdition" used to identify the "man of sin" in 2 Thess. 2:3; and of him [Satan] who is going into perdition [i.e., going into the "Son of Perdition" aka, the Antichrist] found in Revelation 17:6, 11.

Thus, the connection between "perdition/destruction" and Satan is obvious. Our teaming up for the faith of the gospel in this manner whereby we are not in the least terrified by our opponents, exposes their ultimate destruction; and more so, the very one who leads the opposition: The Son of Perdition! *"Your Adversary, the devil"* (1 Peter 5:8). God has a problem: our reluctance to unite together as His assembly and for diverse ministries to team up so as to strike terror into His foe!

Brethren, we are not fooling around here — this is a match that must be wrestled as a tag team — otherwise, we are no "match" with our adversaries; especially, the one Adversary coaching the opposition! Hon's fundamental premise throughout his text has everything to do not only with each member of the Body coming together *"in the uniting bond of peace"* but diverse ministries able to team up for His One Body.

Indeed, throughout the Body of Christ today there are scores of gifted brethren whose ministries operate as a wrestler who hasn't a clue what a tag team is all about; consequently, their opponents, who are plural in number, can easily take them out. When ministries and ministers join together for the sake of His One Body — THAT brings about a profound realization of Ephesians 4 regarding the four-fold ministry of those gifted by the Head of the One Body. Narcissism in ministry, quite frankly, is antithetical to the building up of the Body of Christ. Yes, there are diverse gifts, which in turn, as Hon points out, create *necessary* factions, sects, even divisions in the Body of Christ; however, it is one thing to be associated with a faction, a sect, or a division, but quite another thing to be "factious, sectarian, or divisive" — therein lies the rub!

But, as Henry points out — when such peculiarity arises, then those members of the Body who are truly genuine will earnestly *"keep the unity of the faith in the uniting bond of peace"* — thus expressing a true ekklesia!

"But to you of salvation and that of God" is the result of our teaming up for the Good News. We have nothing to fear . . . we are NOT terrified by our adversaries; to the contrary, our teaming up for the faith of the gospel results in salvation — salvation and/or deliverance for those taking such a united stand; and salvation to those who hear the Good News from those of one spirit and one soul!

Terrifying thought! But not to God's people who are united in Christ alone. No, we're on the offense, proclaiming the Good News, and in NOTHING terrified by our adversaries. This match was won at the cross — now stand in it, brethren!

God bless this noble effort in bringing His people together for such a time as this! Hon does not enlighten us to these truths to "circle the wagons" but through our recognition of the Oneness of the Body whereby we find ourselves standing together for the faith once delivered — then the Good News of His Salvation will be proclaimed to the world around us.

No, we have not been taken out of this world but left in it . . . for the world to believe the Father sent the Son, God's people must find themselves as the answer to the Lord's Prayer, not its impediment. Yes, we cry, as John the Apostle does at the close of the Revelation: *O LORD COME* (Rev. 22:20) – but in the interim may *"the grace of our Lord Jesus Christ be with you all"* (Rev. 22:21) in supplying us all to be His One Body, His New Jerusalem – expressing his Life, Truth and Glory!

> Doug Krieger
> Editor, Tribnet Publications
> Sacramento, California, USA (www.tribnet.org)

Preface

I have never considered that one day I would be a writer and even publish a book until I was almost 60 years old. When I did, I wanted to put into writing all the teachings of the Bible which have affected my life through the lens of John 17, in which the Lord Jesus earnestly prayed that all His followers become one, as one as the Father and Son are one.

My first book is entitled **ONE**. Frank Viola, a noted author, did a rather thorough interview concerning that book. His interview can be read in its entirety at his blog or at www.onebody.life. It provides my clear motivation and proposition among myriads of Christian books on the market today.

Some have told me my book *ONE* was too lengthy and would be a barrier to many people trying to read it. I wholeheartedly agree; therefore, as soon as I finished the book, I knew I would need to start the process of breaking it up into a series.

In practicing the oneness of the Body of Christ, I became clearer and got inspired. Therefore, this first book of a three or four book series will initially focus on ONEness being God's eternal purpose — and how that oneness is put into practice as unveiled through the New Testament.

This issue of becoming "perfected into one," as prayed for by the Lord Jesus at the Last Supper, is not only an awesome guiding vision, but also practical for today. This oneness should be displayed on earth today, positively affecting the daily life of every believer. Likewise, it has a practical manifestation causing the world to believe in Jesus Christ. All believers should aspire to enter this oneness enjoyed within the Triune God, bringing them into fullness of joy while causing the world to believe in Him.

Because of *ONE*'s subtitle, ***"Unfolding God's Eternal Purpose from House to House,"*** many mistakenly think the focus of that book is about "house church," or "organic churches," which was a popular subject among many Christians starting from the late Twentieth Century.

Those with this mistaken opinion of **ONE** may think there is no need for another book to rehash the subject of institutional churches being degraded and promoting the merits of "organic house churches" — where there is a relational community of Christians supporting one another. However, the subject of oneness with God's people is far beyond "house churches." It is so dynamic I find it mandatory to expound upon its merits in ***ONE EKKLESIA.***

Certainly, I support the idea of believers assembling in homes, from house to house, for relational fellowship. However, that in and of itself is not my focus here. It is merely the means in achieving the goal.

The goal is not just having more segregated groups which have "church" in a home rather than in a church building. If a home gathering does not have the vision of the building up of the One Body of Christ, with the practice of extending this one fellowship of Christ to dissimilar believers, then eventually it still will not fulfill God's eternal purpose.

The goal of assembling in homes is for all diverse, dissimilar, members of the Body to function together in oneness for the building up of God's eternal purpose.

Others have informed me that what I am proposing in a way of this vision of ONEness is "unique," "have not heard it before," "too idealistic," "not workable," "honorable," "admirable," "liberating," and "exciting." Notwithstanding, in this first in the series, ***ONE EKKLESIA***, I will endeavor to expound upon further insights bringing about the One Body in answer to our Lord's prayer in John 17.

Readers will have to go before the Lord in prayer concerning what I am asserting here; and determine whether or not the Holy Spirit is speaking this message to their heart. It is critical that the foundation of this vision of ONEness is based upon the revelation found in Scripture alone!

Acknowledgement

Jeremy Tibbets — Born: 06-18-1980 . . . went to be with his Lord: 10-14-2017

I was honored to be asked by Jeremy's wife and parents to give the eulogy at both his funeral and company memorial. I greatly miss Jeremy, for he was like a son to me. For eighteen years until his passing, other than my own children, I have spent the most time with him. The times we ate together, talked, fellowshipped, prayed, and laughed were some of the best memories. When he was 19, a friend of his told him he could come over to my house for a free dinner and he didn't have to stay for the after-dinner fellowship we normally have — so he planned to eat and run. He wasn't going to stay for the "Jesus stuff."

Maybe it was the welcoming atmosphere, but Jeremy decided to stay. Hundreds of young people had come through our home over the years . . . raising four kids tends to generate a crowd at times. However, that night with Jeremy was one of the most unusual.

It was like most Friday nights. We had around 25 in our living room. We started off by going around the circle and having everyone give a thirty-second intro of themselves. Jeremy was sitting in the back row. When it got to Jeremy he said his first name and then just broke down in tears. The Holy Spirit just got a hold of Jeremy and filled him! At that moment, he became a follower of Jesus.

A couple of weeks passed — then Jeremy brought his girl-friend, Paula, to our home. She came armed with skepticism and was ready to argue her way out the door. Yet, she too, after a few weeks, succumbed to the love of Jesus and entered a New Life. Jeremy and Paula were soon married. My wife and I started having fellowship at their home. We commenced weekly meetings there for nearly ten years. Many of Jeremy's friends were brought to the Lord through these home fellowships. Jeremy's love for the Lord was so contagious.

He told others I was his spiritual father and mentor. However, he returned a favor beyond my expectation. He gave me a huge blessing — I'll tell you more about that later.

Jeremy's parents loved their only child . . . offering him to the Lord. Their desire was for Jeremy to serve God. Although Jeremy was led to the Lord when he was a child, he left the Lord for a season while he was a teenager — but his parents' love for the Lord was deeply embedded in him. Eventually, their prayers prepared him for that night at our house.

Jeremy's calling was not to be a full-time pastor like his dad. Yet, he would be a different kind of minister to his family, friends, many employees and associates who were drawn to Jeremy's infectious love for others because of the love spread abroad in his heart by the Holy Spirit. Sharing his faith in Christ with others was his passion — and response to that enthusiasm found many an open heart who likewise embraced the Jesus Jeremy knew.

Jeremy loved his family. He thanked the Lord for his wife and his beloved four children. He would regularly tell me stories about his children with pride and joy.

He accomplished so much in his short 37 years—much more than most people well beyond his age. He started a tree business from scratch and built it into the fastest growing "tree care" company in the nation! He was incredibly innovative in an archaic industry. He became one of the most recognized names in the business — a renowned entrepreneur throughout the industry.

For this eulogy, I asked some of the people who knew him the best to give me a word, an expression, which came to mind in describing Jeremy. From his family: Loving, caring, witty, fun, honest, promise-keeper, principled, contemplative, gifted. From his friends: Leader, counselor, brother, comedian, provider, available, absolute, edifying, trusting and genuine. From his many employees: Inspiring, risk-taker, partner, protective, teacher, sharp, smart, outside-the-box, open, aggressive, and believes in you more than you believe in yourself. These are wonderful characteristics. Jesus Christ lived in Jeremy; therefore, all these words and expressions that are associated with Jesus were lived out through Jeremy. He loved His Savior and enjoyed His presence. He earnestly read his Bible and shared the Words of Jesus with many. He loved to fellowship — he prayed, tithed, and took opportunity to help others. Through these simple practices he lived and expressed the Lord.

Was Jeremy perfect? No. But that is exactly the beauty and wonder of the indwelling Spirit of Jesus Christ. He died for Jeremy's sins so that He can live in him. Through his successes and failures, Jeremy learned to walk with the Lord and went to the Lord. He is with Jesus right now. To us he is merely sleeping. There is no death in Christ. Death is defeated. Jeremy has touched many people in his life, but we believe that his legacy will continue to touch people for God.

Let's get back to that gift that Jeremy gave to me. It is because of his prodding that I became an author and wrote my book: ONE. He was the only one who encouraged me to propagate what I have seen and experienced of the Lord.

He said he has heard many ministers and Bible teachers, and this is what he told me: You have put all the pieces together that made sense like nobody else. How you have integrated regular life with God's eternal purpose is logical and experiential, so others should hear it. Additionally, he told me that I am not just talk, but I am living it. The Lord spoke through Jeremy, so I did something I never thought I could do in my lifetime. I wrote a book and because of this book, my life has been enriched and doors for ministry have opened up around the world.

> "I thank you, Lord Jesus, for giving this gift to Your Body. Now, continue to pour out Your blessing upon Jeremy's family and through the works of his labor, bless so many others."
>
> Jeremy's Company: www.aplustree.com

ONE
EKKLESIA

HENRY HON

ONE Ekklesia

1.
INTRODUCTION TO ONE EKKLESIA

If there is God (and there is), isn't it important for people to know whether God is a God of purpose, or is He trivial with no meaning or significance? Did God just create the entire universe with billions of creatures with the intent humanity could end up in a better place called heaven? If that were the case, He would be a pitiful God. Fortunately, according to the Bible's revelation, He is a God Who is full of purpose and meaning.

If He is a God of purpose, full of resolve, then shouldn't it compel all men and women to know His purpose? What if you can know God's purpose, His pleasure and will, and yet pass up the opportunity to know it? What if it is readily available for humankind to know, and yet people would rather live and die in ignorance, not knowing? In fact, the Bible tells us God has a unique eternal purpose. He has a will which is according to His good pleasure. Have you considered God needs pleasure? Due to His desire and pleasure, He has a will and purpose. His purpose is eternal. That means His purpose started before time and creation; it didn't change over the epoch of time, and it will be the same in eternity.

How awesome is God's eternal purpose! He formulated His unique purpose in Himself before there was anything. He worked it out in Himself according to His plan through creation, the fall of humanity into sin, redemption, regeneration and glorification of humanity. In eternity He will gain His *ekklesia*, a called-out people, to be the increase and expression of Himself. His *ekklesia* is the joining of Himself with humanity in eternal fellowship.

Salvation through the Faith of Jesus Christ
The essence of salvation is when a person is joined to Jesus Christ. When a person comes into a personal relationship with Jesus Christ through

fellowship with Him, then that person is saved. How does a person become joined with Jesus Christ? By faith — to believe and receive Him (John 1:12). Having the faith of Jesus Christ makes a person righteous before God, which is called justification (Rom 3:26). Simultaneously, that person becomes born anew (again) or regenerated as a child of God (John 3:5-7). Union and fellowship with Jesus Christ are realized through the belief of these items of faith:

- Jesus Christ is God, the Son of God, who came in the flesh as a genuine man. (Matt. 1:23; John 1:14; 20:31)
- Jesus Christ died on the cross for the sins of the world and was buried, and He was resurrected on the third day. (1 Cor. 15:1-4)
- In His resurrection and ascension, Jesus Christ became Lord of all. Confessing Him as Lord makes one a believer. (Acts 2:32, 36; Rom. 10:9)
- Jesus Christ indwells all His believers, making His home in their hearts (2 Cor. 13:5; Col. 1:29; Eph. 3:17)

This unique and common faith is possessed by every single follower of Jesus Christ. Believers can differ in so many other doctrinal understandings, but this is the same faith for which all believers must contend — this is their common salvation (Jude 1:3).

Defining Church and Ekklesia (Assembly)

Since the matter of "church" is probably the most significant item of Christianity after faith, generating criticism among both believers and unbelievers, let's start by clearing up the meaning of this word "church." To begin with, the word "church" in the Bible is a mistranslation from the Greek word *ekklesia*.

The Bible speaks of the Lord's ekklesia being the Body of Christ. The Lord will build His ekklesia. It is a word used more than 70 times in the New Testament to describe what God is after for His eternal purpose. In fact, it is impossible to know God's eternal purpose without knowing ekklesia since ekklesia is an integral part of His eternal purpose. This word *ekklesia* in the Greek has been mistranslated in most English versions of the Bible to "church."

The accurate translation of the Greek word "*ekklesia*" is "assembly" or "congregation." Literally, *ekklesia* means the "called-out." The common usage of this word during the apostles' time was for a called-out assembly of people, such as a town hall meeting, whose citizens were "called out" to attend a community assembly. Therefore, the correct translation of *ekklesia* is assembly, or congregation (Thayer's Greek Lexicon).

In fact, ekklesia was invented by the Greeks hundreds of years before Christ. The first record of ekklesia in Athens was dated back to around 621 BC. It was their way to practice democracy where representatives from each sub-group of a community could assemble, voice their concerns and opinions involving any topics relating to the community, and vote for a decision. The ekklesia was the governing body of the community. This practice of ekklesia existed in just about every city throughout Greece. The ekklesia and the city have the same boundaries; meaning there is one ekklesia representing and matching one city.[1] The practice of ekklesia continued and was adopted by the Romans. Acts 19 shows that ekklesia of a city persisted until the time of Jesus Christ and the apostles. Therefore, when Jesus Christ proclaimed He would build His ekklesia in Matthew 16:18, no explanation was needed concerning ekklesia.

The word "church" comes from a very different Greek word. The etymology (etymology.com) of the word "church" is said to be from *kyriake (oikia)*, or *kyriakon doma* meaning, "the lord's house." It refers to an actual place of worship, which included a place to worship idols. This word started being used to identify a Christian place of worship around the fourth century AD, when Constantine established Christianity as the Roman state religion. It was during this time Christians began meeting in dedicated worship buildings, rather than in homes or in public places. The emperor started constructing church buildings, called basilicas, for Christians to gather together in worship.[2]

In 1525, William Tyndale translated the first printed Bible into English. He translated the word *ekklesia* as "congregation" or "assembly." This was in direct contradiction to the Roman Church.[3] At that time, the Roman Church feared the removal of the word "church" from the Bible would threaten their authority and hierarchy. This was one of the major reasons Tyndale was burned at the stake by the Roman Church in 1536.[4] When King

---

1 https://www.britannica.com/topic/Ecclesia-ancient-Greek-assembly
2 http://mymultiplesclerosis.co.uk/da/constantine-christianity/
3 http://www.bl.uk/onlinegallery/sacredtexts/tyndale.html
4 https://en.wikipedia.org/wiki/Tyndale_Bible

James authorized his translation of the Bible in 1611, eighty-four percent of the New Testament was taken directly from Tyndale's Bible. But King James made one translation rule clear: *ekklesia* was to be translated "*church*" and not "*congregation*" or "*assembly*."[5]

King James was the head of the Church of England (the Anglican Church) and all forty-seven translators were members. Once again, for political and control reasons, the King James Version of the Bible purposely mistranslated the Greek word *ekklesia* to "*church*." Since then just about every English version of the Bible has kept to this translation of "*church*."

Consider this: a building must have an ownership by someone or an organization. If Jesus Christ is building His "church" and Christians must go to church (a building), then whoever owns the building can dictate what is taught and practiced in that building. That means whoever controls the building, controls the people in that building. Therefore, by convincing Christians they need to be at "church" if they are to please God, then Christians can be under the control and supervision of the owner of that building. Therefore, it is completely understandable, the Roman church required their members to go to "church" — likewise, King James wanted His subjects to go to his "church."

It is much simpler and honest when words are used exactly for what they mean. Even today the primary dictionary meaning of *church* is "a building that is used for Christian religious services" (Merriam-Webster). Christians who are more advanced in seeing the Body of Christ (Eph 1:22–23) have to constantly clarify and redefine "church" as the believers, not the building.

Considering this, for the sake of accuracy and in support of Tyndale who gave his life for the translation of the Bible, for this book (***ONE EKKLESIA***), the word for *ekklesia* will be translated "*assembly*." When the word "*church*" is used, it will refer to either a physical place for Christian worship or an organized group of Christians associated with one or more dedicated physical buildings of worship.

Additionally, churches are a place for a specific work of ministers, pastors, or priests (the clergy), and because of this, churches are defined by the teachings and practices of their respective clergy. However, the assembly as defined in the New Testament is very different from how churches operate today — the very nature of today's "church" is in counter distinction to the

---

5   http://www.kjvonly.org/other/kj_instructs.htm

nature of an assembly. This is not to denigrate what God may be doing in the various churches and the faithfulness of many of the clergy serving in the churches. However, to come back to the beginning in understanding God's eternal purpose, it is imperative a distinction be made between the assembly as defined by the New Testament and churches as they are known today. In fact, churches as ministries can be many, but the assembly of believers can only be one. The lack of this understanding among Christians is a source of confusion and division.

Many Christian churches in general, as ministries, have been used by God to spread the gospel and to gather believers for teaching the Bible. They have served society with various good deeds, but when compared with the pattern of the assembly of believers (*ekklesia*) as described in the New Testament, institutional churches are entirely different. Some Bible teachers have pointed out various unscriptural practices of institutional churches and have become ultra-critical — to the point that those under their influence would completely alienate themselves from *all* churches and from Christians active in them. This is divisive and damaging to the Lord's Body.

On the other hand, many Christians who have left organized churches and are meeting in homes desiring deeper relational fellowship begin with high expectations and inspiring experiences. Eventually, many of these home groups become ingrown and stagnate, with no outreach and without a higher purpose other than "good fellowship" within their own group. They can become more divisive, controlling, and directionless when compared to Christians in institutional churches. Therefore, one of the most well-known proponents of house churches (also known as "organic churches"), Frank Viola, in his blog dated April 2016 has given a negative assessment to the general state of house churches.[6] Broadly speaking the "organic church" or "simple church" movement also fell short of building up the assembly.

The assembly, as unveiled in the Scriptures, is dynamic, living, fluid, expanding, and proactive. Through gathering in homes from house to house, it is the living Body of Christ with a mission to reach the unsaved, shepherd weaker believers, expand and unite in fellowship with more and more homes thereby building up the practical manifestation of the oneness of all believers. Believers will have complete freedom to be who they are in Christ and function according to their God-given capacity.

---

6   http://frankviola.org/2016/04/21/organicchurch/

There is no separation among God's people, but rather fellowship among all believers no matter how diverse they are. The principal location of the assembly will take place in each other's homes, from house to house. This is the vision of the assembly which God is after — He is building up such a testimony on earth during this age.

Organized churches and assemblies in homes do not have to conflict with each other. Christians do not have to pick one over the other; they serve different purposes. Institutional churches are often set up to further a ministry led by specific ministers with diverse purposes, whereas the assembly existing in homes is for the building up of oneness and fellowship among dissimilar believers who may span various ministries. The assembly is for each believer to function according to the gift the Spirit has given them.

Believers may attend a certain church in support of that ministry and simultaneously gather during the week from house to house with and among diverse believers for the assembly. In fact, **ONE EKKLESIA** is calling upon pastors — the clergy of churches — to encourage those under their ministry to do just that. Their job as gifted ministers is to equip and encourage those under their leadership to be able to unite in fellowship with disparate believers, and to reach out to all.

The author is not advocating an ecumenical movement where all Christian churches work out their differences to come under one umbrella organization. Rather, oneness among believers does not need to be and cannot be organized. Loving one another in the One Body is innate within each believer based on the organic life of Jesus Christ in each one.

While the system of institutional churches of various stripes has been well established for more than a thousand years, the recovery of the independent assembly in homes, house by house, according to the New Testament, is still in its infancy. Ironically, it is the assembly (God's desire) located in homes in which all the apostles labored to build up. Yet two thousand years later, it is still obscure.

However, the Lord Jesus, according to His desire, has not given up and is recovering the assembly back to its rightful prominence. Since it is a fresh discovery by many believers in recent decades, trial and error are still taking place as believers learn and negotiate their way back to assembling as prescribed by the early apostles.

The author hopes that through this book many more believers will be inspired, finding real joy in the building up of the assembly from house to house, according to God's eternal purpose. For those already practicing "assembly" in a home, this book will serve as a way of trading notes so believers can learn and network together in the one fellowship of Jesus Christ. Let's pray and live expecting the next and last revival. Reset to ONE; revival next!

2.
THE LORD'S EKKLESIA IS ONEDERFUL

> "In order that now to the principalities and authorities in the heavenlies might be made known through the assembly [ekklesia] the all-various wisdom of God. This was according to the eternal purpose that he accomplished in Christ Jesus our Lord"
>
> (Eph. 3:10-11 DBY, NET)
>
> "I do not pray for these alone, but also for those who will believe in Me through their word; that they all may be one, as You, Father, are in Me, and I in You; that they also may be one in Us, that the world may believe that You sent Me."
>
> (John 17:20-21)

The entire revelation of God concerning the mystery of His eternal will has been recorded in the Bible. Outside of what is already written in the Bible, no one can add to its revelation or claim to have additional truth that is not already written in the Bible. Neither can anyone remove what is already revealed in God's Word. The Bible is full of mysteries concerning God, Jesus Christ, and God's purpose in relation to His people; yet, it also contains history, stories, laws, parables, including ethical and moral standards. Because of this, readers of the Bible often come away with an assortment of impressions of what this book is really trying to convey. Casual readers, and even many serious students of the Bible can be confused or distracted by what may seem to be a thick forest of topics.

The Scriptures have only one major topic: Jesus, the Messiah — the Christ. Jesus Himself affirmed this in John 5:39: *"You search the Scriptures, for in them you think you have eternal life; and these are they which testify of Me."* The mystery the Bible unveils is Jesus — who He is, His person and work, as well as His "corporate Body."

The Bible speaks of what God is doing today through Christ and through His people. Therefore, though there are tens of thousands of books written concerning the Bible, those which are of greatest spiritual benefit are those that explore and expound on Jesus Christ or the relationship between Jesus and His followers.

Embodied in Jesus Christ is God's eternal purpose, His pleasure, and His will (*"Having made known to us the mystery of His will, according to His good pleasure which He purposed in Himself . . . according to the eternal purpose which He accomplished in Christ Jesus our Lord"* - Eph. 1:9, 3:11). Therefore, to truly know Jesus Christ, one must know more than Jesus' activity in the Gospels; one must also know His purpose, His pleasure, and how He is working out that purpose and pleasure today. Only then will followers of Jesus be able to participate in accomplishing His eternal will. This is absolutely critical.

Notwithstanding, the sad fact is many Christians are too self-centered, trying to figure out what is God's plan and purpose for their own lives. They seek after God's will in order to meet their own personal goals and fortunes. Typically, there is little consideration on God's desire or His need for pleasure and satisfaction. However, God's blessings are upon those who care for His purpose — what's in it for God! When believers live for God's pleasure and purpose, not only are their spiritual lives enriched, God also enhances their well-being in this world.

Certainly, His followers do not have to be anxious about their physical welfare, since God is committed to take care of every one of His children (*"But seek first the kingdom of God and His righteousness, and all these things shall be added to you"* Matt. 6:33.). However, when believers neglect God's purpose and seek to fulfill their own purposes and goals, they are like what Haggai 1:6 described: *You have planted much but harvest little. You eat but are not satisfied. You drink but are still thirsty. You put on clothes but cannot keep warm. Your wages disappear as though you were putting them in pockets filled with holes!*

This is the condition of God's people when they neglect God's purpose in order to pursue their egocentricities. It is counterintuitive: Those caring for God's purpose receive everything in this age and the next. Those caring for their own purposes end up with no satisfaction even when they seemingly have everything.

What about God's Purpose and Will?

In Matthew 16:13 Jesus asked His disciples, *"Who do men say that I, the Son of Man, am?"* The answer to this simple question determined everything for His disciples, and it determines everything for us as well: Faith in Jesus Christ makes the difference in whether someone receives eternal life . . . or not. Some have answered that Jesus was a great teacher, a prophet, or a revolutionary. However, it takes revelation from the Father for a person to recognize *"Thou art the Christ — the Son of the living God,"* the promised Messiah. When Jesus asked Peter: *"But who do you say that I am?"* (Matt. 16:15). Peter answered: *"You are the Christ, the Son of the living God"* (Matt. 16:16) . . . that was life-changing!

Like Peter, people are truly blessed when they see and believe Who Jesus is. As soon as Peter expressed this wondrous revelation, Jesus immediately responded that He would build His ekklesia — an assembly which would crush the gates of Hades. Notice, the assembly is on the offensive here, not defensive since a gate of Hades is immobile. This revelation of the Son of God puts hell on the defensive! Peter received eternal life by believing Jesus was the Son of God (John 20:31; 1 John 3:24); immediately, the Lord explained His mission as the Christ, commissioned by God to mobilize His assembly to defeat the gates of hell.

Half of the revelation Peter received was from the Father, and the other half was from the Son, the Christ. The first part of the revelation was to know Jesus as the Christ, the Son of the living God; the second part was to know Jesus' mission was/is to build an assembly of people who would crush the gates of Hades. Together, the two parts of this revelation make up the whole of Jesus' entire purpose for coming to earth: Recognition by His elect of His Person — the Son of God — the very declaration of His divinity; and through that declaration they would accomplish His purpose and pleasure in defeating the very gates of Hell — the rebellion.

Moreover, this assembly is to be built on the rock. Some have misinterpreted this rock to be Peter. The problem is "Peter" in the Greek means a *stone* that can be moved and thrown about; whereas, "rock" in the Greek means *a solid rock mass* on which a structure can be built. So, in 1 Peter 2:5, Peter declares all believers are similar to him, a living stone. In context, the rock on which the assembly is built can only be Jesus Christ; and more specifically, on the revelation Who is Jesus Christ: *"Thou art the Christ, the Son of the Living God"* (Peter's words: Matt. 16:16). It is this direct revelation from the Father concerning the identity of Jesus Christ. This is the riveting focus on Him alone that is the foundation for the building up of the Lord's assembly — God's eternal purpose. Aside from this revelation of His Person (as Son of God and Son of Man) and work (the ultimate assembly designed to express His purpose in defeating the very gates of hell), there can be no "crushing of Satan" – no mobilization "against the gates of Hades!"

Immediately after revealing His mission of building His ekklesia, Matthew 16:21 states: *"From that time Jesus began to show to His disciples that He must go to Jerusalem and suffer many things from the elders and chief priests and scribes, and be killed, and be raised the third day."* It is from the time Jesus unveiled the building up of His Hades-crushing ekklesia that He began to speak of His death and resurrection. His death and resurrection would be the way for Him to build His ekklesia.

The Prophecy of Caiaphas, the High Priest

We find in John 11 a further amplification of the Lord's eternal plan of the building up of His ekklesia (assembly) in gathering His children "into one." The High Priest, Caiaphas, spoke of the Lord's death to save Judah, the nation (viz., Judea); however, the Apostle John interpreted his remarks as a prophecy, expanding the original prophetic outburst; to wit:

> ". . . nor do you consider that it is expedient for us that one man should die for the people, and not that the whole nation should perish." Now this he did not say on his own [authority]; but being high priest that year he prophesied that Jesus would die for the nation, and not for that nation only, but also that He would gather together in one the children of God who were scattered abroad.
>
> (John 11:50-52)

Caiaphas, though in the position as high priest, certainly would not have believed Jesus was the Christ, the Son of the Living God, coming as the Lamb of God to die for the nation of Judea as the Redeemer — *for this he did not say on his own authority*. If he had believed in the Messiah, he would have been a disciple of Jesus; instead, of instigating His crucifixion. He might have spoken this in a political sense of pacifying and pleasing Rome, that the Jewish nation would give up a troublemaker who claimed to be king within the Roman Empire seems uppermost on his mind.

By giving up such a one to be killed, it would show the allegiance of the Jewish nation to Rome. By giving up a "rebel," it would not just placate the wrath of Rome upon the Jewish nation for raising up such an agitator in their midst, but it would garner favor from Rome for being loyal. Therefore, one man's death for the preservation of Judea was more than "expedient."

In any case, whatever was the reason for Caiaphas to speak these words, the Apostle John extrapolated it into a powerful prophecy. The High Priest might not have known the real meaning of his declaration, but John indicates God still used the "authority" of the office of the high priest to proclaim this timely prophecy. What was John's interpretation of Caiaphas' prophecy? John confirmed that indeed Jesus would die for the nation. In fact, as the Lamb of God, Jesus would take away the sins of the entire world!

But John went much further; there is a second part: He would gather together in ONE the scattered children of God. This, being a prophecy, is forward-looking into the future where believers, as children of God, are scattered and divided. This was not only a physical scattering, but most certainly a spiritual one. The prophecy reveals Jesus' ultimate crucifixion looked beyond human redemption to the very ekklesia — to bringing the children of God, scattered abroad INTO ONE! Obviously, this was ultimately a ONEness in the Spirit, not in physicality.

Matthew's gospel states Jesus would build His ekklesia by going through death and resurrection. John's gospel makes clear that by going into death He would bring God's children into ONE. God's desire looks beyond individual salvation and a passport to glory. The new birth — regeneration — applies the saving work of Christ on the cross for every believer. However, it has in view the bringing together of the children of God into ONE!

A short-sighted view of evangelism may be to save people from damnation so they can go to heaven. Alas! Today we have millions upon millions of believers who are segregated and divided, "scattered abroad." God's purpose is much more than being saved from destruction. God's desire is that His scattered children be brought into ONE. God is against the scattering of His children, He sent His Son to die in order that His scattered children would be brought together in ONE. The Lord's plan is to gather every one of His children into His assembly, His ekklesia. Children scattered equals no building; children gathered in ONE equates to His ekklesia, His built-up assembly.

Becoming ONE Is the Building Up of the Ekklesia

When Jesus said He would build His assembly (ekklesia), it was the first time this word *ekklesia* was used in the New Testament. This word was used in Matthew 16 and again in Matthew 18. After that, the word was not mentioned again until the book of Acts, and then extensively throughout the epistles. The importance of such a word, used by Jesus, is most profound — but why would He use it so infrequently when His very death, and resurrection was the means whereby He would have such an assembly to accomplish His ultimate plan and purpose for the ages?

Ekklesia, by definition, is just a group of people who are called out to assemble, but is that it? What is so special about His assembly, this group of people, for whom Jesus died and rose again? How does this group of people interact with each other? What is this group of people projecting to the world around them?

The night prior to His crucifixion, His "last supper" was held. Here, He unveiled His heart and spoke of extraordinary and mysterious things to His disciples. He was describing and defining the assembly (ekklesia) which He would build. Though the word "assembly" was not used, clearly, Jesus was describing His called-out people and their relationship to the Triune God (Father, Son and Holy Spirit).

The last supper was recorded in John Chapters 13 to 17. Jesus started the evening in Chapter 13 by washing His disciples' feet; a task commonly performed by the lowliest of slaves in those days. Jesus then gave a new commandment: *That you love one another as I have loved you* (John 13:34). This one commandment encapsulated the relationship between every believer in the assembly and was exemplified by Jesus serving His disciples as a slave. What He conveyed by washing their feet was the manifestation of His love; thus, the followers of Jesus should love one another as He loved them — then the world would know this love and would believe on Him (John 13:35). The banner designating the assembly is their love for one another.

Then in John 14, Jesus spoke of His imminent death by saying He was going away. Although the disciples were saddened by Jesus' disclosure that He was leaving them; He, nevertheless, encouraged them, for it was altogether beneficial for His disciples that He die for them. It would be through death He could say: *"I am coming to you"* (lit. *"I will come again* — John 14:3). How? He would come back as the indwelling Comforter — the

Paraclete — the Helper — the Spirit of Christ. If He were not to go away, He would never be able to come to them. But if He leaves by death, then He will come back as the Spirit of Life to *"abide in them."*

Thus, they would dwell in Him and the Father. This is another unveiling of the assembly: It is a group of people with Jesus living in them to constantly help them from within. Now, simultaneously, they would be living in the very fellowship the Father and the Son together enjoy; in the Father's house!

In John 15 Jesus speaks of Himself as the True Vine and all who would believe into Him would be the branches of this one vine. A vine is the sum of all its branches. A vine is not a vine without branches. At best it would just be a stump, but not a vine. By this one description Jesus opened a divine and mysterious reality. Through His death and resurrection, all believers are joined to Him, His One Body. He has expanded and increased Himself from one person in Jesus, the True Vine, to millions as the many branches of the One Vine. The assembly is this vine where His Life ever-expands. The vine is constantly bearing fruit: ever multiplying; ever increasing in number — displaying all the attributes of God in its many branches. When the universe looks at this vine, what is seen is vibrant, divine life coursing through all the Vine's branches; ever-extending, transforming life; love, joy, peace with wondrous attributes of the Spirit expressed as fruit in humanity (Gal. 5:22).

Jesus continues in John 16 to describe the Spirit of Truth Who would guide the assembly of believers into everything real concerning the Trinity. Everything the Father is, and all Jesus Christ has accomplished, will be declared and made real to all believers through the Spirit — this is the supreme expression of the Triune God! The assembly becomes the recipient and the expression of the unsearchable riches of the Trinity. How awesome! Additionally, Jesus revealed His going away to die is like a woman giving birth. His resurrection is the birth of a male child.

This is the new man Paul spoke of in Ephesians 2:14-16. This new man is corporate in nature and comprised of Jew and Gentile, who through His death and resurrection have become ONE. He died as an individual, but He resurrected as a corporate "one new man."

Finally, in John 17, Jesus ended the supper with a monumental and wonderful prayer to the Father. This prayer is the conclusion of that evening as described above. This is Jesus' outpouring from the deepest part of His being on behalf of His followers based upon the eternal purpose of God. His prayer unveils what specifically was wrought through Christ in preparing His One Body. The focus of His prayer was that His people would become ONE. Thrice, He declared: "that they may be ONE."

The Three Gifts for the One Body

In His prayer, He revealed that through His death and resurrection He gave His people three gifts. The result of each gift is that "they may be ONE" — even as one as the Father and the Son are ONE. What a mysterious and extraordinary oneness! God is literally one, though He is distinctly three: Father, Son, and Spirit. The building up of the assembly occurs when millions of distinctively individual believers become one just as the Father and the Son are one.

Since this unity or oneness of His people is impossible to achieve within natural humanity, it is essential to understand and enjoy the three gifts given by the Lord Jesus to all believers through His death and resurrection. It is through these three gifts believers have the same divine and mysterious oneness as displayed in the very Triune God.

The first gift He gave us to accomplish this ONEness is eternal life. This life is not relegated to the future after a person dies, as most people casually understand it, but it is now, today. Knowing the Father and the Son (John 17:2-3) comes from knowing and accepting Jesus Christ as our eternal life at the time of the New Birth. When one is "born from above" (aka, *regeneration*) eternal life enters the spirit of that person.

The second gift is God's Word, which is the truth. It is the truth that makes His people one. Most Christians equate God's Word to the Bible, yet, it is the Bible that has been a main source of countless arguments leading to countless division. It is critical to differentiate between the truth and the Bible. The truth is Jesus Christ. It is the Trinity and His eternal work and purpose. If we leave out this reality, then reading the Bible is simply meaningless. Scriptures, without the truth, will kill and divide us (2 Cor. 3:6), but truth in the Bible will feed and unite us.

The third gift to bring us into ONE is the glory Jesus received as a man after His death, resurrection and ascension. It is this glory which enables His people to be one. Those with worldly glory expect others to serve them, but those who enjoy the gift of His glory will serve others as the Lord did.

His glory empowers His people to be selfless; to be humble servants to all. Pride causes division; His glory results in unity.

The presentation of these three unifying gifts are, in fact, the subject of the book, *ONE* (this author's first book). Later in this book these three gifts will be expanded. The point now is that the Lord Jesus went through death and resurrection in order to achieve oneness for His people, who are the building up of His ekklesia. After the gospels, in the epistles, the assembly was described in more ways: Household (sons) of God, Bride of Christ, Body of Christ, New Man, Warrior, Temple, God's kingdom, and eventually the New Jerusalem. All these descriptions point to God's desire to be one with humanity. His eternal life and divine nature are united together with humankind in a glorious relationship whereby we partake of His divine nature (2 Peter 1:4); ultimately, humanity will have their resource in God alone – The two become ONE. Just as the Father, the Son and the Holy Spirit are perfectly one, God's people will become part of this perfect oneness. As the three of the Trinity are in perfect love, fellowship, and purpose, God's desire is to extend Himself and envelope humanity in this same oneness. His people living in ONEness are the manifestation of their perfect union with God. This is the heart of Jesus, His desire and purpose. God's purpose is fulfilled in this fellowship, this eternal relationship with humanity!

It can then be said this ONEness or becoming ONE as prayed for by Jesus is the consummate definition and description of what He is building – the assembly. The ultimate expression of God's eternal purpose is simply ONE. His ekklesia is ONEderful!

ONEness Experienced and Expressed

> "A new commandment I give to you, that you love one another; as I have loved you, that you also love one another.
>
> (John 13:34)
>
> "This is My commandment, that you love one another as I have loved you.
>
> (John 15:12)

At the beginning of the "last supper" Jesus gave His new and only commandment: *Love one another as I have loved you.* This is the only commandment our Lord owned and claimed for Himself. There is no other commandment Jesus considered to be His. God gave Moses (i.e., the Mosaic Covenant) Ten Commandments at Mount Sinai, but Jesus gave only one. This one commandment embraces all God desires in the New Covenant.

At the end of the supper He prayed for the oneness of His people. However, by the very end of His prayer He brought it back full circle — He ended with: *"... that the love with which You loved Me may be in them, and I in them"* (John 17:26). How could His followers love one another? How could they be one? It has everything to do with the love of the Father and the Son Himself abiding through the Spirit in each believer. The oneness of His people and their love for one another are really two sides of the same coin.

It may be defined this way: the love for one another is what causes all the glorious experiences among these distinctly diverse believers. ONE is the manifestation to the entire universe of the completed work of God within His various people. When God's people are enjoying His love as found in its purist form inherently domiciled in the Trinity, the world, even Satan, will behold this manifestation of ONE. When this happens, God's eternal purpose wrought through Jesus Christ by taking these unique individuals into perfect union, perfect love... found only within the Triune God, is on display to the entire universe!

Although He gave only one commandment: to love one another, there are many "one anothers" in the New Testament. All these "one anothers" can be understood as a description of the various aspects of God's love. Love from a human and secular perspective may only be one dimensional. The definition of love, especially in its worldly context, has suffered a devolution wherein its meaning is virtually valueless. "I love those shoes," and "I love football," makes love trivial and devoid of any concept in relation to the love of God. God's love is eternal, unconditional, sacrificial, and all-encompassing. Therefore, many other "one anothers" are inserted into the Scripture whereby the meaning of God's love in fullness is seen. By considering and praying over this partial list of "one anothers," one will enter into the meaning of the Lord's new commandment:

- Be kind to one another, tenderhearted, forgiving one another (Eph. 4:32)
- No division in the body...have the same care for one another (1 Cor. 12:25)

- Be of the same mind toward one another (Rom. 12:16)
- Building up one another (Rom. 14:19)
- Receive one another (Rom. 15:7)
- Teaching and admonishing one another (Col. 3:16)
- Through love serve one another (Gal. 5:13)
- Not being vainglorious, provoking one another, envying one another (Gal. 5:26)
- Therefore, let us not judge one another anymore (Rom. 4:13)
- Do not complain, brothers, against one another lest you be judged (James 5:9)
- Bear one another's burdens (Gal. 6:2)
- Speaking to one another in psalms and hymns and spiritual songs... Being subject to one another (Eph. 5:19, 21)
- Considering one another more excellent than yourselves (Phil. 2:3)
- Therefore comfort one another (1 Thess. 4:18)
- Always pursue what is good both for one another and for all (1 Thess. 5:15)
- Exhort one another each day (Heb. 3:13)
- Incite one another to love and good works (Heb. 10:24)
- Confess your sins to one another and pray for one another (James 5:16)
- Be hospitable toward one another (1 Pet. 4:9)

Finally, love is very practical: *"But whoever has this world's goods, and sees his brother in need, and shuts up his heart from him, how does the love of God abide in him?"* (1 John 3:17)

All these "one anothers" can clearly define what is included in God's love if believers truly love one another. Love as defined by the Lord is broad and expansive. Loving one another includes all these other elements found in the New Testament. These are exhortations believers should experience between each other: sharing, caring, forgiving, being kind, building up, exhorting, serving, forbearing, speaking kindly, humbly subjecting, graciously considering, admonishing, comforting, praying, being hospitable, not provoking, not envying, not judging, and not complaining about one another.

Through this exhibition of our vibrant love in Jesus Christ the world will discover the Father "so loved" them that He gave His all on their behalf!

This expression of God's love is impossible without the Lord being their life and living it out in His people. The only way to love as the Lord loves is actually living out His love in His followers. He loves others in them and through them. They become one with the indwelling Lord Jesus — through the Spirit of Christ. This is the oneness the Lord prayed for in John 17.

Love and oneness can be experienced and expressed in the work place, on buses and trains, schools, neighborhoods — any place where believers can have a chance to meet one another. Right there in regular daily life, connections can be made, and His ONEness experienced and expressed. Over time, fellowship can continue over the phone, and inviting one another into home fellowships.

You see, the ONEness prayed for by the Lord Jesus is real, practical, and genuine. There is unmitigated joy and rejoicing. Each person can be who they are, just as they are, yet living by the transforming life of Christ, while fellowshipping in the love of God with divergent followers of the Son of God.

Unity Is Not Uniformity

Generally, when the matter of oneness or unity is discussed among Christians, it is related to unity in their own church, denomination, ministry, or group. It is centered on the need for unity within their narrowly defined group. There are an abundant number of ecumenical discussions where various Christian institutions are negotiating, in the main, some sort of organizational oneness between various factions. The ONEness expressed in John 17 is, however, outside any manipulated human organizational effort — for it is the very oneness found in the Trinity. It crosses organizational barriers. It cannot be arranged systematically. It stems from that eternal life within each believer. Being one is not a result of negotiations or human coordination — it is an organic outcome from everyone's own relationship with the Father, the Son, and the Holy Spirit.

Unity in the secular world, and sadly among most Christian churches, is based on uniformity of interest or similar view-points. Oneness in Jesus Christ crosses all boundaries and separations. Anyone with faith in Jesus Christ can immediately enjoy the inherent oneness with every believer because they are in the Son of God, regardless of differing political or even doctrinal differences. There can be immediate fellowship in the Holy Spirit and prayer to the same Father. Fellowship can include testifying of our salvation experiences, illumination from the Word concerning Jesus Christ or sharing the challenges of daily life. This fellowship leads to praying for one another and rejoicing in God's love and mercy. A bond is immediately realized wherein love for one another is instant and genuine.

For too long followers of Christ have allowed divergent doctrinal understandings, Christian practices and personalities, worldly politics, and many other "issues" to divide them. No wonder the world has not believed and instead has mocked the name of Christ. Christians have spent much time and energy in evangelistic techniques, but how many have entered into Jesus' prayer found in John 17 whereby the world will believe when they see His people living out the ONEness found only in the Triune God? The Lord promised when His people are ONE then the world will believe. Wouldn't this be the most powerful evangelistic tool? The verses above are a sampling of experiences of being one. Just consider what the world would see if there were a manifestation of this oneness through these various expressions of His love through those who claim His Name.

Zion Is the Place of ONEness

> Behold, how good and how pleasant [it is] for brethren to dwell together in unity! [It is] like the precious oil upon the head, running down on the beard, the beard of Aaron, running down on the edge of his garments. [It is] like the dew of Hermon, descending upon the mountains of Zion. For there the LORD commanded the blessing — Life forevermore.
>
> (Psalm 133)
>
> For the LORD has chosen Zion; He has desired [it] for His dwelling place.
>
> (Psalm 132:13)

The Lord's Prayer in John 17 corresponds to God's desire in the Hebrew Scriptures. Back in those days there was a mountain in Jerusalem called Zion — the site where the Jewish temple was built. The temple is a pre-figure of the assembly — the dwelling place of God for eternity (Eph. 2:21-22). The assembly that the Lord Jesus is building is called Zion (Heb. 12:22-23). Zion, especially Zion under the "United Kingdom of David" (Acts 15:16 — viz., the "Tabernacle of David"), signifies the place of oneness or unity. It is oneness expressed as God's dwelling place — His Tabernacle, His United Kingdom.

God desires His oneness for His people. He commands the blessing of eternal life on Zion, on a "United Kingdom." Therefore, God's people in oneness, in unity, are joyful, good and pleasant, and at peace. When God's people are in unity, there is the pouring out of the Spirit upon them; signified by the anointing oil poured upon the head of Aaron, down his beard, and running down to the "skirts of his garment" — upon his entire body. Likewise, there is this refreshing morning dew signifying our walk with Christ in "newness of Life" each day.

God wanted His ancient people to keep the center of their worship on Mount Zion — in Jerusalem — to express His oneness; therefore, He commanded all Israel from all the tribal lands to go up to Zion where the temple was located to worship at that place three times every year. They were to make this journey thrice a year with tithing of produce or livestock. On the one hand, the journey for some was an arduous undertaking; on the other hand, it was a joyous occasion as all Twelve Tribes came together to worship, to feast, to be edified in fellowship, and to express to all the surrounding nations they were one people.

How awesome it must have been to witness Israel in their hundreds of thousands streaming from the four corners of the land to God's Holy Hill, Mt. Zion in Jerusalem! As they ascended "the Mountain of the Lord," they would sing the songs of ascent, Psalm 120 to Psalm 134. What jubilation when Israel came together as one in Zion.

Psalm 126 says: *"When the Lord brought back the captivity of Zion, we were like those who dream. Then our mouth was filled with laughter and our tongue with singing."* For a period, Israel was scattered to foreign lands, held in captivity. During that period, they could not come to Zion; yet, they remembered, and wept by the "waters of Babylon" when they "remembered Zion."

Psalm 50 says: *"Out of Zion, the perfection of beauty, God will shine forth."* Oneness is the perfection of beauty. Oneness is where God dwells; where He shines forth. It is no wonder God's desire in ancient times was to build up Zion (Psalm 102:16). Again, Zion under the Mosaic covenant was seen as the precursor to the assembly (ekklesia) in the New Testament. This is why Jesus Christ came; He came to build up the assembly, the oneness of His people in prophetic reality — the very United Kingdom of David (Acts 15:16).

"Those in Zion go from strength to strength" (Psalm 84:7). There is no weakness there, but only strength to even more strength. What a blessing to be in oneness with God's people! Yes, it can be troublesome to seek out this oneness with other believers. When self-pride and self-seeking enter in, it is impossible to be in the place of "Triune oneness" with all kinds of Christians. Nevertheless, if believers do not experience this genuine oneness with those who are different from themselves, they will encounter weakness and impotence. In Zion's oneness, God's people go from strength to strength.

Zion, the place of oneness, is God's desire — even the joy of the entire earth (Psalm 48:2). The entire earth is waiting for the manifestation of the oneness of God's people. This oneness will usher in peace and joy for the whole earth. The nations of the world are hungry to witness living examples of a people who love one another no matter their peculiarities, their individual differences.

Not only so, but this people in oneness will spread out to the "nations, tongues, tribes, peoples and kings" and express their understanding and kindness toward all. Out of this place where God dwells, there is peace and security (Psalm 110:2), for the King's authority is manifested. The response from the people of the world toward Zion matches our Lord's prayer in John 17 — that the world will know and believe Jesus Christ when God's people are truly ONE (John 17:21 — *"that the world may believe that You sent Me"*). No wonder this is the unique calling of every believer: *"endeavoring to keep the unity of the Spirit in the bond of peace"* (Eph. 4:1-3).

The Restoration of the Kingdom of David

At the time of the return to Zion from Babylon as previously mentioned, it was really the return of just two tribes: Judah and Benjamin with some of the Levites and priests. Before their foreign captivity, the "brotherhood" in Israel had already been shattered — the Kingdom of David was split between Judah and Benjamin in the south, and the Ten Tribes to the north known as "Israel, Jezreel, Samaria, and Ephraim." This happened after the northern ten tribes under king Jeroboam rebelled against king Rehoboam who was the grandson of king David.

Eventually, this disunity and division resulted in the Ten Tribes being deported to Assyria and the two tribes of Judah and Benjamin taken into Babylonian captivity (aka, the Seventy Years of Babylonian

Captivity — 608-537 BC). The Assyrian Empire occupied about 120 nations at the time of Ephraim's full deportation (cir. 745-712 B.C.). The Ten Tribes of Israel were scattered throughout the Assyrian Empire and were assimilated[7] — *"Israel is swallowed up; now they are among the Nations"* (Hosea 8:7-8). That is the reason *Ephraim* became synonymous with the *Nations* (Gen. 48:19; Hosea 1:10; 2:23; 8:7-8; Acts 15:14, 17). At this point the United Kingdom of David[8] was completely lost.

The gospel of Jesus Christ first came to the Jews which really refers to those who came back to Jerusalem from Babylon. Then the gospel went out to the Gentiles (aka "ethnos" or "nations") starting with the house of Cornelius (Acts 10); then spread throughout the nations by Paul and Barnabas.

Through the gospel, those being taken out from among the nations believed Jesus and received the Holy Spirit in the same way the Jews did. Some of the Jewish Christians demanded more from Gentile believers — those being called out from among the nations needed to follow the "custom of Moses" (viz., the ordinances of the Law — Acts 15:1, 5; i.e., "circumcision") in addition to faith in Jesus Christ. Due to this confusion, Paul and Barnabas went to Jerusalem to have an assembly with the apostles and elders concerning this matter. This was a crucial convening affecting the relationships between Jews and Gentile believers in the One Body of Christ.

> "After these things I will return, and I will rebuild the tabernacle of David which has fallen; and I will rebuild its ruins and erect it again,
>
> (Acts 15:16)

---

7   https://www.britannica.com/topic/Jew-people
8   The New Century Version (NCV): "After these things I will return. **The kingdom of David** is like a fallen tent. But I will rebuild its ruins, and I will set it up."
    International Children's Bible: "After these things I will return. **The kingdom of David** is like a fallen tent. But I will rebuild it. And I will again build its ruins. And I will set it up.
    The Good News Translation: 'After this I will return, says the Lord, and restore **the kingdom of David**. I will rebuild its ruins and make it strong again.

    The "tabernacle" "tent" or "hut" of David bespeaks of the United Kingdom of David when "All Israel's" twelve tribes were under king David's jurisdiction. The "Breach of Jeroboam" split David's Kingdom in two parts: Israel's Ten Tribes of the North known as Ephraim, Jezreel, Samaria and the Two Tribes of the South known as Judah (Benjamin and Judah).

James made the critical conclusion at this monumental assembly by quoting the above prophecy from the Hebrew Scriptures (Amos 9:11-12). The early apostles and elders in Jerusalem recognized what was taking place between the Jewish believers and *"those scattered among the nations"* (aka, the Gentiles)[9]; it was nothing less than the prophetic fulfillment in the restoration of the United Kingdom of David — the Tabernacle of David — the "uniting bond of peace" through the blood of Christ, was in full view. That means these Gentiles (*"God at first visited the nations to take out of them a people for His name"* — Acts 15:14) are really "scattered Israel." Now, through faith in Christ the kingdom of David is being rebuilt.

King Rehoboam laid a heavy yoke of taxation on the northern ten tribes which was the catalyst which split the United Kingdom of David. As believers now in the rebuilding of the kingdom of the heavenly David, let's not lay any yoke on each other resulting in division (Acts 15:10; 2 Chron. 10:10-11). Back in Acts 15, the yoke was circumcision. Today, Christians can burden one another with any number of things.

The followers of Jesus need to have a deep realization — the oneness of the Body of Christ includes not just the Jews and Gentiles, but all kinds of previously segregated groups (i.e., *"the rest of mankind may seek the Lord ... even all the Gentiles who are called by My name"* — Acts 15:17; Amos 9:12[10]). This is the rebuilding of the kingdom of David, the eternal kingdom of Jesus Christ the King — the Son of David, My Servant David (Ezekiel 37:24-25).

God's Eternal Purpose Fulfilled in ONE

God has an eternal purpose. God had no intention to be alone throughout the ages. His very nature had to be expressed through His creation — the very apex of His creation: MAN — *both male and female created He them.* The pleasure of the Creator was to create an Image or reflection of Himself

---

9 "Gentiles" — when this word is used in this context it stems from the Greek word "ethnos" meaning "ethnic" but alludes to "those scattered among the nations" – viz., Ephraim—the so-called "Lost Ten Tribes" who were "swallowed up of the nations" (Hosea 8:8) ergo Amos 9:11-12

10 Acts 15:17 uses "mankind" quoting from the Greek/Septuagint [translation from the Hebrew Bible into Greek cir. 285 BC] which uses the word ADAM = "Mankind" – whereas the Masoretic text uses the EDOM for "mankind." It is noteworthy that Obed-Edom (the "servant of Edom") received abundant blessing in his household while the Ark of the Covenant rested there. Obed-Edom, along with 69 Edomites who were with him became "gatekeepers" in the City of David at the Tabernacle of David which housed the Ark of the Covenant (See: 2 Sam. 6:11-12; 1 Chron. 15:18; 16:38); therefore, "the rest of mankind" [aka, Edom or Adam] are seen in Obed-Edom and his 68 "brethren" + 1 (Hosah) making a total of 70 of Edom, the "rest of mankind."

who would be the object of His love. This created being would receive and express all the wonderful attributes of God becoming united in relationship with God Himself.

Just as He is three in one, in perfect relationship and harmony, His ultimate intention is to bring millions upon millions of people into relationship with Himself.

Oneness is manifested in His life and character. The expression of so many distinct individuals in unity testifies they are also one with God and in God since the only way people can be *"perfected into one"* (John 17:23) is to display the oneness that defines the very Trinity. Divinity and humanity is domiciled in the Son of God and the Son of Man — Jesus.

Humanity would now be filled with the love of God, the grace of Jesus Christ, and the fellowship of the Holy Spirit. Therefore, oneness is the ultimate expression of God's complete salvation and the state where all of God's blessings are received and enjoyed for eternity.

Believers through the indwelling Spirit of Christ are brought into oneness with the Triune God — into the oneness which from eternity past has always been there. It is only through each person being joined with God in Jesus Christ that diverse individuals are perfectly united in pristine fellowship with God and with one another.

This oneness of believers based upon the Triune God is mysterious, yet practical; divine, yet human; one, yet many individuals; diversity with divine unity. When the people of the world strive for "unity with diversity," the tragic consequence ultimately issues in confusion and division — witness the so-called United Nations or the Tower of Babel.

Conversely, the world's way of having unity is forcing uniformity or conformity. The oneness Jesus prayed for can never be achieved through negotiation, organization, or compromise. Again, the unity found within the bounds of the Triune God is a result of freely receiving and entering into the love of God, through the grace of Jesus Christ, and the fellowship of the Holy Spirit. It is the oneness of the Trinity.

This is the Lord's ekklesia, the glorious assembly of His people established via His Life, His Truth, and His glory!

3.
God's Eternal Purpose: Ekklesia (Sec. A)

God's Two-Step – The Full Revelation

Apart from God revealing just Who Jesus Christ really is — we'll never see Him as the Son of the Living God:

> He said to them, "But who do you say that I am?" Simon Peter answered and said, "You are the Christ, the Son of the living God." Jesus answered and said to him, "Blessed are you, Simon Bar-Jonah, for flesh and blood has not revealed *this* to you, but My Father who is in heaven."
>
> (Matt. 16:15–17)

Jesus asked His disciples, *"Who do you say that I am?"* Today, He's asking the same question. One's answer determines whether eternal life grips the heart. It is the belief that Jesus is the Son of God which gives a person eternal life. *"Who do you say that I am?"* determines one's eternal destiny (John 20:31).

We humans can at least affirm Jesus' humanity — even the most ardent skeptic can come to terms with Jesus in history . . . one of us; but coming to terms with the Son of God — that is an admission of His deity and that takes revelation from above, from the Father!

His title is "Jesus, the Christ, the Messiah" which means He is anointed by God — sent by God — to fulfill God's purpose. The word *Christ* is derived from the Latin word *christus*, which in turn comes from the Greek *christos* meaning, "the anointed." The Hebrew equivalent of the word *christos* is *mashiach* meaning, "messiah" or "the anointed one." This refers to Jesus' work, His mission. Jesus is God in the flesh, and He was sent to fulfill God's purpose. *"You are the Christ* (work), *the Son of the Living God"* (person).

We humans can accept the historical Jesus, the man, but seeing His mission as the Christ and His person as the Son of the Living God; well, without a direct revelation from above, no one can know Who He really is and what He has accomplished.

Building His Ekklesia—His Assembly—The Other Half!

> And I also, I say unto you that you are Peter, and on this rock I will build my assembly, and Hades' gates shall not prevail against it.
> (Matt. 16:18, DBY)

Immediately following His revelation of who He is in Matthew 16:15–17, Jesus said, *"And I say to you ...."* This indicates there is something more than what was just unveiled to Peter. Jesus adds to that revelation the second half — the unveiling of His goal: *He will build His assembly.*

This built-up assembly shall crush the gates of Hades (death), under the authority of Satan (Heb. 2:14). Satan and death will be crushed under the feet of God's people: The Assembly (Rom. 16:20). Wherever Satan's kingdom is crushed and defeated, God's kingdom prevails.

Yes, it is mandatory to know His Person, His Mission. We must consider the other half — the Assembly, His Ekklesia.

The Death and Resurrection of Jesus—why?

For the raising up of the Assembly — that is the reason for the death and resurrection of Jesus.

> "From that time Jesus began to show to His disciples that He must go to Jerusalem and suffer many things from the elders and chief priests and scribes, and be killed, and be raised the third day. Then Peter took Him aside and began to rebuke Him, saying, 'Far be it from You, Lord; this shall not happen to You!' But He turned and said to Peter, 'Get behind Me, Satan! You are an offense to Me, for you are not mindful of the things of God, but the things of men.'
> (Matt. 16:21)

His death, His blood, would be shed for our redemption; while through His resurrection He would impart His Life to us. Through His Spirit — His disciples would become members of His Assembly.

Imagine, Peter makes the most profound declaration one minute . . . *"Thou art the Christ, the Son of the Living God"* and the next minute Jesus is rebuking Peter and telling him: *"Get thee behind me Satan."* Peter had a direct revelation from the Father concerning the Person of Christ — and even the Assembly, His work in defeating the "Gates of Hades" . . . but Peter was sorely remiss on HOW that would be accomplished. It would be through the Cross, not through human manipulation or effort.

Peter, who had just received the revelation from the Father concerning the identity of Jesus, was called *Satan* for objecting to what Jesus needed to do for the building up of His assembly. Even after receiving *the revelation* concerning Jesus, a believer can be an impediment to God's purpose. This should serve as a warning to believers today. Sadly, many believers in Jesus are inadvertently objecting and obstructing the work of God in building the Assembly.

Satan = Adversary . . . often Christians are excited with Scriptural revelations, but when it comes to accomplishing the building up of the Lord's assembly and defeating the Gates of Hades through the cross and resurrection, they become one with the Adversary.

Without the Cross and the Spirit of the Living God — there would be no Assembly, no way to defeat the Gates of Hades.

Just What is the Assembly?

When the Lord used the term "ekklesia" or assembly in Matthew 16 and 18 to be what He was commissioned to build up, He described it as the kingdom of God. Aside from this direct reference to the *assembly* with God's kingdom, Jesus in both John 1:12-13 and John 3:29 alludes to the assembly as "the children of God" and as "the Bride."

The apostles in the epistles give us further descriptions of this ekklesia or assembly. Each depiction can be traced back to the Lord's message at the last supper from John 13 to 17. God's people are perfectly one in fellowship with the Father and the Son — what glorious oneness is this! They are one because they are filled with the Spirit of the Living God . . . they have become the Assembly of the Living God. They have been brought into that intimacy the Son shares with the Father by the power of the Spirit of Truth — now, they know the fellowship of the Trinity (the Father, Son, and the Holy Spirit).

These various descriptions of the Assembly — upon which we will give further elaboration — highlight God's manifold plan and purpose:

> "To preach among the Nations the unsearchable riches of Christ, and to make all see what is the stewardship of the mystery, which from the beginning of the ages has been hidden in God who created all things through Jesus Christ; to the intent that now the manifold (lit. "many sided") wisdom of God might be made known via the ASSEMBLY to the principalities and powers in heavenly places."
>
> (Eph. 3:8-10 FT)

Yes, there are many-sided descriptions in the writings of the apostles which enable us to understand God's intent, His plan and purpose: The Household of Faith, the Temple of the Living God, the Bride of Messiah, the Body of Christ, the One New Man, the Kingdom of God, and the New Jerusalem (to name but a few).

Household, the Family of God – The Father's Increase

> But if I delay, in order that you may know how one ought to conduct oneself in God's house[hold], which is the assembly of the living God, the pillar and base of the truth.
>
> (1 Tim. 3:15, DBY)

> Now, therefore, you are no longer strangers and foreigners, but fellow citizens with the saints and members of the household of God. Being built upon the foundation of the apostles and prophets, Christ Jesus Himself being the corner-stone; in whom all the building, being fitted together, is growing into a holy temple in the Lord; in whom you also are being built together into a dwelling place of God in spirit.
>
> (Eph. 2:19-22)

The word "house" in Ephesians 2:19 in the original Greek is *oikeios*. *Oikeios* does not refer to a physical structure. The word is more accurately translated, "household." *Oikeios* is the family of God, His Household. It is the Father with His many children. This is the Father's pleasure and will: to have many sons. God, now understand me here, is a SUPER FATHER – He has innumerable children. Not only has the Father God begotten them but He has supplied them and cared for them that they might reach maturity. This is the glory of God our Father.

This household, this "family," is the assembly. The assembly the Lord built comprises only of God's offspring. If a person is not born of God, sharing His life, likeness, and nature, that individual cannot be part of this "family" – the assembly. This is totally unique. There is only one way a person can enter God's household – by the new birth.

This is the reason believers in Christ are brothers and sisters to each other. They are all truly from the same Father sharing in His Eternal Life and partaking of His divine nature. It is for this assembly God sent His only Begotten Son into the world that people might believe *into* Him and become part of God's family.

Consider the sons of a human father; they will clearly look like and have the same characteristics as their father (instead of being like a dog or a fish), but the sons and the father are still distinct. The sons can never be the father.

All parents do not want to see their children quarrel or fight among themselves. They want to see their children grow up loving and supporting one another. Instead of fighting each other, they can work together and improve their family for the next generation. If that is the heart of earthly fathers, how much more the heavenly Father? God, as the Father, desires all His children are one, at peace and harmony with each other.

According to Ephesians 2:19-22, the household of God is really His temple, His dwelling place. The emphasis of the building up of His temple with Jesus Christ being the corner stone is that He joins together both Jews and those from among the Nations into the same household. If there is not true oneness between the Jews and the Greeks (aka, the "Gentiles" or "Nations"), then there is no dwelling place for God. God's dwelling place depends on the oneness of all His people. In ancient times God's temple was built on Mount Zion. The Scriptures declare this was the place of oneness for His "chosen people." The "spiritual temple" today is also in the place of true oneness – it is His household.

> "You also, as living stones, are being built up a spiritual house, a holy priesthood; to offer up spiritual sacrifices acceptable to

> God through Jesus Christ . . . Don't you realize that all of you together are the temple of God and that the Spirit of God lives in you?"
>
> (1 Peter 2:5; 1 Cor. 3:16-NLV)

Therefore, there is the need "to grow into this temple." Unlike the temple built in Jerusalem of old with physical stones, the real temple, the eternal one, is built with people, consisting of all those born of God.

People are the "stones." In order to build up this temple, God's children need to *grow*. The followers of Jesus need to *grow into the temple of God*. Growth and maturity are needed in order to be one with other believers who are distinctly different — not all stones are alike! The apostle Paul, in rebuking the Corinthians for quarrelling among themselves, called them babes and fleshly (the fallen sinful nature) for their divisive behavior. This shows that oneness is the result of growth and divisions are due to immaturity. They desperately needed to grow into maturity by being nourished by His Divine Life — so do all believers today.

The Bride of Christ – The Son's Counterpart in Love

> And the LORD God said, "It is not good that man should be alone; I will make him a helper comparable to him." Out of the ground the LORD God formed every beast of the field and every bird of the air, and brought them to Adam to see what he would call them. And whatever Adam called each living creature, that was its name. So Adam gave names to all cattle, to the birds of the air, and to every beast of the field. But for Adam there was not found a helper comparable to him. And the LORD God caused a deep sleep to fall on Adam, and he slept; and He took one of his ribs, and closed up the flesh in its place. Then the rib which the LORD God had taken from man He made into a woman, and He brought her to the man. And Adam said: "This is now bone of my bones and flesh of my flesh. She shall be called Woman, because she was taken out of Man." Therefore a man shall leave his father and mother and be joined to his wife, and they shall become one flesh.
>
> (Gen. 2:18-24)

When God created Adam, He said it was not good man should be alone. God wanted to make man a compatible mate. All creatures of the land and air were created and brought before Adam, so Adam could "check out" each one to see if any were compatible to be his mate. He assigned a different name for each, such as: monkey, lion, eagle, and elephant. But he could not find one matching *him*.

Then God put Adam into deep sleep and took out a part of his inner frame – his rib – and from this piece of man God built another person: WOMAN. When Adam saw this person, he immediately recognized she was out of him, part of him, and completely compatible with him. Therefore, he named her "woman" which is the feminine word for "man" in Hebrew. That means that man and woman are the same species with the same life and nature. Even according to nature, mating to produce offspring can only be achieved among creatures of the same species; consequently, the Hebrew language accords us this understanding.

God surveyed His entire creation including all the angels and did not see any creatures which could match Him as His counterpart, a compatible mate. Therefore, God started a process to gain a counterpart, a mate to match Him. Accordingly, God, as the Son of God, as the pre-incarnate Son of Man, became a man. Romans 5:14 says the "Last" or "real" Adam is Jesus Christ. The story of Adam and Eve in Genesis paves the way for the Last Adam, Jesus Christ. This metaphor portrays Jesus – as the Son of Man – put to sleep (death), from His pierced side came blood and water (John 19:34). The blood signified man's redemption, and the water the Spirit for man's regeneration – life imparting (John 7:37-39). This was the process whereby His "compatible mate" was created. This counterpart is divinely designed, created to complement her groom, the risen, glorified Son of God-Son of Man. Even so: "Come, I will show you the Woman, the Lamb's Bride" (Rev. 21:9).

> Husbands, love your own wives, even as the Christ also loved the assembly, and has delivered himself up for it, in order that he might sanctify it, purifying [it] by the washing of water by [the] word, that he might present the assembly to himself glorious, having no spot, or wrinkle, or any of such things; but that it might be holy and blameless. So ought men also to love their own wives as their own bodies: he that loves his own wife loves

> himself. For no one has ever hated his own flesh, but nourishes and cherishes it, even as also the Christ the assembly: for we are members of his body; we are of his flesh, and of his bones. Because of this a man shall leave his father and mother, and shall be united to his wife, and the two shall be one flesh. This mystery is great, but I speak as to Christ, and as to the assembly.
> (Eph. 5:25-32, DBY)

The real husband and wife, the ultimate "pairing up" in the universe, is Jesus Christ and His assembly (His Woman, His Bride). How great is this mystery! It describes His love leading to His death for the assembly whom He cherishes and nourishes as a man for his wife. The assembly is bone of His bone and flesh of His flesh.

The assembly is just Christ's own Body. This is the real love story of the universe. This is real sacrificial love — willing to die for the person He loves. This portrayal of Jesus Christ and His assembly reflects the real meaning of the Adam and Eve story in Genesis. How mysterious and highly valued is the assembly! It is the very compatible mate of Jesus Christ, the Son of the Living God! In this very real sense, the assembly and Jesus Christ are of the same species.

The great mystery is Jesus Christ as the husband and the assembly as the wife — two persons, joined as one. This supports the earlier statement that the entire revelation consists of knowing Jesus and knowing His assembly. What a profound and wonderful mystery!

Jesus Christ is only joining Himself to one bride. God's ordination is one man, one wife (Matt. 19:4). Jesus Christ is not marrying many brides but just one glorious bride. God is NOT a polygamist! There is not, as some strangely conjecture, the "Wife of Jehovah" for the Old Testament saints, and the Bride of Christ for the New Testament saints — there is only ONE WOMAN throughout the ages, and she is the Bride of Messiah, the Woman of Revelation 21:9.

Divisive brethren who "stand apart" from their fellow brothers and sisters are antithetical to the Woman, the Bride of the Lamb. Ephesians 2:26-27 shows us the "preparation" of His bride through the Lord nourishing and cherishing her. It is by partaking of Christ as her nourishment and rejoicing over His cherishing His assembly grows — is prepared to be His One Bride. His Word, the truth, sanctifies believers so they may be one (John 17:19-21).

This aspect of the assembly being the Bride of Christ displays true oneness which all believers have in their singular relationship with Jesus Christ, the Groom — *"prepared as a Bride adorned for her husband"* (Rev. 21:2).

Christ's Tangible Body—He is NOT a Disembodied Spirit

> There is One Body and one Spirit — just as you were called to the one hope that belongs to your calling.
>
> (Eph. 4:4, ESV)
>
> For in one Spirit we were all baptized into One Body — Jews or Greeks, slaves or free — and all were made to drink of one Spirit.
>
> (1 Cor. 12:13, ESV)

The Body of Christ is the embodiment of the Spirit of God. His One Body is the very expression and manifestation of the Spirit. The Father desires many sons to be His household, or family, as His increase. The Son desires but One Woman, His Bride to be the Groom's Wife. She is His counterpart. The Spirit desires to express Himself through His One Body. These aspects show the prominence, pleasure, and purpose of the assembly of believers in the heart of the Trinity.

The Spirit is invisible. Though He is very real, He cannot be seen; though He is moving and working, the world does not know how He is moving or what He is doing. The Spirit needs the Body to "express" His whereabouts — His move on the earth. Through the body, the world can see His working and moving. How wonderful is the Body of Christ! When Jesus was physically on earth, He expressed the work of the Spirit. He said that the Spirit was upon Him so He could announce the gospel, release those who are oppressed, and give sight to the blind (Luke 4:18). His ministry on earth was one of allowing the Spirit to speak, to move, and to act through Him. Today, the Spirit desires all the members of Christ's Body be His movement upon the earth.

So, what's so significant of the Body? It's ONE! The human body is magnificent and beautiful, but how terrible and tragic if any part of a person's body is severed. There is only One Body of Christ since there is only one Spirit of God. No matter how many millions of believers are members, there still is only One Body. Each diverse member is immersed into one Spirit and drinks of that one Spirit. How can believers not be one? The Spirit is not divided; therefore, the body cannot be divided, and the members cannot be divided.

> ...and has put all things under His [Jesus Christ's] feet, and gave Him to be head over all things to the assembly, which is His body, the fullness of Him who fills all in all.
> (Eph. 1:22–23, DBY)

After Jesus Christ resurrected and ascended, He received all authority in heaven and earth. All things are under His feet including God's enemy, Satan. Then as the Head of all things, He became the Head of the assembly, which is His Body. This Body is the fullness of God Who fills all in all. The assembly is the fullness, the expression of the one who fills the entire universe. How awesome is that? It is hard to comprehend such an assembly with Jesus Christ as the Head, and she — the assembly — God's fullness! This assembly is what Jesus Christ was commissioned to build. What a mission! What an accomplishment!

The verses above show us not only the numerous parts and members of Christ's Body, but His Body is perfectly joined together, under the Headship — under His complete authority. God fills up His Body so that the One Body becomes His very fullness. The Body and God are in perfect harmony with each other and cannot be separated. All the members are one in the Body because each member abides in Christ and Christ abides in each member.

> If the foot should say, "Because I am not a hand, I am not of the body," is it therefore not of the body? And if the ear should say, "Because I am not an eye, I am not of the body," is it therefore not of the body? If the whole body [were] an eye, where [would be] the hearing? If the whole [were] hearing, where [would be] the smelling? But now God has set the members, each one of them, in the body just as He pleased. And if they were all one member, where [would] the body [be]? But now indeed [there are] many members, yet One Body. And the eye cannot say to the hand, "I have no need of you"; nor again the head to the feet, "I have no need of you." No, much rather, those members

> of the body which seem to be weaker are necessary. And those [members] of the body which we think to be less honorable, on these we bestow greater honor; and our unpresentable [parts] have greater modesty, but our presentable [parts] have no need. But God composed the body, having given greater honor to that [part] which lacks it, that there should be no schism in the body, but [that] the members should have the same care for one another. And if one member suffers, all the members suffer with [it]; or if one member is honored, all the members rejoice with [it]. Now you are the Body of Christ, and members individually.
> (1 Cor. 12:15-27)

The second significance of His One Body is the obvious fact all "body parts" are distinct, very different one from the other; yet, still only One Body. This portion of Scriptures stresses on the God-created individuality — even divinely-ordained differences of each of the members. Don't let these distinct "member differences" fool you — it's still One Body because, though many members, they have mutual care for one another stimulated by the same Divine Life which courses through the One Body. They are all members because of His Life, His Spirit — again, their mutuality and care for one another is based upon that same oneness shared within the Triune God.

The fallen nature of humanity is to divide from one another — it is based on differences or a desire to control each other (i.e., coercive uniformity). The reason people do not have an innate ability to avoid such division — to accept and love those who are different from themselves — has everything to do with The Fall in the Garden . . . SIN has left its awful mark. Worldly folks gravitate toward those who are similar. The liberal minded are comfortable around those who have similar dispositions. "Progressives" become judgmental of those with conservative views, and vice versa. Sadly, these dispositional characteristics are carried over into Christianity. Those who have the "Pentecostal" experiences would like all others to have the same. "Calvinists" want to convince all other Christians their understanding of the Bible is the most orthodox. Normally, they become judgmental of those who preach salvation is by one's own will, their choice. Those who believe Christians can lose their salvation due to free will, are critical of the

Calvinists. It is rather easy to write someone off if they have opposing views or experiences.

These verses show there needs to be direct interaction between those who are different from each other. Uncomfortable? Yes. But mandatory. It is natural and comfortable for Christians with similar interest and traits to gather together in likeminded groups. The "eyes" have it — there's nothing like being visual! There's nothing like spending time reading and studying to see more in God's Word. On the other hand, the "mouth" may be those who like to pray, speak in tongues; emphasizing "experience over knowledge."

The "feet" may be those who are always on the go — "Let's preach the gospel any way we can; after all, isn't this the foremost necessity: Hell or Heaven" . . . seems pretty obvious to most on the go. An eye, however, would like to discuss with other "eyes" their latest study of God's Word. They may be critical of the "mouths" that do not like to study. It is so easy to gather with Christians who are similar and criticize those who do not have the same predilection as your group. Paul says clearly in this chapter that we need those who are not like us — that's NOT optional — the eye needs the mouth! It is critical there be a variety of functions, but the same care for one another; the same One Body.

This aspect of the One Body makes clear diversity among believers is actually needed. It is God's will to make each individual different; yet, in the Body they need one another. People are different not just due to their natural characteristics such as whether one is analytical or emotional, extrovert or introvert, but differences are also acquired depending on education, socio-economic levels — scores of factors. The Body of Christ is one despite all the differences — it is truly a testimony that Christ is in each member and each is in Christ. It is precisely these variations of the members make the One Body all the more wonderful. The Body of Christ is where there is genuine celebration of differences because the Body is truly one in Jesus Christ.

4.

God's Eternal Purpose: Ekklesia (Sec. B)

ONE New Man—Expresses God - Crushes His Enemy

> And God made the beast of the earth according to its kind, cattle according to its kind, and everything that creeps on the earth according to its kind. And God saw that it was good. Then God said, "Let Us make man in Our image, according to Our likeness; let them have dominion over the fish of the sea, over the birds of the air, and over the cattle, over all the earth and over every creeping thing that creeps on the earth."
>
> (Gen. 1:25–26)

Genesis 1:25–26 describes every creature in the water, in the air, and on land as made according to "its kind" (Gen. 1:25). Each was fashioned according to its own species. However, when it was time for God to make man, He said, *"Let Us make man in **Our** image and according to **Our** likeness"* (Gen. 1:26). Man is unique. Man was not made according to "its kind" but *according to God's own image and likeness*, according to *God's kind*. When God fashioned man, His "tri-unity" (His triune nature, or the Trinity) was revealed; this is reflected in the use of the pronoun "Us" in Genesis 1:26. God was not simply referring to Himself in the plural as some regal entitlement – e.g., "Your Highness, how are WE feeling today?" No, the use of the plural pronoun was purposeful – perfectly disclosing the tri-unity of the Godhead.

Creating man – both *"male and female"* necessitated a conference within the Godhead of the Father, Son, and the Spirit to design His "likeness and image." It was a "Triumvirate" decision. Man was made altogether distinct; wholly different from all the other creatures. Clearly, before man, there was nothing like man. Man was uniquely formed at that point, after God

Himself, within the counsels of the Godhead — WOW! Man was made to commune with God Himself — the "animal kingdom" may groan for the "*manifestation of the sons of God*" (Rom. 8:19) — but they do NOT have the ability to be in fellowship with the Almighty; in communion with the Everlasting God.

No doubt, God's character and nature are clearly expressed in the vast expanse of the universe and in the minute details of creation. However, human beings express God on a much higher plane. Human ability is to be inventive (to imagine — to create). Along with their ability to express sacrificial love, and to set goals, and to have purpose beyond just existence — all these traits clearly express God in a definitive, unique, and excellent way. Nothing in creation or among all creatures can compare to this. Humanity expresses God's very inner being, His attributes and even His personality.

> So God created man in His own image; in the image of God He created him; male and female He created them.
>
> (Gen. 1:27)

When God created all the other creatures, He spoke the multitude of these creatures into being at His command. Creating man, however, was special. Just as God is distinctly three and essentially one, when God created man in His image and likeness, He didn't create many men. He created only one man, but this one man is made up, not of one individual but two: "man" is both "*male and female created He them*" (Gen. 1:27).

Male is very different than female, but these two form one man. In God's view man is a pair including both male and female. He does not have a preference between the sexes. Just as God consists of Father, Son and Spirit with distinct roles, but not one more important than the other, so too when God created man, He viewed male and female together as "man." (This should be kept in mind when reading the Bible that "man" in the general sense represents humanity; includes both male and female.) Not only so, in God's view, all generations of men after Adam are still just one man (1 Cor. 15:47).

Just as God is singular and yet three, He created one man (singular), and said *"Let them have dominion . . . ."* The man He created is a corporate man, made up of all humanity. He created one man, but within this one man is a multitude of distinct individuals. Therefore, to express God, man must be ONE. Since God cannot be divided between the three of the Trinity, a divided humanity cannot express God in His image and likeness. Just as God is **"three-one,"** man created by God is **"multitude-one."** It is in oneness God is expressed.

After Adam and Eve separated themselves from God by partaking of sin in the form of the tree of the knowledge of good and evil, the very next generation of humanity started dividing against each other. Cain became angry with his brother Abel, and he murdered Abel. This shows that the goal and result of sin is division resulting in death by murder. The history of humanity since Cain and Abel is a multiplicity of divisions leading to war and death. From generation to generation, there have been more divisions, more wars, and more death. Therefore, division expresses sin (Satan), and oneness in diversity expresses God.

To recover oneness among mankind for His eternal purpose, God in the Hebrew Scriptures called out one man, Abraham. Eventually, through Abraham, Isaac, Jacob, the twelve tribes came forth, forming the nation of Israel. God separated them according to His ordinances from the rest of the nations of earth. These twelve distinct tribes would come together as one in Zion to worship and enjoy God.

In God's eyes, these twelve tribes were one man. When they came together, they gathered as "ONE man" (Judg. 20:1). God brought this people back to Himself, and their oneness as His people would express Him. God's glory was in their midst, in the temple built on Zion, the *place* of oneness for Israel. They were able to be one because God was real to them and uplifted among them. When God was pre-eminent in Israel, she was one. When Israel was one, God was expressed, and the enemies of His people were defeated. In Israel's United Kingdom of David, God's desire in creating man to express His oneness was recovered and manifested.

When Israel replaced God with idols, they became divided. After Solomon built the temple on Zion, and Israel was at its zenith, Solomon was drawn off to worship idols. From then on, the "brotherhood" was broken. It was formalized when Jeroboam set up golden calves for Israel to worship in two different places other than the temple in Zion. The tribes split into two states: Israel's Ten Tribes to the North of Zion and Judah's Two Tribes to the South. Eventually all twelve tribes were disbursed to Assyria, Babylon and Egypt. The expression, the glory of God, was lost. Israel became hopelessly divided.

> For he himself is our peace, who has made us both one and has broken down in his flesh the dividing wall of hostility by abolishing the law of commandments expressed in ordinances, that he might create in himself one new man in place of the two, so making peace.
>
> (Eph. 2:14-15, ESV)
>
> ... and have put on the new [man] who is renewed in knowledge according to the image of Him who created him, 11 where there is neither Greek nor Jew, circumcised nor uncircumcised, barbarian, Scythian, slave [nor] free, but Christ [is] all and in all.
>
> (Col. 3:10-11)

By the time Jesus came, the created man was fully divided and the "Chosen Ones" (Israel) were completely scattered throughout the nations. It seems God's purpose in creating man was lost, but God didn't give up His desire to be expressed in a corporate man. Therefore, in the New Testament He created another man, another corporate man in Jesus Christ (Eph. 2:14). This new man is made up of all formerly divided people and individuals (Col. 3:11). People who would not have come together as one are now one in Christ. In fact, in Christ, there cannot be division based on peculiar human differences. The "old man" with its divisive nature is put off and the "new man" is put on. According to Ephesians 2, this new man is the assembly (ekklesia).

The greatest barrier for humanity to come together as one was something God did back in the Hebrew Scriptures when He set apart Israel as a physical example of a people in oneness. Israel was made not simply distinct but also separate from all other nations with a set of ordinances related to the way of worship, diet, keeping of days, ways of living and much more. On one hand, these ordinances kept Israel together as a people. They kept Israel separate for God's purpose, but these very ordinances divided them from all other nations, tribes, tongues and people (aka, Gentiles).

So, in order to create the One New Man, God abolished the "enmity" (the antagonisms) wrought by these commands and ordinances – and tore down the *"middle wall of separation"* created by these same divinely-given commands and ordinances which existed between the Jews and the Gentiles (aka, "the nations") through the blood of Christ (Eph. 2:11-17). God brought together those known as the "circumcision" with those called "uncircumcised" (Eph. 2:11) through His death upon the cross, and raised up One New Man, through His resurrection! The "middle wall of separation" has been smashed to smithereens!

Whatever hostility there was between people was eliminated through the death of Jesus Christ. If the death of Christ terminated the hostility, animosity, ill-will, THE EMNITY between Jews and Gentiles — an animosity and separation divinely generated over centuries — why then would believers allow Christian practices and lifestyle (which can also be justified as ordained by God) to divide the followers of the Lamb?

It seems so easy for Christians to set up various ordinances based on their understanding of the Bible, including the New Testament. Christian ordinances can include ways to worship, ways to pray, ways to baptize, ways to dress, ways to live, and especially "Christian belief systems" embedded in various Christian theologies. God, through the blood of the cross, demolished that "middle wall of separation" wrought by these "commandments contained in ordinances" (Eph. 2:15), terminating the enmity created by these divinely-ordered ordinances among the Israelites that would keep His people separated and divided.

Since God terminated this former enmity, then believers should also lay aside all their newly-created ordinances for the sake of the One New Man — "*so making peace*" (Eph. 2:15). Yes, in and of themselves, such commandments and ordinances can readily be justified by their divine origins — but swirling behind them are enmities with their divisive appeal to the same flesh which created the enmity in the first place. Nevertheless, praise God: *"For He Himself is our peace, who has made both one, and has broken down the middle wall of separation, having abolished in His flesh the enmity!"* (Eph. 2:14-15).

The New Man, though made up of all kinds of different and diverse people, is one because Christ is "*all and in all*" (Col. 3:10). The followers of Jesus Christ should fully embrace His people since all these individuals are "in Christ" (2 Cor. 5:17; 1 Cor. 1:30); and "Christ is in them" (Rom. 8:10; 2 Cor. 13:5; Col. 1:27; Eph. 3:17) — they are His One New Man. Though distinct, they are absolutely and inseparably in Christ. The assembly as the new man then fulfills God's purpose in creating man to express Himself. If you would: Multitude-One; thus, making peace.

Peace is not just an objective fact between believers and God, it has to be real and experiential between assorted believers. It is in the New Man peace is realized and expressed.

> The God of peace will soon crush Satan under your feet. The grace of our Lord Jesus Christ be with you.
> (Rom. 16:20, ESV)

When God created Adam, the first man (male and female), God said man would have *"dominion over the fish of the sea, over the birds of the air, and over the cattle, over all the earth and over every creeping thing that creeps on the earth."* *". . . over all the earth"* should have covered everything on earth, but God added another category of things that is not of the earth: *"creeping thing."*

This must refer specifically to Satan, the serpent, the "king" of *"every creeping thing."* God's intention was not that He would defeat His enemy Satan by Himself; He ordained *man* to be the one to defeat Satan. The first man, Adam, did not fulfill this commission; rather, the first man became a partner with Satan. Adam's defiance was expressed as *"one man's DISOBEDIENCE many were made sinners"* (Rom. 5:19).

Jesus said in Matthew 16:18 His built-up assembly would crush the gates of Hades. The oneness wrought in the One New Man is vital in the defeat of Satan. It makes sense, then, Satan's main tactic today is to divide believers, because it is a built-up oneness that defeats God's foe. Consequently, the prayer for oneness in John 17 was paramount in the heart of Jesus: AN ARMY OF ONE.

No wonder the crushing of Satan's head is reserved to Romans 16 where believers were charged to greet one another and specially to greet those who were not in their own "comfort zone." (This will be discussed at length in later chapters). At the end of Romans 16, it says *the God of peace will crush Satan under their feet shortly*. God does not crush Satan directly, but under the feet of those in peace and in fellowship with one another in oneness. Brethren — we've got to come out of our doctrinal dogmatism, cultural and racial prejudices — you name it — to "meet and greet" other brethren for the express purpose of CRUSHING THE HEAD OF SATAN! Most Christians have no idea they are commanded to so meet and greet one another. No, it's NOT optional; it's mandatory!

It is under the feet of those who are actively one that Satan is crushed. This fulfills what the Lord promised would be accomplished by the built-up assembly — the very Gates of Hades would be destroyed. We're not waiting around to be attacked by those gates . . . No, no, no — WE'RE ON THE ATTACK, THE OFFENSE. God's army is not on garrison duty — we're on the front lines — pushing back the Gates of Hell . . . come on brothers, come on sisters, let's move out! We're God's One New Man — designed to crush Satan's head!

> …in order that now to the principalities and authorities in the heavenlies might be made known through the assembly the all-various wisdom of God.
>
> (Eph. 3:10, DBY)

When Satan rebelled against God, he had no concept of the depth and height of God's wisdom. Satan could have easily thought he was wiser than God. Alas! It is through the built-up assembly that Satan, and the cohort of angels that were loyal to him, will finally know God's wisdom in His glory. Consider that the assembly is made up of human beings who were once corrupted, deadened, and divided by Satan. They were sinful enemies against God and full of animosity toward those who are different. It is out of this hopeless people who God came to redeem, to recover, to enliven, and build them into ONE — the ONE NEW MAN — to defeat Satan.

What manifestation of wisdom! The more challenging the problem, the more wisdom is manifested when the problem is solved. Each believer was a big problem — a challenge — to God; yet, all have become living members in this wonderful assembly. The "manifold wisdom of God" is at work today . . . isn't it time to join in the ARMY OF ONE?

The Kingdom of God

> Being asked by the Pharisees when the kingdom of God would come, he answered them, "The kingdom of God is not coming in ways that can be observed, nor will they say, 'Look, here it is!' or 'There!' for behold, the kingdom of God is in the midst of you."
>
> (Luke 17:20-21 ESV)

> And He said to them, "Assuredly, I say to you that there are some standing here who will not taste death till they see the kingdom of God present with power." Now after six days Jesus took Peter, James, and John, and led them up on a high mountain apart by themselves; and He was transfigured before them.
>
> (Mark 9:1-2)

There are these two definitions of a kingdom according to dictionary.com:

1) a state (domain) where a king rules (have sovereignty) and
2) a realm or province of nature; such as, animal kingdom, plant kingdom, etc.

When these two definitions are applied to the kingdom of God, it is very significant to find the phrase "kingdom of God" or its synonym, the "kingdom of heaven," was not used throughout the entire Hebrew Scriptures. The first time it was used was when John the Baptist introduced Jesus and He proclaimed *"Repent, for the kingdom of heaven is at hand."* Then Jesus told the Pharisees the kingdom of God was not a physical place, but it is He, Himself, who is in their midst.

In Mark 9, He told His disciples some of them will see the kingdom of God before they die, then in the very next verse He transfigured Himself, shining as bright as the sun, in front of them. He was the very manifestation of the kingdom of God with power.

It seems before Satan became the adversary, when he was the top angel leading worship to God (See chapter 9: "God, Man, Satan" in the book *ONE*), he was given the earth as His kingdom (Luke 4:6). He was like an administrator of God's creation. When Satan tempted Jesus by offering Him all the kingdoms and the glory of this world, Jesus accepted the fact Satan had the right to give them to Him. Of course, Jesus would not bow down to worship Satan as the condition to receive his offer. From this and other indications, it is understood this world is Satan's domain, his kingdom, and not God's. The entire worldly system is under the rule of the evil one (John 12:31). All human beings born on this earth are automatically born into Satan's kingdom, under bondage.

Although this is Satan's kingdom, he cannot arbitrarily damage God's people. When it came to hurting God's people, he needed God's permission as seen in the case of Job. It is like God has the veto power to restrain Satan from causing too much destruction. Nevertheless, God didn't have the right to simply take people out of Satan's domain just because He is God. Therefore, the kingdom of God was not yet on earth, and God's realm was not yet available for people to enter. God didn't have His kingdom until the coming of Jesus Christ. God by Himself, no matter how powerful, may be the *king*, but He is without a *kingdom* on earth.

Through the Person and Work of Jesus Christ, God gained His Kingdom, His ruling, His domain where He has full authority on earth. In Jesus Christ as a genuine man, both definitions of the kingdom of God were realized and expressed. Jesus as a man completely submitted Himself to God. God had full authority as the King in Jesus Christ. Additionally, Jesus being born of the Spirit and baptized by the Spirit has the same life form and attributes as God. He was truly the same as God in life and nature. Jesus was the true King in the line of David because not only was He an offspring of David, but He was also in the lineage of God.

> "Rejoice greatly, O daughter of Zion! Shout, O daughter of Jerusalem! Behold, your King is coming to you, He is just and having salvation, lowly and riding on a donkey, a colt, the foal of a donkey. I will cut off the chariot from Ephraim and the horse from Jerusalem, the battle bow shall be cut off. He shall speak peace to the nations; His dominion shall be from sea to sea and from the River to the ends of the earth."
>
> (Zech. 9:9-10)

Jesus Christ as the kingdom of God was similar to God establishing a beachhead for His kingdom on the earth. Ever since Satan's rebellion, God had been locked out of having His kingdom on earth. God is a righteous God, so even in His dealing with Satan, He could not simply take back the authority and the domain which was once granted to this top angel. God needed to do all things properly so He could be declared righteous when He judges (Rom. 3:4). Jesus Christ, being the Kingdom of God on the earth, bears His authority.

> But Jesus knew their thoughts, and said to them: "Every kingdom divided against itself is brought to desolation, and every city or house divided against itself will not stand. "If Satan casts out

> Satan, he is divided against himself. How then will his kingdom stand? "And if I cast out demons by Beelzebub, by whom do your sons cast [them] out? Therefore they shall be your judges. "But if I cast out demons by the Spirit of God, surely the kingdom of God has come upon you.
>
> (Matt. 12:25-28)

God didn't just want one man in His kingdom. He wants many men to be rescued from Satan's kingdom. Humankind were created as vessels to be filled up with God, to express God (Rom. 9:23); but due to the fall of man, humanity became an integral part of Satan's kingdom. People became filled with all the things of Satan's kingdom including evil spirits to enslave and possess them (Rom. 1:29). In turn, they became Satan's possessions in his house, his kingdom (Matt. 12:29). Therefore, Jesus, by the Spirit of God, is in the business of casting out the demonic forces from people so they can be immersed in the kingdom of God. It was a testimony and a declaration that with the coming of the kingdom of God, there would be release and deliverance for humanity that was under the dominion of Satan. Jesus, by casting out demons, gave us a foretaste of the coming kingdom in fullness where the Satanic kingdom is no more (Rev. 11:15).

Throughout the gospels when Jesus was physically on earth, no matter how many demons and evil spirits were cast out of people, there was no indication anyone actually entered into the kingdom of God. They witnessed the kingdom of God in action and they tasted the power and freedom of the Kingdom of God to come, but no one actually entered it to become a part of the kingdom of God. Jesus Christ's mission with His coming to earth was not just to be the kingdom of God Himself, but that He would open the way for humanity to be transferred into the kingdom (*The Father has delivered and drawn us to Himself out of the control and the dominion of darkness and has transferred us into the kingdom of the Son of His love*) (Col. 1:13-Amplified Version).

> Jesus answered, "Most assuredly, I say to you, unless one is born of water and the Spirit, he cannot enter the kingdom of God. ... "Do not marvel that I said to you, 'You must be born again.'
>
> (John 3:5, 7)

> For the kingdom of God is not eating and drinking, but righteousness and peace and joy in the Holy Spirit.
>
> (Rom. 14:17)

Jesus, in the Gospel of John, clearly spoke of how a person is to enter the kingdom of God: He is to be born of water and the Spirit. "Water" referred to baptism which signifies the old fallen man, who was in the bondage of the Satanic kingdom, is dead and buried. And "Spirit" is the new birth to bring in God's life and nature.

The person is to be born again — from above — or regenerated. When a person is born again, that person is freed from Satan's kingdom and has entered into God's kingdom. That one, through birth, has the same "life form" or DNA, if you would, as God the Father. Jesus spoke of this in the Gospels, but this could not transpire until after His death and resurrection. The death of Jesus Christ paid for the sins of humanity and terminated the old man (Rom. 6:6). It was the "old man" who found himself in Satan's kingdom. The resurrection of Jesus Christ provided the means whereby God's life could enter into man. It is His resurrection which made the new birth or regeneration a reality (1 Pet. 1:3).

With Christ's death and resurrection, God increased His kingdom from one man to a multitude of people; a people who have submitted to God by obeying the gospel (1 Thess. 1:18); and a people who possess God's eternal life and partake of His divine nature. That's how the Kingdom of God grows and is built up — by the growth of Life.

> And I also, I say unto you that you are Peter, and on this rock I will build my assembly, and Hades' gates shall not prevail against it. And I will give to you the keys of the kingdom of the heavens; and whatsoever you may bind upon the earth shall be bound in the heavens; and whatsoever you may loose on the earth shall be loosed in the heavens.
>
> (Matt. 16:18-19)
>
> "Assuredly, I say to you, whatever you bind on earth will be bound in heaven, and whatever you loose on earth will be loosed in heaven. Again I say to you that if two of you agree on earth concerning anything that they ask, it will be done for them by My Father in heaven."
>
> (Matt. 18:18-19)

> "Or how can one enter a strong man's house and plunder his goods, unless he first binds the strong man? And then he will plunder his house."
>
> (Matt. 12:29)

Immediately after Jesus Christ revealed He would build His assembly ("ekklesia"), He spoke of God's kingdom to reign on earth. Remember: the Greek ekklesia was a governing body where decisions were made for the city. The keys to bind and to loose on earth were not just given to Peter, but to all believers in oneness (Matt. 18:18-19).

God's desire for the assembly is to bring in His kingdom, His rule, and authority. According to His plan, God does not bind and defeat Satan's kingdom directly. Rather, He needs someone, a corporate man, a people on earth, to exercise His authority directly against His enemy. The problem is not in heaven where God is surely in control as the king. The problem is on earth where Satan's kingdom persists.

God needs His people in oneness as the assembly to bind and to loose: to bind the strongman and to loose the vessels that are held in his house. The strongman is Satan, his house is his kingdom, and the goods in his house are the people, the vessels who need to be rescued in order to be filled with God (Rom. 9:23). In a way, God's hands are tied on the earth, but with the built-up assembly, His kingdom has increased on the earth.

The oneness of the assembly is not oneness for an event or action. This kind of oneness is selective and temporal. This is not the true oneness the Lord is building; rather, true oneness is a state of being and living which expresses continual oneness found alone in the Trinity. Thus, for the assembly to be the kingdom of God, the assembly has to be ONE, and the assembly has to be a people who are filled with God. The assembly in this aspect has to be fully standing as ONE in the "uniting bond of peace" — filled with the Life of God, in full expression of His authority upon this earth going on the offensive against the Gates of Hades.

The assembly will be the one which will finally terminate Satan's kingdom and bring in God's kingdom in fullness and manifestation. *"The kingdom of this world has become the kingdom of His Christ. And He shall reign forever and ever." (Rev. 11:15)*

New Jerusalem – Describes the Union of God & Man

> Then I, John, saw the holy city, New Jerusalem, coming down out of heaven from God, prepared as a bride adorned for her husband. And I heard a loud voice from heaven saying, "Behold, the tabernacle of God is with men, and He will dwell with them, and they shall be His people. God Himself will be with them and be their God."
>
> "Come, I will show you the bride, the Lamb's wife." And he carried me away in the Spirit to a great and high mountain, and showed me the great city, the holy Jerusalem, descending out of heaven from God, having the glory of God. Her light was like a most precious stone, like a jasper stone, clear as crystal.
>
> (Rev. 21:2–3, 9–11)
>
> And He [God] who sat there was like a jasper and a sardius stone in appearance; and there was a rainbow around the throne, in appearance like an emerald.
>
> (Rev. 4:3)

In eternity the ekklesia is called the "New Jerusalem." The New Jerusalem, though a "city," is far and above anything confined to physicality. She is the Bride, the Lamb's wife. The Lord Jesus is not marrying a physical city; rather, He is marrying His assembly for whom He died. This city, being the Lord's wife, is bone of His bone and flesh of His flesh. The two are inseparably one in eternal union – they are MADE FOR EACH OTHER; sharing the same Life. The New Jerusalem is the last and greatest symbol to describe the mysterious and profound union between God and man.

Jesus was called the tabernacle of God in John 1:14. Herein the Revelation, the entire city is the tabernacle of God. The tabernacle is the dwelling place of God. In the Hebrew Scriptures, the tabernacle was in the wilderness. When Israel went into the good land, the temple replaced the tabernacle as God's dwelling place. In the New Testament, God was in Jesus Christ reconciling the world unto Himself commencing at His incarnation (2 Cor. 5:19). That habitation has expanded to include all of His people; therefore, the assembly is the temple of God (Eph. 2:21-22). This is the New Jerusalem. God found His eternal dwelling place within the assembly, the eternal tabernacle.

The New Jerusalem is the consummation of the Body of Messiah. Although the city is one, the distinctiveness of each member is still clearly expressed as shown by the twelve patriarchs or tribes of Israel, and the twelve apostles of the Lamb. It was through the apostles' teaching believers were brought into the fellowship of His One Body (1 John 1:3) — into the very Commonwealth of Israel (Eph. 2:12); therefore, these "twelve gates" and "twelve foundations" comprise His Glorious Bride, His Holy City — His One Body.

The New Jerusalem's foundations are made up of twelve layers. Each layer represents one of the twelve apostles, and each layer is a different precious stone, with its own characteristics and color in expression. This shows that though they all preached only one message of Jesus Christ, they are still distinct individuals with their own characteristics and expression. This is the One Body of Christ made up of all distinctly different individuals.

Moreover, in line with the eternal plan and purpose of the Almighty the tribes of Israel were literally arrange in camps to surround the Tabernacle in the Wilderness — 3 tribes on each side, representing the gates of the New Jerusalem (Rev. 21:12-13).

The New Jerusalem is also the new man, who is MULTITUDE-ONE, expressing the very Triune God. Although the term "new man" was not used to describe the city, it is indeed the new man since it is one entity composed of all of God's people. This oneness expresses God; therefore, the City shines with the glory of God and her appearance is like a jasper stone (Rev. 21:11). Interestingly, God's appearance — on the throne — is also described as a jasper stone. This indicates the very nature and appearance of God permeates the city. The city and God are *one*, and all of God's people are one.

Finally, the New Jerusalem is the eternal kingdom of God. The throne of this kingdom is clearly described as the pinnacle and center of the city.

> And he showed me a pure river of water of life, clear as crystal, proceeding from the throne of God and of the Lamb. In the middle of its street, and on either side of the river, was the tree of life, which bore twelve fruits, each tree yielding its fruit every month. The leaves of the tree were for the healing of the nations.
> (Rev. 22:1-2)

Although the New Jerusalem is laid out as "four-square" (Rev. 21:16) and can readily be considered a cube; yet, it is described in multiple passages as a huge mountain (about 1,500 miles high). The New Jerusalem is truly multi-dimensional — though a four-square cube it is described as the Mountain of the Lord.

On top of this mountain is the King of this kingdom, the throne of God and the Lamb. Flowing out of the throne is the River of Life that spirals all the way down the mountain until the base is encompassed. The Tree of Life, laden with fruit, also originates from the throne, grows like a vine from the middle of the river, and courses down along both sides of the banks. What a wonderful sight of life is this last descriptive sign of the assembly. This is the eternal kingdom of God!

The throne of God and the Lamb symbolize the Father and the Son within each other. For eternity, the Son is the Lamb, the Redeemer, with both divinity (Son of God) and humanity (the glorified Son of Man). The River of Life is the Spirit flowing out from God, becoming an integral part of the city. The Tree of Life, which is just God Himself, is the continual supply for the assembly, for eternity.

The Triune God (Father, Son and Spirit) is completely intertwined, disbursed, and everywhere with His people — the assembly.

Careful observation of the Holy City reveals the Trinity, yet there is still a distinction. God is still the one on the throne — but the closer you look, the more you see the Lamb is on that throne; and He is still the Spirit flowing out with the Tree of Life to be the City's unique source of supply. Even though the assembly of His people is one with God in life, sharing and partaking of His divine nature (2 Peter 1:4), and expression (and will be for eternity), God is still the One on the throne to be worshipped by all and the Source for all in perpetuity. No wonder then, her description is both four-square and a triangular mountain, the Creation with the Creator. . . a multi-dimensional marvel.

Perfect Oneness between God and Man

> At that day you will know that I [am] in My Father, and you (plural) in Me, and I in you (plural).
>
> (John 14:20)
>
> But he that is joined unto the Lord is one spirit.
>
> (1 Co 6:17 ASV)

From the descriptions of the assembly as described in the Scriptures, it is clear that God's eternal purpose is the building of His assembly. This assembly, composed of all His people since the creation of Adam, is a perfect union in eternal relationship with God — sharing in the wondrous oneness the Father, the Son, and the Holy Spirit have always shared — but now the pinnacle of His Creation, in Jesus Christ, shares in that Oneness.

How mysterious is this unity with God in Christ! How can one describe "you in Me and I in you?" This is like an intrinsic union; nevertheless, there is still "you" and "Me" — a perfect inextricable unity between two: The Lord Jesus and His people. This is the union and oneness within the Trinity. Jesus said in John 14:10, *"I am in the Father and the Father is in Me."* The best word to describe this relationship may be "coinherence" where the two exist within each other for eternity. There is a clear distinction between the Father, Son and Holy Spirit; yet, they are ONE within each other. The relationship between believers and Jesus the Son is exactly the same as between the Son and the Father.

In such a relationship, Paul says in 1 Corinthians 6:17, the believer and the Lord are ONE. The "join" in that verse is referring to two parties joining together. The result of this joining is simply one. Paul in that verse did not use the preposition "with." He didn't say "one *with* the Spirit." One *with* the Lord or one *with* the Spirit can be comprehended more easily. That would be typically what Christians might say, "we are one with the Lord" since in their consideration they are still two separate persons. In fact, Paul's description of believers and the Lord being one is so intense and striking that some Bible translator added in italics "one spirit *with Him.*" However, Paul simply said: he who is joined to the Lord is ONE SPIRIT. Everyone who is joined to the Lord through faith is one spirit. Millions upon millions of people who are joined to the Lord are one spirit both individually and as a body. How mysterious!

This is the same language the Lord used when He said, "*I and the Father are one*" (John 10:30). They are two, but they are also simply one — not figuratively but numerically one. The fact is that God being both three and one simultaneously and eternally is mysterious and beyond our earthly understanding, so also believers and their Lord together with the Trinity are also mysteriously and wondrously one. All believers are literally one because they are all joined to the Lord.

Throughout history Bible teachers have used various words in an attempt to describe this oneness in relationship between believers and their Lord. Such expressions as *union, united, blended, mingled, merged, connected, grafted* are some of the attempts to explain this relationship. Throughout this book some of these same words may be used; however, all human language fails at defining the mystery and awe as described by the words in Scripture as stated.

Although there is such a mysterious oneness whereby we participate and possess God's divine nature, eternal life, His glory and expression, there is still distinction. The Trinity is still the only God to be worshipped and His followers are to give Him all adoration and praise — no one else is worthy. Though His people have the distinctiveness of being the many sons of God, God is still the Father, Jesus is still the Only begotten and the Firstborn within the Trinity, and the Holy Spirit continues to be the unique source of fellowship. While the Bride of Christ, God's ekklesia, is the very Image of Christ, she will never be the fourth person of the Godhead.

Glory! God is in us, we are in Him, and all together we are ONE. This is the reason the highest, fullest, ultimate, and consummate manifestation of the ekklesia (assembly) is ONE. Just as Jesus Christ's mission is to build the assembly, all believers, no matter their ministries, are to serve toward the building of that one assembly. Since the assembly is esteemed so highly, it is critical to know who the members of this assembly are.

5.
DEFINING THE LORD'S EKKLESIA

In our previous chapter we disclosed some of the most prominent Biblical descriptions of the assembly (ekklesia) of the Lord Jesus. Obviously, the dominant theme of such an assembly is this: ONE. Again, if we do not have a life-changing revelation of this vision, like Peter . . . *"I will build My assembly* (ekklesia) *and the gates of Hades will not prevail against it,"* then divisions among genuine followers of Jesus will continue.

This vision motivates a person to pursue Christ; seeks out other relationships in the Body of Christ; transforms our professional goals; and dynamically alters our daily life. Once you see the vision — your life's goals take a back seat to fulfilling this vision of His assembly.

The following chapters attempt to make the assembly more practical. How should believers live from day to day to participate and contribute to the building up of the Lord's assembly on earth? The assembly the Lord is building can be expressed on earth. She was not described as one in the future kingdom since she has the authority to bind and loose on earth today. By seeing her oneness, unbelievers will accept Jesus as Lord and Savior. Jesus did not pray in John 17 that in the "sweet by and by" we would all be one somewhere off in heaven. No, He prayed that His believers are kept in the world and the world would believe when they become one in the here and now!

The assembly can be understood using three words: *constituent, reality,* and *manifestation*. The constituent of the assembly is the sum of its members. This prompts an initial question: What makes a person a member of the assembly? Secondly, once in the assembly we all share our experiences — here daily struggles and victories with the Lord should define the reality of His assembly. Finally, the manifestation of His assembly is NOT something hidden away from society — no, a true assembly impacts the world in which we live.

Constituents of the Ekklesia are all Believers

The primary utterance as to who are the members of the assembly is when the word "assembly" (ekklesia) was first used by the Lord Jesus:

> And Simon Peter answering said, You are the Christ, the Son of the living God. And Jesus answering said to him, Blessed are you, Simon Barjona, for flesh and blood has not revealed [it] to you, but my Father who is in the heavens. And also, I say unto you that you are Peter, and on this rock I will build my assembly [ekklesia], and hades' gates shall not prevail against it.
> (Matt. 16:16-18 DBY)

> Yourselves also, as living stones, are being built up a spiritual house, a holy priesthood, to offer spiritual sacrifices acceptable to God by Jesus Christ.
> (1 Pet. 2:5 DBY)

As soon as Peter recognized Jesus was the Christ, the Son of the living God, Jesus changed His name to Peter which means a stone. His personal revelation as to Who Jesus is made him a stone — material for the building up of the assembly. To build up His assembly, God needed construction material or "constituents."

Peter understood he was just one of the many stones in the assembly. Later in his epistle he identified all believers as "living stones." Even newborn babes in Christ (1 Pet. 2:2) are called living stones for the building up of the spiritual house, which refers to the assembly. There is no time gap between having faith in Jesus Christ and becoming a member of the assembly. As soon as one declares faith in Jesus Christ as the Son of God (His deity), who came to die for our sins, and rose from the dead, that one becomes a living stone for His building — construction material!

The New Birth

Faith in Jesus Christ is the unique qualification in becoming a member of the assembly. Each member, as a consequence of their newbirth experience, is able to reach out in mutual love for one another, thereby building up the assembly. Wherever this assembly is, it will always be comprised of God's children — those who have called upon the name of the Lord.

> ...to the assembly of God which is in Corinth, to those sanctified in Christ Jesus, called saints, with all that in every place call on the name of our Lord Jesus Christ, both theirs and ours.
>
> (1 Cor. 1:2, DBY)

Anyone who has believed into Christ Jesus is sanctified or "set apart." Believers are no longer common, as is everyone else outside of Christ. A "saint" is someone who has been set apart. Catholicism defines a saint as someone extraordinary. No, a saint is simply a person sanctified in Christ Jesus — every believer is defined by that God-given title. Therefore, God's assembly is made up of people beyond Corinth — people everywhere and in every place.

> But as many as received Him, to them He gave the right to become children of God, to those who believe in His name: who were born, not of blood, nor of the will of the flesh, nor of the will of man, but of God.
>
> (John 1:12)

The assembly consists of everyone in God's household — they are His sons and daughters — the Father's children. It is clear from John 1:12 that the unique way to become a child of God is through faith, by believing in Jesus Christ and receiving Him. At that moment of faith, a person is reborn (born anew, from above), regenerated . . . indwelt by the Spirit of the Living God. The "new birth" is not something self-generated. A person cannot "buy" the new birth. The only way to become a child of God, a saint, a member of His assembly — is to have your human spirit regenerated by the Spirit of Christ. That's faith in action. Faith has an object — that object is Jesus Christ.

> Jesus answered, "Truly, truly, I say to you, unless one is born of water and the Spirit, he cannot enter the kingdom of God. ... 7 Do not marvel that I said to you, 'You must be born again.' ... 16 "For God so loved the world, that he gave his only Son, that whoever believes in[to] him should not perish but have eternal life.
>
> (John 3:5, 7, 16 ESV)

In the previous chapters, we discovered the assembly is the kingdom of God. The point highlighted in the verses above demonstrates it is only through the new birth one enters the kingdom of God. When you enter the kingdom of God, you enter His assembly. Jesus made it clear: The new birth, giving believers eternal life, is simply through believing into Him. John 3:16 may be the most famous verse in the Bible. It is often quoted to show us faith is the only requirement for salvation and eternal life. However, it is rare to hear additional exposition, using this verse in context, to show belief in Jesus Christ also brings a person into the kingdom of God, the assembly.

To have eternal life and become a member of the assembly, there are no classes to take, no requirements to change life-style or character, no waiting time, and no membership dues. The only requirement is the living faith of Jesus Christ. Because it seems too easy and simple, people with a religious mindset add requirements. It can be in the form of taking classes, committing to stop sinning, having to attend church, go through certain rituals, donate money, etc. Any additional requirements to faith are simply not in the Scriptures.

This is not to say when a person believes and becomes a member of the assembly, the person will not change. In fact, there will be a lot of transformation, but it is due to the eternal (divine) life which is received through faith in Christ. Changes in life-style and character happen after the new birth, after regeneration.

Sanctification takes place in the believer AFTER regeneration. The more a new believer nourishes the new birth through daily repentance, feasting on the Word of God as spiritual nourishment, living by the Life of Christ, sharing Christ with others, and relying upon the finished work of Christ — His death and resurrection — the more this person will grow and be transformed. Sanctification continues for the entire life of the believer. This process of transformation takes place after one through faith enters the kingdom of God, the assembly. Don't pursue sanctification or being made worthy so you can be a member of the assembly; no, you enter the assembly through faith in His finished work on the cross. Now the work of sanctification can take place.

> That if you confess with your mouth the Lord Jesus and believe in your heart that God has raised Him from the dead, you will be saved. ... For there is no distinction between Jew and Greek, for the same Lord over all is rich to all who call upon Him. For "whoever calls on the name of the LORD shall be saved."
>
> (Rom. 10:12-13)

Paul is straightforward: *everyone* who calls on the name of the Lord shall be saved. There is no distinction between persons. As long as one calls on His name for salvation, "Lord Jesus Christ" with a believing heart, they are saved. The salvation experience makes the believer a member of His assembly. Notice that this simple way of salvation through faith extends to both Jews and what the New Testament calls, *those called out from the nations* (other ethnic groups).

This unique salvation brings the two previously divided and segregated peoples to become one assembly. Ethnic groups have serious differences; but these differences do not have to be ironed out to become His assembly. At the moment of salvation, the Jews and the Greeks (aka, the nations) become one. The biggest division with the deepest animosity (enmity and separation) between two people groups was erased by the same salvation in Jesus Christ.

At the moment of faith, whether Jew or Gentile (i.e., "taken from among the nations"), bond or free, male or female, people from every tribe and tongue automatically comprise the assembly. All differences, all what divides individuals from each other, are no longer relevant because through faith in Jesus Christ, these individuals are now "born again" into the same Family or Household of God, the Temple or Dwelling Place of God, the Bride of Christ, the Body of Christ, the New Man, the Kingdom of God, the Holy City — the New Jerusalem!

These passages make clear those who constitute the assembly. The assembly is God's eternal purpose made up of people who have become her constituent through simple faith in Jesus Christ. Without faith, there is absolutely no way to become a part of God's assembly; no amount of money, effort or behavioral modification can make a person a member of the assembly. Conversely, once a person is regenerated through faith, no one, no organization — not even Satan himself — can nullify a person's membership in God's assembly. A person is part of the assembly because he or she is brought into relationship with the Living God. When a person receives Jesus Christ, is "found" in Christ, then this person is automatically in the assembly.

Since faith in Christ is the only prerequisite in becoming a member of the assembly, imagine all the assorted types of people who now comprise the assembly — her constituents. They are not just from every tribe, tongue and nation (Rev. 5:9); they occupy every socioeconomic grouping on the planet — the rich and poor; the slave and free (Col. 3:11), and of course in that mix would include people of various political persuasions and educational levels.

Certainly, among these people, there will be some who are spiritually weaker and some stronger; some with certain doctrinal understanding and others with contrary understanding; some who have already gravitated to certain Christian practices and others, quite frankly, who are clueless as to any type of so-called Christian tradition. Yet, here is God's assembly composed of such a variety of people called out for Himself. It is among such diversity God will have an expression of one assembly. What a challenge! With the "natural man" (aka, human endeavor without Christ) this is an impossibility. But it is precisely in such a humanly impossible situation that God's multi-faceted wisdom will be made known to both heavenly and earthly entities through the oneness of His assembly (Eph. 3:10).

Reality of Ekklesia Is in Fellowship of the Holy Spirit

It should now be clear the assembly is made up of every single person regenerated through faith in the Son of the Living God, the Lord Jesus Christ. Now consider what and where the reality of this assembly is. How does a believer experience and participate in the assembly? According to Ephesians 1, the assembly is the fullness of God.

> And has put all things under his feet and gave him [to be] head over all things to the assembly, which is his body, the fullness of him who fills all in all.
>
> (Eph. 1:22-23 DBY)

How awesome is the assembly! The assembly is the Body of Christ, the fullness of God. Everything related to the Trinity is in His One Body. When Jesus was on earth, all the fullness of the Godhead indwelt Him bodily (Col. 2:9). Jesus Christ was not only the Son of God, He equally expressed and represented the Father (John 14:9), and He also is called the Life-Giving Spirit or Spirit of Christ (2 Cor. 3:17; Rom. 8:9).

When Jesus died, resurrected, ascended and the Spirit was poured out during Pentecost, the members of His Body radically increased. Before His death and resurrection, His body on earth was only in one man, Jesus Christ, but now His Body is a corporate man made up of all His followers. The fullness of the God-head now dwells in the corporate Body of Christ with many members, His ekklesia (assembly).

Believers are really missing out and come far short if they do not take advantage of their rightful place in the Body. Everything God intends for every believer is found in this One Body: love, joy, peace, deliverance, the unsearchable riches of Jesus Christ, the termination of all problems related to sin and death, resurrection, ascension, anointing, and so much more with an unlimited supply beyond all human endeavor — all are now available to the assembly.

All of God's children should be in this reality, the reality of the assembly. May I be so bold to state: This reality is the very purpose of the universe!

Believers are not meant to be isolated or divided from the Body of Christ, the assembly. They are to enjoy all the riches of the Trinity which have been transferred to the assembly. When believers are isolated from one another, the Lord is still with them because of His indwelling Spirit — but the fullness is missing. They can still pray, read the Bible and have fellowship directly with God, but the spiritual supply is but a trickle — here a little, there a little — but very little. The Christian life becomes a struggle and a chore. The full enjoyment of Christ is missing. Why? Because the fullness can only be found in the assembly — that's why the Gates of Hades can't stand it!

Many Christians have earnestly sought the Lord through various methods and practices: special ways to pray, fasting, Bible research and study, missions, discipleship programs, worship music and so much more. No doubt many of these ways and practices are helpful, but because the fullness is missing, their search persists from method to method. What about the Body of Christ? What about just simply entering the reality of the assembly in order to receive and enjoy everything God has already poured out? Know this: You're a stone. You've been designed for the building, the dwelling place of the Living God. Is it not time to enter into the reality of God's program, His building? Let's enter into fellowship.

The Fellowship of the Holy Spirit

The reality of a genuine assembly is in fellowship with all kinds of believers. There is only one fellowship in the assembly: it is the fellowship of Jesus Christ, the fellowship of the Holy Spirit.

> The grace of the Lord Jesus Christ and the love of God and the fellowship of the Holy Spirit be with you all.
> (2 Cor. 13:14 ESV)

How to articulate in words the marvelous nature of the Triune God — we just fall so short! Though God is uniquely one, He is distinctly the Father, the Son and the Holy Spirit. Each of the three has their own attributes and functions; yet, they are absolutely, perfectly, inseparably one. Distinction YES — Separation — NO! Some of the main attributes that describe the relationship within the Trinity:

- The Father loves the Son (John 5:20); the Son loves the Father (John 14:31);
- They have an intimate knowledge of one another (John 10:15);
- They support the work of each other (John 5:36; 6:44);
- They glorify each other (John 17:1);
- They have the same purpose and will (John 5:30).

The Person of the Holy Spirit provides their means of perfect community. The Holy Spirit facilitates the fellowship within the Triune God. It is the Spirit Who binds and joins the three in one since God is Spirit (John 4:24), the Son is Spirit (Gal 4:6) and the Spirit, of course, is Spirit.

Fellowship in the original Greek is the word *koinōnia*, which means, "share which one has in anything" (Thayer's). It is also translated communication, community, participation, distribution and communion. This Greek word is derived from *koinōnos* which means "having in common" (Vine's). It has the meaning of partnership (join together) or participation. So, fellowship can mean "sharing something that is in common" or "due to sharing, there is commonality." The sharing of what one has can be both physical and spiritual.

Although the word *koinōnia* was not used in the Scriptures to describe the relationship within the Trinity, clearly this word does describe the relationship among the Father, Son and Holy Spirit. Truly, the three Persons of the Godhead are united together as co-equal partners. Furthermore, they have perfect communication. The sharing or communication within the Triune God is absolute, total, without defilement — it is altogether generous.

The riches of God in His Trinity are unlimited; therefore, in His eternal purpose, He desired a people called out to be His assembly to receive His riches to become a part of His pristine fellowship. His desire was to create an image and likeness of Himself; yes, a vessel, into which He could pour Himself. He chose the pinnacle of His creation: MAN (male and female) to be that vessel to contain His very presence, His Life! The apex of His creation would in turn freely respond to Him, interact with Him, and be joined to Him in fellowship. The consummate result is the Creator and His Creation — MAN — would celebrate their relationship of fellowship for all eternity!

When believers participate in the fellowship of the Holy Spirit, then God's love and His grace wrought in Jesus Christ become real to them. God's love includes all of God's goodness and kindness towards humanity. The grace of the Lord includes all He has accomplished for humanity through His death and resurrection. All these unlimited riches of love and grace are real to believers when they are in "the fellowship of the Holy Spirit." When fellowship is absent, love and grace are but mere knowledge or memory of past experiences. The fellowship of the Spirit in the life of the believer makes real the freshness of His love and grace; and causes the believer to enjoy the fellowship the Father enjoys with the Son!

When did this Fellowship Begin?

Let us consider when the word "fellowship" or *koinōnia* was first used in the Scriptures.

> And they devoted themselves to the apostles' teaching and the fellowship, to the breaking of bread and the prayers.
> (Acts 2:42 ESV)

It is significant to note such a wonderful word as "fellowship" was not used in any of the gospels. In fact, the first time this word was used in the New Testament is found in the verse above. This happened immediately after the Day of Pentecost when the Spirit was poured out upon 120 followers of Jesus. Immediately, they shared the gospel; they shared the riches of Christ to all who in Jerusalem would hear the "good news." As soon as they were empowered by the Holy Spirit to declare the gospel of the Savior — the fellowship commenced!

Although the disciples and many others followed the Lord for up to three-and-a-half-years, and even recognized and believed Jesus was indeed the Christ, the Son of the Living God; yet, according to the Scriptures, they did not have "fellowship." They spoke with Jesus and He spoke to them. Yes, they communicated, but *koinōnia* did not happen.

It is certain they shared their food and drink, but it was not *koinōnia*. No matter how tight a friendship they had with Jesus, how much Jesus loved them, how much they witnessed the miracles He did, and how much the Lord opened His heart to them, the word "fellowship" or *koinōnia* was never used.

It seems "fellowship" or *koinōnia* is much more than what is defined by the Greek lexicon: communication, community, participation, distribution, and communion. It needs enlightenment to understand and participate in fellowship. *Koinōnia* or "fellowship" is of the Holy Spirit. Without the Holy Spirit being active and moving among people, there is no fellowship. Therefore, even though the Lord Jesus was physically communicating and sharing with the disciples, the Holy Spirit was not yet able to share or flow into and out of the believers until after the Lord's death, resurrection, ascension, and the Spirit's outpouring.

Although Jesus spoke of eating and drinking Him (John 6), and that the Spirit is like a flowing river gushing out of believers (John 7:38-39), such an experience among His followers did not actually happen until after Jesus' death and resurrection. The following verses should make clear that something universally impactful happened at the monumental events of His death and resurrection:

> But because I have said these things to you [concerning His going to death], sorrow has filled your heart. Nevertheless, I tell you the truth: it is to your advantage that I go away, for if I do not go away, the Helper will not come to you. But if I go, I will send him to you. ... When the Spirit of truth comes, he will guide you into all the truth, for he will not speak on his own authority, but whatever he hears he will speak, and he will declare to you the things that are to come. He will glorify me, for he will take what is mine and declare it to you. All that the Father has is mine; therefore I said that he will take what is mine and declare it to you.
>
> (John 16:6-7, 13-15 ESV)

It was after the Lord's death and resurrection He, as the Spirit, would be able come inside His believers — to indwell them forever (John 14:16-18). Before this, Jesus could only be *with* His disciples but not *in* them; but when the Helper, the Spirit of Truth, came, then He could live in them.

Moreover, as the Spirit of Truth, He was able to both speak and make known all that the Father is and has to the believer. Everything the Son is and has accomplished would also be known by the Spirit of Truth. This describes how one initially receives the Promise of the Spirit, the Comforter, the Paraclete, and how one is brought into the enjoyment of that fellowship. The Spirit Who provides the fellowship within the Triune God is now enabled to grant to all believers the same rich fellowship enjoyed within the Trinity.

This is not a cerebral understanding — it is experiential knowledge based upon the regenerating power of the Holy Spirit. Now, the Spirit can actually guide and lead the followers of Jesus into the very truth and experience of the Trinity and the riches shared in their fellowship. Believers through the Spirit are brought into the reality of the Father's life and nature; and the Son's terminating death, life-giving resurrection, and His all-subjecting-Lordship through His ascension. It is through the Spirit's indwelling believers may experience the expanse found alone within God.

What is described in these verses is the commencement of the fellowship of the Holy Spirit — the out-flowing of the Spirit to humanity. How awesome is this! Through the Spirit, everything of the Father and Son are made available to all believers. As believers, we can proclaim: "I am His and He is mine!"

Receiving the Spirit of Truth by believers happened right after resurrection when Jesus met His disciples. John 20:22 recorded the event: *"He breathed on them and said to them, receive the Holy Spirit."* At that very moment, what the Lord promised in John 14 and 16 concerning the Helper (the Paraclete, the Comforter), the Spirit of Truth being in them, was fulfilled. From then on, the Spirit of Christ indwelt them. Jesus who once was physically with them became the Jesus Who was spiritually in them. Jesus who could physically leave them became Jesus who would be with them and in them forever. This is the beginning of the fellowship of the Spirit Who was not yet available before Jesus' death and resurrection.

Shouldn't the word "fellowship" be used by the end of the Gospel of John after the Spirit was breathed into the disciples? Even while they prayed together in one accord for ten days, the word "fellowship" was still not used. It seems the Spirit needed to take one more step before *fellowship* could take place. Let's consider these verses relating to the outpouring of the Spirit.

> When the day of Pentecost had arrived, they were all together in one place. Suddenly a sound like that of a violent rushing wind came from heaven, and it filled the whole house where they were staying. And tongues, like flames of fire that were divided, appeared to them and rested on each one of them. Then they were all filled with the Holy Spirit and began to speak in different languages, as the Spirit gave them ability for speech.
>
> (Acts 2:1-4 HCSB)
>
> Then they were all amazed and marveled, saying to one another, "Look, are not all these who speak Galileans? And how [is it that] we hear, each in our own language in which we were born? Parthians and Medes and Elamites, those dwelling in Mesopotamia, Judea and Cappadocia, Pontus and Asia, Phrygia and Pamphylia, Egypt and the parts of Libya adjoining Cyrene, visitors from Rome, both Jews and proselytes, Cretans and Arabs — we hear them speaking in our own tongues the wonderful works of God."
>
> (Act 2:7-11)

In Acts, after the Lord Jesus breathed into the believers, they were together for ten days praying in one accord. Then on the Day of Pentecost (the fiftieth day after the Feast of Passover and 10 days after His ascension), the Spirit was poured out to fill them with power and the ability to speak, to share, to communicate to people the things of God and Christ. It is interesting to note the sign of the Spirit *upon* them was "tongues" — showing that the outpouring of the Spirit empowers believers to speak, to communicate. This is the outworking for the building up of God's one assembly. Instead of the Spirit being breathed *into* them in John 20, the Spirit here came like a violent rushing wind. Breath for breathing is designed to sustain life. On the other hand, wind is for working and moving. The stronger the wind, the quicker a windmill can turn and the faster a ship can sail.

Certainly, without the indwelling Spirit, there would have been no way they could pray in one accord for ten days! However, after the Spirit was poured out, their speaking was radically transformed. By speaking the magnificent works of God, they were able to transmit and distribute the riches they had received from the Trinity to anyone who was listening. Undoubtedly, it was a miracle Galileans could speak the various languages of the people from all over the world, but the ongoing and bigger miracle was people could now distribute and communicate the riches of the Trinity to others. When believers speak concerning Jesus Christ, they not only impart understanding, but now the life-giving Spirit is imparted to the hearer as well. ***Believers were no longer just receivers, they became dispensers.*** They became partners in the fellowship of the Holy Spirit.

Fellowship is communication on a completely different level, even in a different realm. The speaking concerning Jesus Christ didn't just relay information, it transmitted the Spirit as well. With the transmission of the Spirit, the love of God and the Grace of Christ, reached the hearer. Yes, the hearer received information for understanding, but even more, they received faith, and the things of God — the person and work of Jesus Christ became real to them. They were brought into the reality of the Trinity. How awesome is this, as believers speak the things of Jesus Christ, the Spirit Himself is being transmitted from person to person — that's the way it should be today.

Yes, it is altogether significant, after the outpouring of the Spirit which gave believers the ability to speak and communicate the riches of Christ, then the word "fellowship" or *koinonia* appears. It takes divine enlightenment and the unveiling of Scriptures to fully understand the matter of the fellowship of the Holy Spirit. Everything has been accomplished: death, resurrection, ascension, and the outpouring of the Spirit of God. People everywhere can receive and dispense the riches of the Trinity. This is fellowship. This is *koinonia*.

How to Enter into Fellowship?

In 1 John 1, the apostle John explains how people are brought into fellowship.

> That which was from the beginning, which we have heard, which we have seen with our eyes, which we have looked upon, and our hands have handled, concerning the Word of Life — the life was manifested, and we have seen, and bear witness, and declare to you that eternal life which was with the Father and was manifested to us — that which we have seen and heard we declare to you, that you also may have fellowship with us; and truly our fellowship is with the Father and with His Son Jesus Christ. And these things we write to you that your joy may be full.
>
> (1 John 1:1-4)

In John's gospel, He started also with the beginning, He said in the beginning was the Word and the Word became flesh. This Word Who became flesh was Jesus Christ. Here in his epistle (letter), he didn't name Jesus Christ as the One from the beginning, but he used the phrase: "Word of Life." John described the object of the apostles' intimate relationship as *the Word of Life*. The Word of Life was manifested to them. It is this Word Who they declare. By declaring and communicating this Word, the hearer is brought into fellowship. Everyone who hears this Word is brought into this same fellowship — the fellowship that is with the Father and with the Son, Jesus Christ.

In the Gospel of John, Jesus Christ came to them in the flesh, as a man. At this point, He could not be in His followers nor could they be in Him. Therefore, it was impossible to have the fellowship of the Spirit. In John's epistle, referring to the period after the Lord's death, resurrection, and ascension, He is now the Word of Life.

The Lord said the flesh profits nothing; because, His words are Spirit and Life (John 6:63). As the Word of Life, He could be declared, communicated, understood, disbursed — He could enter His believers by this very Spirit of Life. The apostles received the declared Word of Life. Now, through their declaration, their speaking, people who were once alienated from God were brought into fellowship. They were brought into fellowship not just with those declaring the Word, but with the Trinity Himself. Now those brought into this fellowship with the Father and the Son through the apostles are also handling and receiving the Word of Life, so they too can declare this very Word to bring others into the same fellowship of eternal life in which they now share. Thus, the "circle of Life" is ever-expanding — millions upon millions are now brought into the fellowship the Father has eternally shared with the Son!

The Word of Life declared by the apostles was the person and work of the Lord Jesus. The Word or *logos*, was God manifested in the flesh. He is both God and man. He has both divinity and humanity. He is a sinless, perfect man. In His humanity, He manifested unlimited love, righteousness, holiness, and God's glory. God was manifested in and through Him. His name is WONDERFUL — the MIGHTY GOD (Isa. 9:6).

As such a person, He came to fulfill His mission. He was anointed to complete God's eternal purpose. After His incarnation (when He became flesh), He lived and died as the God-Man on the cross to terminate, to purge all the negative things in the universe. His death achieved the impossible: washed away the sins of humanity, enabling people to be justified before God (Rom. 5:1, 9). Through His incarnation, life, and death, He destroyed the devil and made him of non-effect (Heb. 2:14). He terminated the "old man" — the "First Adam" — who through disobedience became the source of human strife.

On the cross, He demolished the enmity between Jew and Greek [aka, the Nations] in His very flesh — that "wall of separation" created by God-given commandments and ordinances which had kept the Jews separated from all the nations surrounding them (Eph. 2:14-15). Praise God, He put to death that enmity and reconciled both Jew and Gentile into *"One Body through the cross"!* (Eph. 2:14-16).

Through His resurrection we have become a New Creation (Gal. 6:15). As the *"Last Adam or Second Adam"* He *"became a Life-Giving Spirit"* (1 Cor. 15:45). He enlivened His people and brought humanity into God. Moreover, God and man are brought into eternal fellowship. As a man, in His ascension, He was made both Lord and Messiah to complete God's eternal purpose. Finally, He poured out His Spirit so all the members of His One Body now share in the same anointing whereby His built up ekklesia is able to display to all the world God's eternal plan and purpose throughout all the ages.

The above is a very short summary concerning the Word of Life. It will take eternity to fully discover the depth and height of the Word of Life. What can be spoken of Him is unsearchable, utterly inexhaustible. As the apostles declared this Word, something mysterious and wonderful happened; the hearers were brought into fellowship.

This may surprise many Christians, but Jesus as the Word of Life (1 John 1:1) is much more accessible to us than Jesus walking on earth 2000 years ago. As the Word of Life contained in the Scriptures, He can be replicated through the printing and distribution of Scriptures. When people read and handle the Scriptures, the Word of Life is communicated and enters one's understanding in a way that is logical and reasonable — but it does not stop there.

Since it is the Word *of Life,* something mysterious of God's Life affects those hearing this Word. It is that Life which enlivens the spirit of man. When a person's spirit is awakened, made alive by the Word of Life, then one so enlivened has an immediate, direct contact with God. They enter into fellowship with God. They are brought into the oneness with God. Not only that, they can immediately speak to those around them the Word of Life that they have received and are presently enjoying. They can share that Life with others. This is the power of the Word of Life.

Certainly, only God can forgive sins (Mark 2:7) and give life (Acts 17:25); yet, due to the fact the Word of Life has entered into believers becoming one with them, believers now have the same authority as the indwelling Holy Spirit in them to forgive sins as written in John 20:23 *"If you forgive the sins of any, they shall be forgiven them."* They can also pray and give life to others as written in 1 John 5:16 *"If any man see his brother sin a sin which is not unto death, he shall ask, and he shall give him life…"* (KJV). What a privilege and responsibility given to all those who have become one with God through receiving of the Word of Life by faith.

In the sequence of these verses in 1 John 1, there were no requirements for anyone to fulfill other than to hear and receive the declared Word of Life in order to enter into fellowship. When a person opens their ears to hear and receive the Word of Life into them, their spirit is regenerated, resulting in immediate fellowship.

Again, this shows the Word of Life is not just information and understanding, but the possession of eternal life, the love of God, and the grace of Christ. Yes, mysterious, because something altogether wonderful happens to a person as they hear the Word of Life. The eternal, unconditional love of God, and all that Christ has accomplished on the cross for the forgiveness of sins, His resurrection in total triumph over all His enemies – all becomes real and experiential. Then as fellowship ensues, all the attributes of the Trinity – such as divine love and the ability to forgive one another, joy, peace, purpose, righteousness, holiness, humility, and so much more, continue to refresh and renew the believer. This is fellowship: a continual receiving and sharing of the Life found alone in the Triune God.

Where and When Should Fellowship Happen?

"For where two or three are gathered together in [*into*] My name, I am there in the midst of them."

(Matt. 18:20)

Redeeming the time, because the days are evil. Therefore do not be unwise, but understand what the will of the Lord [is]. And do

> not be drunk with wine, in which is dissipation; but be filled with the Spirit.
>
> (Eph. 5:16-18)

The Lord Jesus Christ is in the midst of two or three believers gathered together for fellowship. *"In My name"* in the Greek should be translated, *"into My name."* *"In My name"* to most people is understood as "one being a representative of the Lord," such as saying, "I am doing this in the name of the king." That means the king is not actually there, but the representative stands in for the king. A gathering "in" His name, then, would mean that the gathering is with a formal intention of representing the Lord's name. That is not bad, but where is the Lord Himself?

However, "into" the Lord's name means the gathering is inside the sphere of or inside the person of the Lord Jesus. That is why the Lord is in their midst — the gathering is *inside Christ*. The gathering is enveloped in all Jesus Christ *is* and *has accomplished*.

The "name of the Lord" is actually the very person of the Lord Himself. That is why there is no other name given to men whereby they must be saved (Acts 4:12), and why when men call on the name of the Lord, they are saved (Rom. 10:13). The name can save because behind the name of Jesus is the very person of Jesus. His name is just Himself; otherwise, the name "Jesus" by itself, separated from the person, means nothing; it cannot save.

The gathering *into* the Lord's name has a clarity of direction or focus — the gathering is committed to the very person, presence, and Spirit of the Lord Jesus. This can and should happen anytime or anywhere when "two or three" believers are together; they should direct their conversation toward the person and work of the Lord Jesus. In doing so, the Lord is in their midst, and they are in the Spirit of the Lord with all His *"riches in glory"* (Phil. 4:19).

Most Christians only consider going to church, or going to an organized Christian event or meeting, to be a time for "fellowship" with other believers. If believers would consider fellowship can occur "where two or three" are gathered *into* His name, all sorts of opportunities throughout the day and week would open up! Fellowship can be short periods of time, even for five minutes. It can happen while commuting to work. It can occur over a coffee break, at a restaurant, or while shopping with another person. Understanding this, every believer can find opportunities to fellowship by meeting with another person or two, during the normal activities of life.

Today, with the availability of mobile technologies, it's even easier. A phone call or a video chat is accessible with a push of a button. Immediately, two to three people can be gathered into His name though they may be spread across the globe. The Lord is in their midst while they are in fellowship over the Internet. Amazing!

This verse cannot be emphasized enough. Understanding and practicing this verse will liberate believers to meet others anywhere, anytime, and for any length of time. There is no need for set events or a special place like a church building. No agenda, schedule, or material is required. What freedom to be able to gather and have the Lord Jesus in their midst, wherever they are! Without this understanding, believers may always think they need to be somewhere special or do something extraordinary in order to have fellowship.

According to the Pew Research Center (http://www.pewforum.org/2015/04/02/christians/), about 75% of the USA population identifies as Christian (including Catholics). Even for an African country such as Nigeria, about 50% of the population consider themselves Christian. That means 3 of every 4 people in the USA, even if they do not have a personal relationship with Jesus Christ, accept the foundational faith: Jesus Christ is both God and man; He died for the sins of humanity, and He resurrected on the third day.

Let's imagine these Christians, all having the same faith in their daily living, would put aside their differences as to what church they may or may not attend and the minutia of the various Christian doctrines and practices and then fellowship in twos and threes. Since, wherever people are located, half the people claim some faith in Jesus Christ; therefore, they are of the same faith who can fellowship. If fellowship happens, then the ekklesia is real to all these people. Those Christians in name only, who have not experienced the Holy Spirit, when they gather together in this manner with those having a personal knowledge of Jesus, are more likely than ever to have a personal encounter with the presence of the Living God.

Ephesians 5 says believers should redeem the time or buy back the time. In other words, don't let time get wasted because the days are evil. How do they make time profitable? By speaking to one another in psalms, hymns and spiritual songs . . . this generates true fellowship (Eph. 5:19).

Back when the New Testament was written, the Scripture as a book or a scroll was rarely available; therefore, words concerning the person and work of Jesus Christ and the believers' experiences were memorialized in long and short poems put to music. These then were sung and spoken to one another. The Word of Life was transmitted through speaking and singing of these songs which in turn brought in the fellowship of the Holy Spirit. How rich was the Trinity in those kinds of fellowships! By this simplicity, they were filled in their spirit with the Spirit of God. They were filled with joy, freshness and even excitement. It had a similar effect as being filled with wine, but it was profitable in every way.

Based on this thought of redeeming the time, even one minute of interaction in fellowship (which includes prayer) is profitable. If fellowship is no longer limited to a planned event at a certain location, then time can be redeemed — 5 minutes here by the water cooler; 3 minutes there between classes; 20 minutes of fellowship can take place at a coffee shop after shopping; 10 minutes can happen while taking a bus; 30 minutes can be redeemed by visiting or having a neighbor over. In such fellowship with all kinds of believers here and there, time is redeemed, and spirits would be filled up. With the reality of ekklesia taking place everywhere, the assembly with all the riches of the Triune God are realized.

Since believers are now in both the Father and the Son, they jointly participate in all that is in the Father and Son. What all believers "have in common" is Jesus Christ; therefore, spiritual and even physical blessings should be shared among them.

This is the result of receiving the gospel. Every believer enters into this fellowship that is in the Father and the Son. Once a person believes, experientially, he or she feels connected to every other believer in Christ. Initially, there is no thought of, "What kind of a Christian am I?" Or, "To what Christian group do I belong?" Why? Because we're all sharing in the same eternal life. There is a feeling of connection and belonging with every believer throughout time and space.

It is not until corrupt thoughts enter the believer's mind that Christians begin to consider segregation among believers. The fullness of joy is not in division, but in one fellowship with all believers in the Father and the Son.

This fellowship brings in the love of God and the grace of the Lord Jesus into the life of every believer. One does NOT have to "change churches" or even "go to church." The only requirement to enjoy this unity with other believers is a desire to reach out in fellowship with Christians all around you. Lay aside any impediment that divides to solely focus on our mutual faith in Jesus Christ. Christians need to forget about "what church do you go to" as a way of segregating each other and just learn to pray and fellowship together concerning the wonderful person and work of Jesus Christ. This is the reality of ekklesia which brings us into the fullness of the Lord.

Start Sharing and Receiving!

> And they continued steadfastly in the apostles' doctrine and fellowship, in the breaking of bread, and in prayers. ... Now all who believed were together, and had all things in common, and sold their possessions and goods, and divided them among all, as anyone had need.
>
> (Acts 2:42, 44-45)
>
> For it pleased those from Macedonia and Achaia to make a certain contribution [*koinōnia*] for the poor among the saints who are in Jerusalem.
>
> (Rom. 15:26)

Firstly, there is the apostles' doctrine or teaching; then, comes fellowship. Fellowship is a result of the apostles' teaching. Within this fellowship there is community. Community is part of the definition of *koinōnia*. In this community everyone shares their material blessings. Fellowship is not just a sharing of spiritual riches, but also physical. Believers in Acts 2 willingly sold their possessions and goods in order to share with other believers. This practice of having everything in common and dividing their physical possessions so no one had lack started right after the day of Pentecost, but it only lasted a short time.

By the time Paul started writing his epistles, the practice among the followers of Jesus had changed: They kept their own possessions but gave according to their prosperity. They did not have all things in common; rather, they kept ownership of what they had earned, but willingly shared according to the needs of others. The word for "contribution" (Romans 15:26) is a translation from the word *koinōnia* (i.e., fellowship). That means sharing physical things was part of fellowship, and it is in this fellowship community is realized.

In human societies, there is a form of government where the law of the land is to have all things in common. The rich are to give away all their riches to the poor so everyone is equal. That political system is called "socialism" or "communism." Since it is a matter of law, people are forced to turn over their riches to the government for distribution to the poor. It can be considered as a counterfeit to Acts 2.

History has shown this form of government is mostly unworkable because a large part of the citizens are demotivated from working hard, thinking any excess from productivity will be taken by the government. It also encourages laziness since the *"non-productives"* will receive their equal share of sustenance no matter what. Trying to duplicate equality without the reality of divine fellowship has been a societal disaster.

Since God's love and grace is found spontaneously in divine fellowship, there is a supernatural desire to share one's spiritual and physical blessings. It is not forced. Once it is forced upon a person, it is no longer fellowship. But when believers are in fellowship, there is a communion of people who are willing to help one another by all means. Mutual caring and bearing of each other's burdens is the hallmark of community — the needy are cared for where there is fellowship and community.

Fellowship brings in a love and care that bridges all barriers. In Romans 15:26, the Gentile believers contributed their material riches to Jewish believers in Jerusalem. The greatest cultural enmity at the time was between the Jews and Gentiles; yet, when there was the fellowship of the Holy Spirit, there was a willingness to share, to contribute to those in need. Many of the Jewish believers might have become poor due to persecution or a famine in the land, not because of their laziness — but their "natural enemies" who had become their brothers and sisters stepped up and came to their rescue.

When there is fellowship, community is immediate. As soon as there is fellowship in the Holy Spirit between believers, community shows up. Instantly, there is mutual care and a willingness to share and help each other. Time is not needed to build community. Community can be among believers who may go to different churches or not attend any. The identity of this kind of community is the Lord's assembly, the ekklesia. Certainly, it is good to have friends with whom one can consistently be in fellowship, but at the same time, just because the same few Christians are together all the time, do things together, and even pray together it's not necessarily a sign of fellowship. If these individuals can freely "fellowship" among themselves but are unable to fellowship with other believers not in their group, then their "fellowship" is questionable. It may be but a friendly clique — it's not fellowship.

In the same way, there certainly can be fellowship among those in the same ministry or church, but that fellowship is also dubious if those in that ministry or church do not or cannot fellowship with other believers not in their church or denomination. Often when a person finds themself outside of a particular church identity, he or she is no longer in "fellowship" with the members of that church. If a person leaves a church and the church rejects that person from their "fellowship" and support, then the sharing and camaraderie that exists among the members of that church is more akin to that of a club, a fraternity, or a sect and not the one fellowship of the Holy Spirit within the ekklesia.

Building Christian Community

Many ministers and believers are desirous of building a Christian community. "Organic churches" or house churches are normally comprised of Christians who have left institutional churches due to their desire for community. These communities are intended to be relational, communal, sharing, and mutually supportive of one another in their daily lives. They see Acts 2 as the model of ekklesia for them to emulate today. This is of course admirable and understandable for seeking believers to leave organizational and hierarchical structures and enter the simplicity of the ekklesia.

This noble goal of Christian community has been pursued in earnest by believers over the past few centuries. Moving closer together, rather than being so scattered; some even to the point of communal living. This was the aspiration of the monastic communities of the past and the many Christian communes during the Jesus People Movement in the late '60s and '70s.

Due to the many legitimate complaints and criticisms against hierarchical, impersonal, and divided system of institutional churches, those desiring Christian community can have an overzealous negativity toward institutional churches. In their passion to advocate such "Biblical" communities, their condemnation of institutional churches becomes normative; this then develops into a barrier of fellowship with believers who are still active in institutional churches. Thus, inadvertently, their desire to come back to the simplicity of Biblical community becomes a barrier to fellowship with other believers still within organizational structures.

Let's say a particular Christian community starts off with a pure motive, full of the joy of sharing and fellowship; yet, over time, an exclusive element develops. If the same group of people can indeed maintain a community, a culture will develop that is their own. That means it becomes difficult for believers to come and participate as equal members without adopting their culture which could include a dominant Christian doctrine or practice. There will be "outsiders" who will need to become "insiders." Furthermore, if this community becomes successful with increases in the number of members spreading to other locations and growing, then it is inevitable organizational structure will set in. Soon a hierarchical leadership will be formed. The leadership will then place "safe guards" to protect the community's culture. When it becomes institutionalized, then, it has come full circle. Alas! That which they feared the most has come upon them! They have just repeated history and morphed into another well-defined group or division among the many sects of Christianity.

The caution is that if the effort is placed on building a community patterned after various models — including Acts 2 — and that effort neglects the fact the definition of true fellowship is universal, then eventually those communities will become segregated from other believers. They'll become just another sect among the tens of thousands of divisions in Christianity.

In Scripture there is only one fellowship and one community which is the ekklesia consisting of all believers. The vision of the oneness of all believers is simply those who have faith in Jesus Christ freely fellowshipping and sharing with each other through their daily lives, whether they see each other regularly or meet for the first time. It is an open community which is the reality of God's ekklesia.

It is critical in our understanding that fellowship is universal. There is only one fellowship. This fellowship is of the Holy Spirit. The ability to fellowship is innate in every believer. Fellowship is always reaching out to others. It is not bottled up but extends and spreads. Everyone entering fellowship is immediately an equal member. Yes, community will be formed due to fellowship, but this community has no boundaries; it is fluid, it can easily spread from one household to the next.

In fellowship, what a community looks like can be different with those at work from those in a neighborhood. There can be one set of communal relationships with people at work or at school and another set with those who gather in a home, but if fellowship is genuine, then believers in the various communities can easily and quickly blend with each other and fellowship as one ekklesia. This testifies to the truth there is only one fellowship resulting in one ekklesia.

Consider again the situation in Romans 15:26. Believers in Macedonia and Achaia (Greece) freely contributed to Jerusalem's poor Jewish believers even though they were in two different places and under two different ministries (Paul in Greece and Peter in Jerusalem). It is certain most of the "saints in Macedonia and Achaia" had never met Jewish believers in Jerusalem; yet, because of fellowship, there was contribution and community.

Therefore, it is commendable for believers to be willing to move within proximity with others to build a strong and close-knit community; yet, prudence is needed they do not become isolated from other believers in the Body of Christ — even ones they've never seen. The genuineness of fellowship within such a community is constantly tested by whether that fellowship is fluid, open, boundary-less, and ever reaching out to others.

6.
WHAT DOES EKKLESIA LOOK LIKE?

In the last chapter, the *constituents* and *reality* of the assembly (ekklesia) were covered. The one assembly comprises all genuine believers with faith in Jesus Christ — whose human spirit has been regenerated by the Spirit of the Living God. The reality of this one assembly is domiciled in the *fellowship* of the Holy Spirit.

Sharing in the fellowship of the Triune God provides believers with pristine unity which cannot be achieved by any other means — its basis is the very fellowship enjoyed within the Triune God. The omnipresence of the Trinity sustains in time and space this unique oneness among believers. In this chapter we will present what the ekklesia looks like — its *manifestation*.

Matthew 18:20 shows when two or three are gathered at anytime, anywhere *into* the name of the Lord Jesus Christ, He is in their midst. This verse gives a solid basis concerning the need for believers to fellowship with each other whenever the opportunities are presented throughout one's daily life. Likewise, in Matthew 18, it says if the same two or three cannot solve a problem between themselves they are to take the matter to the ekklesia/assembly. The ekklesia is the final arbiter of disputes among believers.

Matthew 18 exposes the fact no matter how often two or three are gathered together — they still do NOT constitute the ekklesia. Great fellowship between two or three may have the presence of the Lord in their midst but something is lacking — they need to "bring it" to the ekklesia. I hear folks say when they get together: "We're having church together." True, there is reality in fellowship wrought by the Triune God — Jesus is in their midst . . . but Jesus still wants us to understand that the "assembly" is where God's fullness abides. There is a significant difference; therefore, having the reality is not enough — the manifestation of ekklesia is needed.

The Meaning of Ekklesia

> Therefore, if the whole church [ekklesia] comes together in one place, and all speak with tongues, and there come in [those who are] uninformed or unbelievers, will they not say that you are out of your mind? But if all prophesy, and an unbeliever or an uninformed person comes in, he is convinced by all, he is convicted by all. And thus the secrets of his heart are revealed; and so, falling down on [his] face, he will worship God and report that God is truly among you.
>
> (1 Cor. 14:23-25)

In Matthew 16:18, the Lord Jesus said He would build His ekklesia. In previous chapters, it was explained the Greek word *ekklesia* had been mistranslated to "church" in most English translations. The accurate translation of *ekklesia* in the Greek means to be *called out for an assembly* (Vine's). The etymology of the word "church" is literally referring to a physical building for religious worship. The Lord Jesus is not building a physical building, He is calling out a group of people and gathering them together to be one in order to express or manifest the multi-attributes of the Trinity. This group of people called the assembly is described as: God's household or family, the Bride of Christ, the Body of Christ, God's Kingdom, and the Holy City, New Jerusalem.

The word *ekklesia* in the Greek was already in use for at least 600 years before the birth of Jesus Christ — before He said that He would build His own ekklesia, or assembly. A quick research on Google shows *"ekklesia"* literally means "called out" and it refers to an assembly of the citizens of a community. It was an assembly of citizens in a city coming together for civil matters — akin to a town hall meeting. The practice of ekklesia started with the Greeks and continued by the Romans. A city or a town would have various sub-groups of citizens: Jews and Gentiles, rich and poor, tradesmen and farmers, etc. When there were matters which affected the entire city, then the citizens were called out of their sub-groups for an ekklesia, there would have been representatives from every sub-group since a city-wide decision could affect everyone in a city. It would not be an ekklesia if only the rich people would have been invited or if only the farmers were represented.

An ekklesia would have included all the various sub-groups so everyone would have the opportunity to voice their interest and concerns relating to matters at hand. One or even two sub-groups could not make city-wide decisions affecting all the diverse subgroups; therefore, any exclusion of a sub-group of citizens could not be classified as an ekklesia. Greece was the birthplace of democracy; therefore, ekklesia was their democratic method for people of a community to make decisions. One can imagine that these ekklesia with conflicting interests represented were quite boisterous and confusing; such an ekklesia happened in Ephesus and it was recorded in Acts 19.

In Acts 19, a typical assembly (ekklesia) of the secular world is described: A silversmith who was making money from crafting idols for the goddess Diana stirred up the entire city against Paul for preaching the gospel of Jesus Christ. The silversmith guild of the city was afraid of losing their livelihood if people ceased their idol worship. These idol-makers instigated a riot. They called out the people of Ephesus; created a work stoppage; and, gathered an assembly to bring things to a head!

They didn't gather to listen to an orator, they gathered because they were stirred up for action where everyone wanted to express their opinions concerning the situation at hand. Acts 19:32 says, *"Some therefore cried one thing and some another, for the assembly (ekklesia) was confused..."* This event, this gathering, was called an ekklesia. This was purely a secular assembly designed to settle some matters related to the citizens of the city.

Therefore, it is interesting, almost anti-climactic, that Jesus would use such a secular word, *ekklesia*, to describe His eternal purpose. *"I will build my ekklesia,"* Jesus proclaimed; yet, His ekklesia would be spiritual, universally high, extraordinary — but be practical enough where if there were insurmountable problems between community members, they could bring their disputes to the assembly (on the earth).

> And they sang a new song, saying, "Worthy are you to take the scroll and to open its seals, for you were slain, and by your blood you ransomed people for God from every tribe and language and people and nation, and you have made them a kingdom and priests to our God, and they shall reign on the earth."
> [Rev. 5:9-10 ESV]

When Jesus said He would build His ekklesia, there was no question among the disciples as to His meaning. He didn't redefine or change the basic structure of ekklesia. The only thing is this ekklesia would be His and not belong to any worldly community. It is of great interest the Lord picked a secular assembly to model His eternal purpose. On the other hand, one can argue the ekklesia was modeled after God's eternal heart's desire. In the verse above, the Lord redeemed and brought together an assorted and diverse people from every sub-group on earth. They were brought together into one kingdom where every one of those called out ones would function as priests to God, to serve, and to enjoy God. They shall reign forever. Here is ekklesia where there is representation from every sub-group assembled and where each member is an active participant. Their function is to make decisions as rulers over the entire earth.

So, when Jesus said He would build His ekklesia in Matthew 16, it would have been well understood He would be calling out a people from wherever they were found; from whatever preoccupation involved them, and from a divergence of sub-groups. These called-out ones would assemble in one place; everyone functioning, having fellowship; interacting with one another and the world around them... dealing with matters pertinent to their newly-found community in the new creation. Here they could participate; enjoy living fellowship around the Lord; and from that community reflect their testimony as His assembly to the world.

The fact the disciples did not question the Lord's use of the word *ekklesia* means they accepted it according to the common usage of the day. It is critical to recognize why the Lord didn't use a religious gathering to describe His eternal purpose: a gathering where there is solemnity, rituals, homogeneous adherents, spectators observing the performances of a few, and submission to the leader-priest of that religion. It is crucial Christians come to an understanding why the word *ekklesia* is intrinsic to God's plan and purpose. In Acts 2:42-47 there is a short account of what the Lord's ekklesia looks like in action. There is only one other portion found in God's Word which describes what the Lord's ekklesia looks like in practicality when His people are called out to be an assembly.

It is described in detail from 1 Corinthians 11:17 through the end of Chapter 14. If believers are interested in God's eternal purpose worked out on earth, it is imperative they consider and study this portion of Scripture. Here are some of the main points of the Lord's ekklesia shown from these passages:

- It was a calling out of divergent believers to be an assembly: Jews and Gentiles, slaves and free, rich and poor, male and female, those who are honorable and those who are not (1 Cor. 11:21, 12:13, 22-23).
- Believers would come together in one place. It was a specific place at a specific time the assembly took place (1 Cor. 14:23).
- The faithful would come together for a common meal (1 Cor. 11:21,33).
- They would participate in the bread and the cup (the body and blood of their Lord) in remembrance of Him until He came again (I Cor. 11:23-28).
- The spiritual gifts given to each member of the Lord's Body were freely operating and expressed (1 Cor. 12:4-14).
- Love for one another would be the dominant atmosphere and the basic foundational connection between all these diverse believers (1 Cor. 13).
- Everyone would speak and contribute what was in them through prophesying: teaching, testifying, singing, or praying (1 Cor. 14:15, 26, 31).
- No one would be able to dominate the gathering; there would be freedom to interrupt each other in the middle of someone speaking (1 Cor. 14:30-31).
- The purpose of gathering was to build up the assembly by encouraging one another, comforting; edifying one another through sharing their experiences of Christ (1 Cor. 14:3-4).
- The "unbelieving" and "uninformed" who might find themselves in such an assembly could witness the living God among them. Being convicted and convinced by the Body of Christ in action, they would fall down and worship God (1 Cor. 14:23-25).

Difference between "Secular" and Lord's Ekklesia?

It is not a coincidence the Scriptures gave two examples of ekklesia. One is secular which took place in Ephesus recorded in Acts 19, and the other is the Lord's, which was described in detail in 1 Corinthians. Let's first look at the similarities:

1. People were called out and came together as an assembly;
2. They assembled for a purpose;
3. Everyone had equal opportunity to speak out what mattered to them; they were all eager to participate.

These characteristics are common between both a secular and "spiritual" ekklesia. That is why no questions were asked by the disciples when the Lord said He would build His ekklesia. When people heard about the Lord's ekklesia, they immediately understood its structure would have similar characteristics as that of a secular one. Now let's consider the differences:

1. The first overt difference was a meal with the bread and cup associated with the Lord's ekklesia. No doubt it mirrored the last supper the Lord had with the disciples before going to the cross. He ate a meal with them and after the supper He broke bread to symbolize His body broken and passed the cup to signify His shed blood. The Lord's assembly continues the remembrance of having a meal together with a focus on all Jesus accomplished through His death and resurrection.
2. The atmosphere of the secular ekklesia in Acts 19 is one of fear, confusion, with a goal of uplifting idol worship and destroying people; whereas, the Lord's ekklesia is one of love, encouragement, no confusion — the goal was the building up of God's eternal purpose resulting in encouragement and comfort to all in attendance.
3. The Trinity within and upon all those "called out" by God was fully manifested in the Lord's ekklesia. Each member was gifted by the Triune God in order to function and participate in the assembly. A variety of gifts were given to match the diversity of the assembly. Each participating member would find their place, from the greatest to the least significant. All were fully welcomed, encouraged, and accepted. Those members who were weaker or less attractive received even more honor so that the fullness of Christ would be displayed.

Due to the common understanding of ekklesia in those days, the Lord's ekklesia was similar in structure to a common gathering of community members; as well as resembling the participatory relationship among attendees. At the same time, since it was the Lord's ekklesia, the Trinity would be completely engaged: He is integrated among them, joined in union with all the members, so the atmosphere is one of loving and building up one another. The focus of the conversation is the Lord Jesus Christ; the result is the building up of God's eternal purpose on the earth. No wonder unbelievers or the "unlearned" coming into such an assembly would see God in their midst, fall down, and worship by declaring: *"God is among you of a truth!"*

Truly, the manifestation of the Lord's assembly is awesome, inspiring, convicting, and convincing since she displays all the previously mentioned attributes: The Body of Christ, the Bride of Christ, the Kingdom of God, etc. Even if the reality of the ekklesia is present with all kinds of "twos and threes," without an actual assembly of believers according to the description given in 1 Corinthians, there would still be a deficiency. Where can the ekklesia be seen, where can people come and see God with man, where can the members gather to exercise their God-given gifts, where can all kinds of believers display their oneness? It is in the gathering of saints according to the pattern of the Lord's ekklesia that such a manifestation takes place.

This manifestation fulfills the Lord's prayer in John 17. He prayed for the oneness of His people so the world would believe in Him. The assembly with God's presence and the Lord's unveiling among His people was to be so powerful, it would cause the unbeliever to fall down in worship to God. It seems preaching was not all that necessary. There was no need to argue or to convince anyone. The revelation of God and His presence were so formidable people just got convicted and believed. This is what you call a prevailing gospel! Every believer, exercising their gifts, being who they are in Christ, loving one another — this is truly the love of Christ among His people.

Churches Versus Ekklesia

> Some indeed preach Christ even from envy and strife, and some also from goodwill: ...What then? Only [that] in every way, whether in pretense or in truth, Christ is preached; and in this I rejoice, yes, and will rejoice.
>
> (Phil. 1:15, 18)

When an ekklesia (assembly) as defined and described is compared with how churches operate today, they are obviously very different. Since "church" is defined in all major English dictionaries as "a building for public and especially Christian worship" (Merriam-Webster), Christians should stop redefining "church" as the people and start describing it as the building. "Church" is literally the building and not the people. At best it is an organization using a certain building. In any case, it is not ekklesia according to the definition of the word.

In fact, how Christians function within a church today is completely different from the Lord's assembly. That is why there is so much confusion among Christians concerning the ekklesia which the Lord is building. Christians should just be accurate — stop calling the Lord's ekklesia "church"; stop using the word "church" to describe the Body and Bride of Christ. I know, it may sound rather harsh — but God's people need a paradigm shift in their thinking concerning what a "church" really is.

Ministries take place in "Churches"

Consequently, a good question to ask would be: Why are there churches today and what are their benefits? Churches today are places where ministries operate. Various ministers, according to the gift they have received, gather people in their respective churches in order to preach the gospel, encourage God's people, and teach the Bible. This is similar to Paul renting the School of Tyrannus in Ephesus for two years in order to preach and teach daily (Acts 19:9), or when the apostles taught at the public square of the temple in Jerusalem.

The Bible clearly did not call these places utilized by specific ministers an ekklesia (assembly). Since a church is used to represent the teaching and practice of a particular ministry, then all the churches by definition are different: they express the various views and practices of their respective ministers.

People go to a church of their choice based on where they get the most help and inspiration. Just as Paul was an apostle to the Nations, today a minister may be drawn to ministering to ethnic Chinese. In this case, his church, quite naturally, will be a convening place where Chinese meet.

Another minister may be inspired by Pentecostal experiences; through his/her ministry, a "Pentecostal" church would be raised up. Another minister may have a heart for urban youth; therefore, he or she may have an approach which will reach that target audience. His or her church will be a gathering place for young people. We now find tens of thousands of various kinds of churches since each minister has a unique calling and various ways or styles to present the Scripture. Each church represents a different take or emphasis on Christian doctrines, practices, music, demography, style, etc.

According to Philippians 1:15-18, as long as Christ is preached, all followers of Christ should rejoice. Some in Paul's day preached out of selfish ambition and others out of love, but, either way, Christ is preached, and Paul rejoiced.

Most pastors and ministers in different churches today try their best to preach Christ in their own way. Through all these various practices which target various demographics throughout the earth, millions upon millions of people have come to believe in Jesus Christ. For this, all Christians should rejoice.

Although some Christians object to using "rock music" to worship in church, it is still undeniable — myriads of people have come to believe the gospel through their attraction to this genre of music. Even among churches using contemporary music, there are ministers who will use country music and others will use rap. Some believe preaching Jesus with an emphasis on predestination is the way to turn people to God, and certainly thousands upon thousands have come to know Christ through this teaching. Contrarily, others preach Jesus Christ with an emphasis a person has a choice to believe and can even lose their salvation if they stop believing. They too, have brought thousands upon thousands to Christ. If Paul were alive today, he would rejoice and so should all followers of the Lamb. There should be rejoicing that so many millions of believers are on earth today . . . *"so that by all possible means I might save some"* (1 Cor. 9:22).

Due to all these various ministers building their own churches around their ministries, Christians have become segregated based on their preferences; such as: doctrinal emphasis, methodologies, political persuasions, ethnic groupings, demographics, liturgical issues, personalities, and just about anything else that can be used as a niche for ministries — especially, the "style of the preacher."

Even those who have left the institutional church to gather in homes as "house churches" eventually, even unconsciously, gravitate in separating themselves from other Christians. Many of these believers view themselves as another church with a defined group of believers gathering as a "house church." Just because the gathering is in a home without an organizational structure does not necessarily mean that this home group is manifesting ekklesia. They can simply be another form of ministry that emphasizes personal interactions.

Churches Are Homogeneous – Ekklesia is Diverse

> For there must also be factions among you, that those who are approved may be recognized among you.
>
> (1 Cor. 11:19)

Churches today are simply gathering places of homogeneous groups of people. They may have sameness in ethnicity, in doctrinal understanding, in Christian practice, or share common political views. Therefore, it is useless and unreasonable to disturb or object to the brand of ministry associated with a church. If a particular church becomes a gathering place for those who are inspired by its music ministry, it would be silly to tell that church to stop using that brand of music to attract people to Christ. If a church teaches that speaking in tongues is a way to have the presence of the Holy Spirit, it would be counter-productive to go into that church and tell them otherwise. The ekklesia or the Lord's assembly, however, pools together all believers comprised of ones called out from different backgrounds, ministries, practices — from all sorts of segregated ministry circumstances.

Churches today are normally designed where a dominant person (e.g., the "senior pastor" or one style of speaking takes place); whereas, the ekklesia or assembly is defined by everyone having the freedom to express what they have seen of the Lord and to function according to the gifts of the Spirit they have received — we're not talking about a free-for-all here — *"let all things be done decently and in order"* (1 Cor. 14:40). No matter how little their contribution is, everyone coming to an assembly should come having the freedom to speak about their experience with Jesus Christ. Contrariwise, those attending a "church" go to listen to a specific ministry and rarely is it permissible to interrupt or openly dissent; unless, of course, audience participation is encouraged by the pastor or leadership regarding the topic at hand.

Today's churches, if understood as ministries, cannot handle division and contrary opinions in their ranks. As a ministry, they need everyone to be on the same page; otherwise, the ministry will lose its effectiveness, even disintegrate. When there was a sharp disagreement between Paul and Barnabas in Acts 15, they split up their ministry. They could no longer carry out the same ministry together. They split over personalities — sound familiar? In this case it was over John Mark who Paul said was unprofitable for the ministry; but who later became *"profitable to me for the ministry"* (2 Tim. 4:11). There was no judgment as to who was right or wrong. Due to this insurmountable contention, Paul went on his own ministry without Barnabas. Barnabas continued his ministry without Paul, and apparently headed off to evangelize Cyprus.

Certainly, Paul was clear about the One Body and the one fellowship; therefore, though they went their separate ways, it did not mean they were divided in the body and no longer had fellowship with each other. It just meant they now had two different ministries since they had two different methods of carrying out their ministry.

When it comes to the ekklesia, though the goal is the building up of the One Body; yet, ***there will always be factious elements*** while the building work is on-going — count on it! An ekklesia consists of a variety of people being called together for an assembly, it is normal that there will be people with differing, even opposing views. An assembly, by definition, is going to have people from different backgrounds, experiences, doctrinal views, and Christian practices.

Paul said in 1 Corinthians 11:19 there must be factions in the ekklesia; otherwise, those who are approved will not be manifested. The word "must" in the Greek means "necessary" or "there is need of" (Thayer's). So, Paul was saying when the ekklesia comes together, it is necessary there are factions so those who are "approved" will be manifested. We know that factions and divisions in the Body of Christ are negative — something condemned by the Lord.

Therefore, those *who are approved* must be referring to those who are not factious. Evidence that they are not factious can be seen by the fact they have no problem fellowshipping and blending in with everyone in the assembly no matter which faction shows up in the gathering.

Moreover, an approved person is one who can reconcile the factious and bring them together into the oneness of the fellowship

Conversely, in a ministry or a church, factions are not allowed. If a person speaks out with a contradictory opinion concerning the ways of a particular ministry, that person will no longer be welcomed — the person will be "fingered" and/or isolated, even asked to leave. Whereas, the ekklesia of the Lord is constantly increasing with diverse individuals who have differing and often opposing doctrinal understandings, practices, and a host of other conflicting views similar in today's world. The fact is the assembly does not represent any one view other than Jesus Christ being the foundation and cornerstone for the building up of the assembly. ***The person and work of Jesus Christ is the only constant in an assembly***, and that is what is portrayed by the participation of the bread and the cup.

The assembly is a safe and welcoming place for believers to share what the Lord has shown them and what they have experienced of Christ no matter how peculiar to some, different, or marginal to others. It is so safe that even if one is unattractive in anyway, that one is to be honored all the more. The level of love and acceptance in an assembly is incomparable. Simultaneously, it should be a place where promoting a view — with the intent of building up a faction to cause a division would not be welcomed.

Bread and Cup—Blessing or Judgment?

Since the ekklesia is not an organization, the risk of judgment is not from any hierarchy, "leadership," or from the majority, rather, it is directly from the Lord who is building up His assembly. There is judgment on those harming His assembly.

> Whoever, therefore, eats the bread or drinks the cup of the Lord in an unworthy manner will be guilty concerning the body and blood of the Lord. Let a person examine himself, then, and so eat of the bread and drink of the cup. For anyone who eats and drinks without discerning the body eats and drinks judgment on himself. That is why many of you are weak and ill, and some have died.
> (1 Cor. 11:27-30 ESV)

> Because there is one bread, we who are many are One Body, for we all partake of the one bread.
> (1 Cor. 10:17 ESV)

When a person comes into an assembly to partake of the Lord's bread and cup, that person is reminded Jesus died not just for the sins of the world but more so, to build up His ekklesia, His One Body.

The significance of the bread is not only its representation of the physical Body of Christ being broken for us, but in resurrection His Body now consists of many members. He now has a corporate body; therefore, the bread partaken in the assembly also represents the entire Body of Christ (1 Cor. 10). When believers partake of that bread, they are not just declaring they partake of Jesus alone, but they are partaking of His corporate body with all other members around the world.

Yes, believers are "feeding on Jesus Himself" (*"This is My body"* — John 6:53); but you are discerning you are doing so with all the members of His One Body. Everyone is needed. There is only one bread, One Body — all division is excluded. Factions and divisions are anathema in the Body of Christ.

Those in various factions may have started in such a state when they first came into the assembly — since they were called from where they were, but Paul warned them not to stay in a factious or divided state. Each member needs to *examine* himself/herself when partaking of the bread and the cup relative to the One Body . . . let me explain.

The word *"examine"* here is the same word in Greek as *"approved"* found in 1 Corinthians 11:19. Those who are *approved* are those who are not caught up in a faction, but rather they can fellowship with everyone. Many Christians have mistakenly believed the word *"examine"* here is related to whether one has any "unconfessed" sin or failures during the week; therefore, they're not worthy to partake of the Lord's Table. The Lord's death on the cross for the forgiveness of all sins has made every believer qualified to partake of Him at any time, all the time — in other words you don't eat and drink "unworthily" heaping up damnation to yourself because you're such a wretched sinner; rather, examining here is related to whether a person is discerning His One Body. This is not a time to confess your "sins" to the Lord — it is a time to DISCERN HIS One Body.

To be unworthy, is not discerning Jesus Christ died to have One Body. Participating in the bread and the cup declares all believers are ONE in Christ. Therefore, a person who practices division is not discerning the body and will come under God's judgment. Indeed, Christ died for your sins; now, examine your heart and see if you are standing apart from other believers!

This is a serious matter of which most Christians today are oblivious: being factious in the body brings in God's judgment. Sickness, weakness, even death can be a result of divisiveness. On the one hand, when believers partake of the bread and the cup in the assembly, a huge blessing awaits them because they enjoy all the Lord has done and completed in accomplishing God's eternal purpose for His One Body; but on the other hand, "the table" can be taken in judgment if an individual continues in his/her sectarian ways. Yes, believers in an assembly may have differing views and experiences. Such diversity is a beautiful mosaic showing off God's masterpiece of His ekklesia. What is not acceptable in the assembly is for someone to form a party or a faction based on differences where those in one faction will not or cannot fellowship with those not in their faction.

If you're going to "examine your own sinfulness" or "unconfessed sin" — cut to the chase and *"see if there be any divisions among you"* . . . that's what we should be confessing and repenting from such.

For example, let's say a believer really got blessed by speaking in an unknown tongue for prayer. Sharing that experience in the assembly would be a blessing; and may even encourage others to open up for such a blessing. However, it's totally another matter if the person then tries to build up a faction of believers who define themselves as those who have this blessing in order to cause a separation with those who do not. That "blessed group" may now have a goal of increasing their faction by having more believers join their ranks.

Their gospel will not just be Jesus Christ and Him alone, but Jesus Christ plus the need to speak in tongues as a "prayer language." Yes, something given by the Lord can divide the brethren if we do not "discern the Body." This can be seen in various doctrinal squabbles: Brethren who ascribe to a pre-tribulational rapture of God's people as the "Blessed Hope of His Coming" normally find themselves at odds with folks who maintain a post-tribulational position where God's people will not see the Glorified Son of Man until "after the tribulation of those days" (Matt. 24:31).

Each member in the assembly has the freedom to share their doctrinal conviction to the glory of God . . . but building a faction around that doctrine would be detrimental to His Body, His ekklesia. This can be applied to all kinds of various teachings and practices found in the Bible where each of these items can be a help to someone; yet, not necessarily to others. This kind of diversity can either manifest genuine oneness in the body or it can be used for divisiveness, bringing in God's judgment. Confusion enters the assembly when factions evolve around, quite frankly, what appears to be the soundest of teachings.

As soon as someone says that so-and-so is "into OSAS" (i.e., "once saved always saved"), you can write 'um off; they're in error or those same OSAS look upon those who can "lose their salvation" as a "works-oriented" group building on sand — they need to get clear, otherwise we can't have "fellowship" with them. The "disputes" are endless. Again, only in the ekklesia are BOTH opinions welcome — Christ is our salvation; the doctrine of OSAS or losing one's salvation never saved us in the first place!

It is through participating in the Lord's Table when the whole assembly of believers comes together that we should examine ourselves and discern His One Body. If we repent from any divisiveness and become one to manifest God's ekklesia — then we will be "worthy" to participate in the bread and cup.

The Gifts of the Spirit Operating in the One Body

A beautiful picture of the Lord's Body is seen in 1 Corinthians 12 and 14. All members have different gifts — each has the freedom to function according to their gift. The totality of what is expressed is not any specific gift or ministry, but the One Body of Christ. What an awesome description of the Body of Christ in action. What we are witnessing is the *manifestation* of the ekklesia or assembly.

Believers are called together as an assembly. While some may be in a faction; they come into an assembly to be one by serving and loving one another. The churches representing various ministries are the basis of these various factions, but saints in these various churches need to know and experience ekklesia . . . not forming another defined group as another church, but purpose to become one and practice that oneness as the Lord's assembly. All believers in the various churches are being "called out" to be the Lord's assembly — breaking bread from house to house: The unique place where believers from various factions can come together.

Compelled to Be in Christ Alone

> For as the body is one and has many members, but all the members of that One Body, being many, are One Body, so also [is] Christ. For by one Spirit we were all baptized into One Body — whether Jews or Greeks, whether slaves or free — and have all been made to drink into one Spirit.
>
> (1 Cor. 12:12-13)

All the various people starting out from various backgrounds and divided in various factions are now all immersed (baptized) into Christ. Positionally, they are in Christ, they *are* One Body. Although they are still individual members with their own individual characteristics; they are One

Body in Christ. They are not uniformly the same, but they are all drinking of one Spirit. This is the assembly: they are called out of various factions, whether natural or secular (slaves or free), or ethnic or religious (Jews and Greeks), to become One Body in Christ.

Though such distinctions are obvious; yet, instead of forming factions, they are now using their distinctiveness to serve one another — they refuse to be separated. Not everyone has the same gift; therefore, Paul used the metaphor of the human body in saying not all are eyes or ears. The One Body needs the eyes, the ears, the mouth, the feet, every part of the One Body (1 Cor. 12:14-27). The only way this can happen is when distinct believers recognize the reality they are all immersed in Christ — together they drink of the SAME Spirit. Jesus Christ is the only way; He is the only way whereby the building up of the One Body can take place.

Christians who have not witnessed or participated in the Lord's ekklesia as described in these chapters will be concerned with such diversity and openness for anyone to speak — this "thing" will "get out of control!" There will be "wrong" teachings and believers in these assemblies can be led astray by wolves which come in "unawares."

Many who are familiar with the practice of going to church to listen to a sermon from a minister or preacher have accepted them to be trained in the Bible; therefore, there's a greater level of "trust." Since they are professionals, most of the Christians who attend their respective churches will automatically trust in what is being taught from the pulpit. Tragically, such trust can put the congregant at risk; since in the main, they have given up their discernment whether or not the preaching or teaching is from the Lord and according to Scriptures. Far too often, disappointment due to moral failure, or idiosyncrasies among the "leadership," or strident disputes among the congregants splits the "church" and off we go again.

In the Lord's ekklesia (assembly) in which there is sharing from disparate believers, the listeners are encouraged to exercise discernment in considering each of those sharing — is it beneficial to them and according to Scripture (1 Cor. 14:29). Listeners will not automatically accept what is spoken without considering the matter before the Lord and searching the Scriptures "whether these things be so."

Additionally, since no one person dominates the speaking over the course of an assembly gathering, even if a few do speak something not according to Scripture, their speaking is only for a short period. There is not enough time for any unscriptural teaching to overshadow the assembly. Instead of causing damage, questionable utterances will generate more fellowship from others that may want to pivot from any error to the truth. Since no one is the "authority" with the final interpretation or understanding, the Lord becomes the Head of the assembly. Everyone will have to look to the Lord Himself as the Head of the Body instead of to any man.

When believers in the assembly recognize there are contrary views relative to the various doctrines and practices, then the assembly, instead of breaking down in argumentation, will focus on Jesus Christ alone. They will experience Jesus as truly the only unifying factor in the Body. Believers will learn to promote anything other than Jesus will cause unnecessary issues in the assembly. Over time, believers will come to understand the ekklesia is not built upon any extraneous doctrinal view, but upon Jesus Christ alone. Jesus Christ alone is uplifted. He, together with the Father and the Holy Spirit, is the only one worthy of the assembly's undivided attention, focus, and praise.

Hosting the Lord's Ekklesia

> Gaius, my host and host of the whole assembly, greets you. Erastus, the treasurer of the city, greets you, as does Quartus, the brother.
>
> (Rom. 16:23 HNV)
>
> The assemblies of Asia greet you. Aquila and Priscilla greet you much in the Lord, together with the assembly that is in their house.
>
> (1 Cor. 16:19 HNV)
>
> Greet the brothers who are in Laodicea, and Nymphas, and the assembly that is in his house.
>
> (Col. 4:15 HNV)
>
> But Saul ravaged the assembly, entering into the houses one after another, and dragging off both men and women delivered them up to prison.
>
> (Acts 8:3 DBY)

Over the last few centuries, though ministries have flourished and churches have multiplied, where is the Lord's ekklesia, the assembly? How much are believers, though having the same faith, fellowshipping together in their daily living without letting church membership or non-membership become a barrier? Where is the manifestation of the assembly according to Scripture? The fact is the Lord's ekklesia has been neglected; even deprecated.

Not only is it rare today to participate in an assembly, the very meaning and essentialness of ekklesia has been, in the main, buried and lost. That is why there is a need to RESET — back to what God originally intended in building up, through the death and resurrection of Jesus Christ, the manifestation of His Assembly.

In the beginning of Acts, the ekklesia was the goal for the apostles' ministry. The formation of the ekklesia went into immediate action after the day of Pentecost. What they were practicing was described in 1 Corinthians Chapters 11-14. They were having meals together as the Lord's ekklesia from house to house.

When Saul (before his conversion to Paul) was persecuting the ekklesia (assembly), he went from house to house to affect his persecution. The only way to devastate the assembly was to go to all the homes of believers where ekklesia was taking place (Acts 8:3). The gathering place of the ekklesia was in the homes of believers. The Lord called out people to assemble in homes to have meals, fellowship, and to build up one another in love.

Read the entire New Testament and you will find the only location mentioned for the Lord's ekklesia was in someone's home. Ministers, such as the apostles, may use different venues for their ministry: at the temple, in a public square or open market, in a school, in an upper room, in a rented house or apartment. The only spot where an actual ekklesia (assembly) was cited was in a home, someone's living space. The so-called "primitive" model of the "church" was, and should be today, the "standard model" for ekklesia — i.e., the home.

It is in the informal, unreligious, family atmosphere of a home the assembly of the Lord is associated. It is in a home where folks gather for meals, relaxation, entertainment, friends, and family — this is where the assembly is housed. This shows the normality and humanity which is intertwined with the heavenly, spiritual, yet pragmatic, where the ekklesia of the Lord flourishes.

Today, a minister who preaches the gospel or teaches the Bible would prefer a large audience. Yet, there were many instances during the preaching of Jesus and the apostles where they ministered to just one person, such as the woman at the well in John 4, or Paul and Silas leading the jailer to salvation in Acts 16, where ministry was very intimate. Of course, there were also instances where Jesus spoke to a large crowd such as in Luke 8 or when the apostles spoke to thousands in the temple in Acts 2. The point is ministries can be carried out to thousands or to only one person.

Although a secular ekklesia often took place in a public arena such as the one in Acts 19, the Lord's ekklesia (assembly) in the New Testament was found only in homes. This is not to say ekklesia cannot take place in other venues other than in a home, but there is no record in the New Testament other than in homes so designated where ekklesia took place.

Based on the descriptions of the assembly given in 1 Corinthians 11-14, where believers had meals together and where they manifested their God-given gifts, the ideal location was, again, in a home. The narrative was clearly a gathering of more than two or three people. At the same time, since everyone was expected to participate and share their testimonies or insights of Jesus Christ, the number of people assembled could not have been too large.

A home automatically limits the number of people assembled; therefore, allowing everyone to have opportunity to participate and contribute is the norm. If there are more people than the number that can fit into one house, then the assembly would spread to another home. This was the case with the ekklesia in Jerusalem where thousands of believers ate their meals and assembled from house to house, in every home. Additionally, unlike a public place, the homes of believers are normally available for assembly with the environment relatively freed from distractions — even children who are normally found in a home can be included in such an ekklesia.

It is natural to have ekklesia in a neutral location such as a home rather than in a church (building) because a church usually belongs to an organization with a specific ministry. Believers that have an issue with a certain church will have a difficult time going to that church to practice ekklesia without a certain amount of reluctance and discomfort.

For example, it would be difficult for a typical Protestant believer to go into a Catholic church to practice 1 Corinthians 11-14. Likewise, it would be challenging for a Catholic believer to enter a Pentecostal church. However, a home is neutral and relaxing. It does not represent any religious organization; Therefore, unthreatening for those with religious sensibilities which include unbelievers who may be averse to going into any church at all.

Paul wrote the epistles to the Romans from Corinth. While in Corinth, he was hosted by Gaius who was also the host of the assembly in Corinth. Gaius not only gave hospitality to Paul, he equally opened his home for the saints to assemble as the Lord's ekklesia. Paul used the word "host" to describe the relationship between the assembly and Gaius.

The Greek word for "host" is *xenos*. This word literally means a foreigner or stranger (Thayer's). In fact, this word was used 14 times in the New Testament. In the King James Version, this word was translated 13 times as either "stranger" or "strange." Only one time, in this verse, was this word translated "host." When Gaius hosted the ekklesia, he welcomed strangers into his house. It is clearly consistent with the definition of ekklesia: God is calling out His people from all directions and diversity; therefore, a believer opening his/her home to have the Lord's ekklesia is going to expect strangers. There will be people in his house who he will not know. They may have views and understandings which are quite different from his.

When a person hosts the ekklesia, he or she gives up the right to exclude believers due to different teachings, practices or political views; and welcomes all those who God has received — even if they are strangers. To have an ekklesia in your house, or to be a host of the assembly, means it is a gathering of "strangers."

Certainly, it does not mean that literally everyone coming to Gaius' house were all strangers who didn't know each other. What it does indicate is Gaius as a host was expecting strangers to show up — they were all welcomed. What it also indicates is Gaius did not view the gathering at his house to be his "church" in the sense he was building up a defined group of regular attendees under his pastoral supervision. Rather, he merely opened his house to host, to be used by the Lord and His saints allowing all those who the Lord was calling to assemble in his house.

Gaius recognized it was the Lord's ekklesia. He was simply letting the Lord and the called-out saints use it for assembly. Finally, what it also means is there is only one class of people; they are all considered to be "strangers." No one has any seniority over another. Other than the person and work of Jesus Christ, there is no specifically defined doctrine or practice based on "insiders" or those considered to be "family." No, everyone is a stranger in the sense everyone has equal opportunity to speak forth what the Lord has given them without permission from an insider. Everyone is on the same level since everyone has the same status as a "stranger." Yet, over the course of an ekklesia, all strangers experience the real family of the Lord, the commonwealth of Israel, the One Body of Christ, and all the other wonderful descriptions which manifest various aspects of ekklesia, the assembly.

In an ekklesia, it is normal and expected to have strangers. Even when strangers are there for the first time, they are in an atmosphere where they have the complete freedom to share their realization and experiences of Christ. No doubt there will be some in the assembly who are more experienced in the way of assembly. They will manifest themselves as "approved" since they can fellowship freely with everyone, draw out the gifts of strangers, and bring people who are factious together.

The matter of hosting is a critical point. It shows: Gaius was not building another defined group of people in his home. He was not trying to turn his house into another church. He was not trying to create a following. He simply opened his home to be the place of the Lord's assembly where 1 Corinthians 11:17 to 14 could take place.

This is not what most Christians commonly consider to be a "house church." If a house gathering has the same people together month after month and year after year, it would not qualify as an assembly as described in 1 Corinthians. Instead, it would just be another category of church such as Baptist, Pentecostal, Catholic, or a House Church. It would be someone's house church just as all the other churches belong to some ministers/pastors. If the gathering in a house results in weeding out believers over time who do not conform to the majority, until those gathering become homogeneous in some way, then that home gathering is not the Lord's ekklesia. It doesn't mean they are not serving the Lord or providing benefits to believers in the group, but it just means that in nature they are no different than all the other churches as ministries big or small.

Blessings and Challenges of Being a Host

What a privilege it must be for the Lord's ekklesia to be in someone's home! God's eternal purpose is being fulfilled right in a home, someone's dwelling. The psalmist in Psalm 8 pondered: *"When I considered the heavens . . . what is man that You would be mindful of him and visit him. ...*" Humans seem so insignificant in the midst of the universe; yet, the God of the universe has chosen to join Himself and live in such lowly human beings.

All believers should have this reality, this unfathomable wonder, at the time they received the faith of Jesus Christ. Similarly, what is a house, a home of a believer? Compared to the fancy and expensive buildings housing the many ministries, how insignificant is a home, a small house or apartment! Compared to the opulence of Solomon's temple, a home for the Lord's ekklesia seems so trivial: people sharing a meal, being who they are in Christ, loving one another, speaking, and unveiling the wonder and mystery of Jesus Christ.

Nevertheless, it is the location of God's eternal purpose. His eternal purpose is being fulfilled and God is being manifested in their midst. This is so real and convincing that unbelievers become instant worshippers of the God of the universe. Just as believers should surrender their hearts to God, for Him to dwell and have His way in their midst, believers should surrender their homes to God for a place of ekklesia. In a way, a person's home is really the fortress of one's life.

A home is someone's protected place, a place of privacy; therefore, how can believers speak of surrendering their heart without surrendering their home for the Lord to use? Surrendering a heart is unseen, whereas, surrendering a home is practical and observable. God needs both the heart and the home of believers for His eternal purpose to be established and manifested on earth.

In the Old Testament the tabernacle and the temple were types foreshadowing the ekklesia in the New Testament. The ark of the testimony in the Old Testament — a type of Jesus Christ being the testimony of God — was to be housed first in the tabernacle and then in the temple. Consider the following to show the blessings of housing or being a host to the ark of the testimony of God.

> So David would not move the ark of the LORD with him into the City of David; but David took it aside into the house of Obed-Edom the Gittite. The ark of the LORD remained in the house of Obed-Edom the Gittite three months. And the LORD blessed Obed-Edom and all his household. Now it was told King David, saying, "The LORD has blessed the house of Obed-Edom and all

> that [belongs] to him, because of the ark of God." So David went and brought up the ark of God from the house of Obed-Edom to the City of David with gladness.
>
> (2 Sam. 6:10-12)

At one point in the journey of the ark, King David placed the ark in the house of Obed-Edom the Gittite. One can say Obed-Edom's house became the tabernacle or the temple. The ark of the testimony, the glory of God, was there at his house, and his household was blessed. *"The Lord blessed the house of Obed-Edom and all that belongs to him."* His entire household was blessed due to the ark being there. His home became the "dwelling place" — the tabernacle of God.

What is also of interest is Obed-Edom was a descendent of Esau whom, according to Romans 9:13, God hated. Additionally, he is from the city of Gath which is the same city from where Goliath hailed. So, Obed-Edom's lineage was hated by God; and he was from a city that was the birthplace of the most notorious mocker of God's people.

Yet, Obed-Edom (lit. meaning "the servant of Edom") housed, hosted, the ark of God. In New Testament terms, his house was a place of the Lord's ekklesia where Christ as the testimony of God is found. This story shows anyone, even the least with a most dreadful background, can be a host of an ekklesia. Additionally, it was an abundant blessing to be such a host. The entire household was blessed. Likewise, hosting the ekklesia today is a real blessing. The Holy Spirit's anointing, the freshness of the revelation and experience of Jesus Christ; indeed, all the blessings related to eternal life are upon a house of ekklesia, a house for the assembly of the Lord. Of course, not the physical house, but the household, all the folks within that home are related to this household are considered in the environment of blessing.

It certainly is a blessing for a family to host an ekklesia. However, to host such an assembly of the Lord is not naturally easy. Those who are willing to open their home to be a host will need a certain amount of maturity of the indwelling life of Christ, a solid foundation of the truth, and a heart to serve in humility — willing to become as nothing.

As described in 1 Corinthians 11, the host will need to be an "approved" person who is not in a faction. He or she, husband and wife, could form a team such as Priscilla and Aquila. They will have to be able to receive, accept, and fellowship with all kinds of believers. They'll be able to cross all factious barriers. If a host is factious in any way, they will automatically side with various factions and have conflict with other factions who gather with them. If this is the case, the ekklesia will not be able to continue in their home because, over time, those whom they have conflict with will not feel welcome to function in their home. When that happens, then the gathering in such a home will no longer be an ekklesia of the Lord. At best, it will become a ministry with a point of view to help other believers or unbelievers. There is nothing wrong with that per se, it's just not an ekklesia.

A host must have an attitude and spirit of a servant, a slave. If a host seeks self-glory, recognition, or attempts to exert control over a group of believers, they will be disappointed. Eventually, they will not be able to host any more. Rather, they need to be hospitable, ready to be a servant in food preparation or housekeeping.

Although all believers meeting at the host's home should certainly contribute to all the practical areas in sustaining the ekklesia; notwithstanding, the host might be left "holding the bag" in the area of clean up, food preparation, furniture deterioration, misplaced items, and such things are to be expected when "strangers" have the freedom to assemble in their house. Yet, for what is a home for believers if not for God's house? What a privilege that God can build up His glorious ekklesia in the modesty of every believer's home.

The Scriptures seem to indicate that homes hosting the Lord's ekklesia are a regular place of assembly. Paul could say the ekklesia at so and so person's house — that is why Peter knew where to go after getting out of prison (Acts 12:12). So, a stable and permanent home where the Lord's ekklesia is hosted is preferred over moving the location or the assembly from house to house. However, with today's ease of communication and travel from one house to the next, it may work just as well to move a location for gathering from house to house. The objective is people know where to go when they want to go to the Lord's assembly.

Nevertheless, what a freedom and release from a heavy burden it is when one does not have to consider hosting an assembly means one must build and maintain a following or grow and sustain a defined group of believers.

It is challenging to build, maintain and grow a group of people to become a "church." Even with resources of funding and personnel, today's churches in the West are still losing membership. When the thought is trying to do the same in one's home, few can bear such a burden. If institutional churches cannot hold on to members, over the long run, it will be more challenging for house churches.

Truly, the Lord's ekklesia (assembly) is His. It does not belong to any person or group. No one can claim ownership or be the head of the Lord's assembly. The best a follower of Christ can do is become an "approved" member of the assembly, be a peace maker, participate, receive the wealth of Christian experience from other members, or be an example by allowing the Lord to use them for the building up of God's ekklesia.

The Lord needs to raise more believers with this vision and motivate them to open their homes to host an ekklesia. It seems when there is persecution, such as what happened in China during the Cultural Revolution, believers were forced to meet in homes. They spontaneously opened their homes to host the Lord's ekklesia without considering denominational affiliation. Christians in the West have the freedom and luxury of going to "the church of their choice"; therefore, it's easy to stay segregated into various sects or ministries. Let's pray that the Lord will bring back ekklesia in the homes among more followers of Jesus without the need of persecution. Let's be those with a vision of the ekklesia and do it willingly.

Let's Reset to One!

In a locality or a region, as the Lord spreads His ekklesia through "meeting and greeting" one another, there will be more homes becoming host to an assembly. Different individuals can participate during each day of the week. Multiple gatherings can take place simultaneously during weekends.

Believers in a given area will have an increasing number of choices to participate in as an ekklesia in various home environments. The followers of Jesus can follow the Spirit's leading, or based on how convenient it is, decide which home to go to for an assembly. They would have the freedom to go to multiple homes in any given week. Perhaps half the participants in any one home have the same people attending from the previous week. The other half are those who have never been there before. Nevertheless, everyone starts as "strangers" with some in factions, but over the course of the assembly, they grow into unity; thus, oneness is manifested.

More unbelievers are being added — such as should be saved. In this way, the Spirit has the freedom to gather exactly the right combination of people in any given home hosting ekklesia throughout the entire week. This was the situation in Acts 2 when believers gathered daily from house to house, breaking bread, fellowshipping, having favor with all the people around them. In such oneness people daily came to Jesus for salvation — God was glorified!

This is the exact opposite of how Christians have been taught to stay put in one place; they need to be committed to one church or one group of Christians. The problem with that understanding is simple: Where in Scripture do we find that?

Yes, believers should be committed to building up an ekklesia, but the ekklesia is manifested and spreads from house to house. Should Christians then just commit themselves to going to the same house if there are multiple homes to choose from in an area? If they do, they will no longer follow Paul's command to go greet. If they stay with the same group of people year after year, then a distinct identity will be formed other than simply being members of Messiah's Body, they would become a faction. The fact is after centuries of following the advice to commit to a church; overall, Christians are still lacking in maturity — there is now more divisiveness than ever.

Let's follow this more Scriptural pattern for the building up of the ekklesia: Go and greet, host an ekklesia, expect strangers and factions to come together, then watch the transformation into the manifestation of the oneness of His Body for God's glory and the demise of His enemy, Satan. This is the new paradigm; yet, this was the way it was in the New Testament. It is time to RESET TO ONE!

7.
Paradigm Shift: "Church" to Ekklesia

How Christians understand and practice "church" today is very different from the practice of the Lord's ekklesia in the New Testament. Although most Bible teachers may find this a radical shift compared to how Christians understand "church," it is as old as what is described in the New Testament.

New Testament Ministers Building Up One Ekklesia

In the days of the New Testament, there were multiple independent gifted ministers such as Paul, Peter, and Apollos. We also know they may have had different methods, approaches and burdens as to how, where, and to whom they preached Jesus Christ as the gospel (Gal. 2:7). Nevertheless, it is indisputable their ultimate objective was to build up the one assembly, the Body of Christ. Their goal was not to build their own group, sect or church, but for believers to be united in one fellowship. Their ministries, though different, were for all believers practically meeting in various localities to be One Body in Christ, to be in one ekklesia (assembly). This is what we find among the Corinthian believers.

> God [is] faithful, by whom you were called into the fellowship of His Son, Jesus Christ our Lord.
>
> (1 Cor. 1:9)
>
> Who then is Paul, and who [is] Apollos, but ministers through whom you believed, as the Lord gave to each one? I planted, Apollos watered, but God gave the increase. So then neither he who plants is anything, nor he who waters, but God who gives the increase. Now he who plants and he who waters are one, and each one will receive his own reward according to his own labor.

> For we are God's fellow workers; you are God's field, [you are] God's building.
>
> (1 Cor. 3:5-9)
>
> Therefore let no one boast in men. For all things are yours: whether Paul or Apollos or Cephas, or the world or life or death, or things present or things to come — all are yours [the assembly].
>
> (1 Cor. 3:21-22)

Paul was the first apostle who went to Corinth to preach the gospel to the Corinthians (Acts 18). Through his preaching and teaching, many people believed, including both Jews and those from among the nations (aka, Gentiles). Therefore, it can be said the assembly in Corinth was planted by Paul.

Despite this, he did not consider Corinth, which included all believers who came to faith in Jesus Christ through him, to be his. He left it open for other ministers to come to the assembly he planted to minister to every saint in Corinth. Those who came to minister were not just brethren who supported and extended his ministry, such as Timothy, Titus and Silas; rather, they were ministers who were independent from him with burdens and methods which in all probability were different from his. In fact, there were teachers who taught in Corinth things which were downright distracting from the gospel preached by Paul.

By neither claiming any ownership nor establishing any safe-guard to keep the assembly in Corinth under his ministry, the Corinthians had full freedom to receive all sorts of diverse ministers to the point where they formed divisions based on preferences for Paul, Peter (Cephas), and Apollos. Moreover, they received some who came and preached a different Jesus, a different gospel with a different spirit (2 Cor. 11:4). Regarding such, Paul warned the Corinthian Christians these were false apostles and deceitful workers; nevertheless, it showcases the open nature of the Lord's assembly. In fact, regarding these individuals who were bringing believers back to keep the laws of the Old Covenant, there was no indication Paul asked the assembly to remove these kinds of people.

Now, let's just consider the other two *genuine* workers who were named: Apollos and Peter. Apollos was one who needed to be taught by Paul's disciples, Priscilla and Aquila, the way of God more accurately (Acts 18:26).

Thereafter, Apollos went to Corinth and ministered to the assembly in Corinth. Although his teaching was inferior to Paul's (Acts 19:1-6), he had complete freedom to minister in the ekklesia in Corinth.

Apollos was a minister not quite up to the standard in revelation of the planting apostle; yet, he had the full liberty to speak and teach all believers in the Corinthian assembly. Since Apollos worked independently from Paul, he was not under Paul's direction (1 Cor. 16:12); nevertheless, Paul considered him a co-worker, working together in unity for the building up of the assembly (1 Cor. 3:6-9).

Let's consider Peter (Cephas). Certainly, he was one of the twelve disciples and the first one who preached the gospel on the day of Pentecost where 3,000 souls were baptized. Later, he was the first to bring the gospel to a Gentile household, the house of Cornelius (Acts 10). He must have had a powerful reputation among all Christians in those days, both Jews and Gentiles. It is possible that the approach of his ministry was more favorable to Jews since his mission was for the Jews (Gal 2:7-8).

Although there is no record Peter visited Corinth; nevertheless, he had enough influence among believers to generate a division around himself. While Paul was in Corinth, he wrote a letter to the Galatians. In that letter, he spoke of how he rebuked Peter openly for not walking according to the truth of the Gospel when Peter withdrew from eating with the Gentiles for fear of Jewish believers who came from James in Jerusalem.

Indeed, if Paul did not disparage Peter to the Corinthians, he could have at least spoken a word of warning concerning Peter's hypocrisy. The fact the Corinthians felt the freedom to form a party around Peter demonstrates Paul did not criticize Peter to the Corinthians.

These facts illustrate there was no such concept among the early apostles wherein anyone of them would purposefully gather members of a local assembly around themselves; this was most notable in Paul's case as a "planting apostle." It seems he purposefully delimited himself to this task and gave the task of watering and/or care to other ministers . . . and concluded that "God made it grow!"

Although Paul was more advanced in revelation concerning Jesus Christ than Apollos, and he was more steadfast than Peter in regard to the truth, Paul did not blame either Apollos or Peter for causing divisions among the assembly he founded in Corinth. Rather, he blamed the Corinthians for being babies in Christ and being fleshly like unbelievers (1 Cor. 3:1).

Paul told them all the ministers are nothing. They were merely servants to serve the faithful, the assembly (1 Cor. 3:22). They worked together in planting and watering so that they, the assembly, would grow to become God's building. These ministries, of course, did not include false and deceitful ministers mentioned in 2 Corinthians 11 who preached another gospel.

The point that needs to be emphasized is the openness of the assembly and the diversity of ministries that were active among the saints within the assembly. No matter how independent from each other the ministers were and how different their approaches to carry out their individual missions, they all focused on the building up of one assembly in a locality.

Their view was straightforward: All believers are in the same unique assembly (ekklesia). The ministers may have rented their own individual places for ministry such as Paul did in Ephesus and in Rome, but all members of the assembly in Corinth gathered in one place as His One Body (1 Cor. 14:23). This fact is indisputable with the revelation of this manifestation of His One Body abundantly clear in Scripture.

The above scenario has been illustrated with a few diagrams to aid our understanding. The first diagram shows the situation in Corinth where three gifted ministers were named. They were for the building up of one fellowship in Jesus Christ among all believers in the one assembly. This diagram shows the proper relationship of the assembly based on 1 Corinthians:

The large circle – the one assembly (ekklesia) with the constituents consisting of all believers in a locality.

The open dots – the gifted ministers such as Paul, Apollos and Peter.

The solid dots – all the believers.

The dotted lines – the ministry of planting and watering in service to believers that they will grow.

The solid lines – The one fellowship taking place between all the believers.

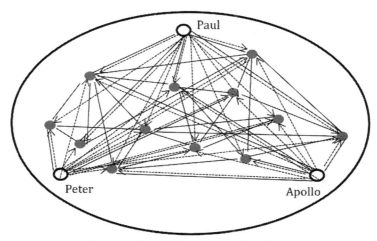

Figure 1- One Ekklesia, one fellowship

Fleshly Believers dividing the Body

> Now I plead with you, brethren, by the name of our Lord Jesus Christ, that you all speak the same thing, and [that] there be no divisions among you, but [that] you be perfectly joined together in the same mind and in the same judgment. ... Now I say this, that each of you says, "I am of Paul," or "I am of Apollos," or "I am of Cephas," or "I am of Christ."
>
> (1 Cor. 1:10, 12)
>
> For you are still of the flesh. For while there is jealousy and strife among you, are you not of the flesh and behaving only in a human way? For when one says, "I follow Paul," and another, "I follow Apollos," are you not being merely human?
>
> (1 Cor. 3:3-4 ESV)

Although these gifted ministers were for the building up of the One Body of Christ, their Corinthian benefactors started forming groups around ministry preferences. They were dividing and contending as to who was a better minister. They started defining themselves according to the minister from whom they received the most help. In application, Christians today not only group themselves around ministers, but also group themselves around the teachings of ministers they promote. Paul didn't blame Apollos or Peter for causing this division; rather, he blamed the baby Corinthian believers for being fleshly, according to their base human nature.

Some may have considered themselves to be more spiritual; therefore, saying they were of "Christ." This sounds superior and Scriptural, but Paul included them among the divisive and contentious. It is very possible to espouse "sound doctrine" — even the doctrine concerning being "of Christ" — yet, they can become divisive. This happens when various individuals in a group define themselves as those who are "of Christ" in a way whereby they separate themselves from those who are of Paul and Apollos.

There is nothing wrong with being "of Christ." It is certainly in accordance with God's purpose. However, if a group so self-defined excludes and divides from those who likewise are centered around another minister, then the "of Christ" group is also divisive. The group that is "of Christ" can be more divisive, because they are blinded by their spirituality and superiority in being those who are "of Christ."

Today, there are groups which are for the oneness of the Body; however, they have become extremely divisive and sectarian based on this same principle.

If a group of believers come together and define themselves to be for the oneness of His Body in a way of excluding or dividing themselves from those who are not "for oneness," then this "oneness" group is equally divisive, and more so, since they can be blinded due to the correctness of their position.

In the next diagram the Corinthian believers started grouping themselves in divisions based upon their preferred ministers.

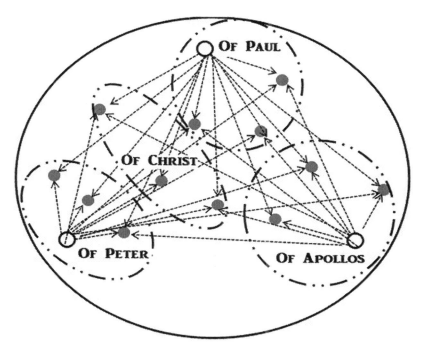

Figure 2- Corinth's Ministry Preferences

Today's Ministers Building Their Own Ministries

Here we are 2,000 years later. Today's ministers (be they pastors, evangelists, or designated leaders of various Christian organizations) are mostly building their own ministries normally expressed in the form of a "church."

Earlier we pointed out that churches traditionally find themselves within the confines of a ministry: Catholic, Lutheran, Baptist, Pentecostal, etc. Each church expresses the doctrines and practices of a specific minister or ministry. Where is the ekklesia God desires? Where is the assembly the Lord is building? She has faded into obscurity. It is easy to simply say the assembly can only be found in a "spiritual realm" or she will be manifested at the second advent of Jesus Christ.

To simply push the building of the assembly into a futuristic, unseen realm or into an ultimate prophetic fulfillment is to ignore, bypass, the Lord's prayer in John 17 which demands the world may believe NOW. Additionally, in the early assemblies, during the New Testament period, they were loving one another in oneness so much so unbelievers fell down to worship God because God was manifested in their midst (1 Cor. 14:24-25).

Today, almost every minister/pastor evaluates and measures their effectiveness or success based on numbers — who has the largest group. Even a home church would consider their success in a similar way. If not a church, then at least the number of followers they can count under their influence.

Therefore, the more ministers/pastors there are, the more the number of defined groups found among God's people. No wonder there is an explosion of segregated Christian groups and churches. According to the World Christian Encyclopedia, there are now over 33,000 denominational churches in the world and still increasing[11]. Building a defined group of believers, large or small, has become the goal of just about every minister/pastor. As soon as someone gifted is called and inspired to serve as a pastor, another group can be expected to form.

Even among the so-called parachurch groups who do not have their own church, such as Intervarsity, Navigators, YWAM, etc., their mission typically does not include the building up of oneness among believers as the ekklesia. Mostly, they fulfill their mission to preach the gospel, to teach the Bible, to help society with social missions. Then, they leave it up to the people who are helped by them to then find the "church of their choice."

Throughout history gifted ministers have replicated more ministers. In the New Testament, Barnabas brought Paul into the ministry. They both started out in the same ministry. Eventually, they split into two separate ministries. It is natural to have a multiplication of ministries as more ministers are being trained and inspired.

Here what's problematic in today's primary objective of service — more ministers mean more divisions; since, generally, all ministers today grade their success by the size of the group they can muster. Does that mean division is God's fault since He inspires and motivates people to serve Him, which in turn causes more divisions? Not at all. Rather, it is Satan's scheme to prevent gifted ministers from seeing and building up the Lord's ekklesia.

In a way, some have argued Satan cannot stop people from salvation since those who are chosen and predestinated will be saved. However, salvation alone does not end the reign of God's enemy on earth. Today, there are a number of nations on earth where more than 50% of the population would claim they believe in Jesus Christ, but the effect on society is minimal. Satan continues to corrupt and destroy humanity in those nations just as in "non-Christian" countries.

---

11   http://www.philvaz.com/apologetics/a106.htm

The reason is it is the Lord's ekklesia who defeats the gates of Hades, the Satanic kingdom. It is the oneness of believers that would cause the world to believe. It is the built-up assembly who will bring the Lord back for His prepared bride to end this age (Rev. 21:2). It is the new man with the full armor of God who stands against all the stratagems of the devil.

Certainly, every person who comes to Jesus Christ in faith is a defeat for Satan, but from a strategic point of view, as long as Satan can keep believers from building up the one fellowship, the ekklesia, he is still in charge, he wins on earth. Chapter 9 of this book will delve into Satanic tactics and his full-time job focusing on dividing the Body of Christ.

This diagram illustrates today's divided Christian environment. Indeed, most of the churches today have specific ministers directing them; likewise, there are groups who have rejected the traditional institutional church format to become "house churches" or "organic churches" to practice the priesthood of all believers creating a relational community.

Notwithstanding, if these house churches function as another defined group in a sea of segregated groups, then in principle, they would be like those in 1 Corinthians who say they are "of Christ." Now, there are a proliferation of defined groups of Christians large and small, but the one ekklesia, the Lord's assembly, has mostly disappeared from the understanding and consciousness of believers.

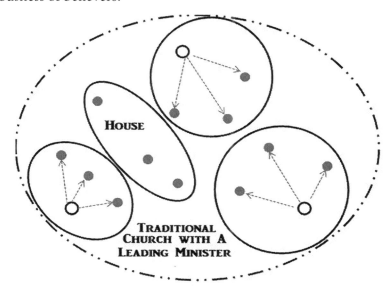

Figure 3- Traditional Churches and House Churches

8.

GREETING—VITAL FOR SPREADING EKKLESIA

Solving the Most Divisive Problem: Jews and Gentiles

> For He Himself is our peace, who has made both one, and has broken down the middle wall of separation, having abolished in His flesh the enmity, [that is], the law of commandments [contained] in ordinances, so as to create in Himself one new man [from] the two, [thus] making peace, and that He might reconcile them both to God in One Body through the cross, thereby putting to death the enmity.
>
> (Eph. 2:14-16)

It is a fact Christians today are splintered and divided into a multitude of pieces. The general sentiment is sectarianism will continue with not much hope for reversal anytime soon. Unity among God's people is a mere dream of utopia. Therefore, it is crucial to consider from the Bible whether unity can indeed be realized among believers while they are still living in this world.

It is important to realize the most divided groups of people throughout ages are between the Jews and the Gentiles (aka "the nations" or *"ethnos"*). It was a God created division. God literally gave laws to keep these two peoples separated. Therefore, hatred developed between these two groups. This division and enmity could not be reconciled until the cross of Jesus Christ. He terminated the enmity (hatred) created by the ordinances given by God in keeping these two peoples partitioned in order that He could create in Himself One New Man, the Body of Christ. It is in the Lord's ekklesia where there is now peace between these two estranged enemies.

Although the enmity separating Jews and Gentiles had been abolished, yet the centuries' divide between these peoples persisted in their subjective experiences and dispositions, so great was this deep animosity.

One of the main points of division was diet. According to God's law, the Jewish people cannot eat unclean (non-kosher) food eaten among the nations. That law guarantees Jews and Gentiles cannot have meals together. They literally must eat separately. One of the most common social interactions of eating together cannot be contemplated between these two peoples. In other words, these two peoples are divided down to the basic social fabric of community.

In preparing Peter to preach the gospel to the Gentiles — joining together Jew and Gentile — God came to Peter three times while he was in a trance. Peter saw a sheet coming down from heaven with all sorts of unclean animals and creeping things. God unequivocally told Peter to kill and eat these unclean animals.

Peter said "no" to God three times (Acts 10:14). He would not partake of anything unclean even though God explicitly said He cleaned them. This vision was a precursor letting Peter know he was not only going to preach the gospel and bring those from among the nations into the kingdom of God, but he would simultaneously dine at table with them. Specifically, he would now need to eat what the Gentiles eat without distinction and separation. They would now interact and become one with those considered unclean, including eating together.

However, the partition between the Jews and Gentiles was so ingrained, Peter would rather disobey God than to join himself in a meal with the Gentiles. Nevertheless, despite Peter's resistance, he did preach the gospel to the house of Cornelius, the Roman centurion, whereupon God did fill them with the Holy Spirit ushering these Gentiles into the Kingdom (Acts 10:45).

God opened the door, calling out from among the nations a people for His Name. Thus, the gospel started to spread throughout the Gentile world through the missional journey of Paul and Barnabas. Jewish believers continued to have an issue with Gentile believers — as shown in the epistles. It was extremely challenging for them to be one. Jewish believers could not accept Gentile believers as equals in the One New Man. They wanted those called out from among the nations to convert to Judaism in addition to believing in Jesus Christ.

Jewish Christians from Jerusalem went out to the Gentiles in Asia Minor in an effort to "Judaize" these new converts from among the nations through circumcision — trying to convince them this was mandatory in order to be saved; they needed to be circumcised according to the "custom of Moses" (Acts 15:1) — it was Christ plus the "customs of Moses."

Due to this dispute, Paul and Barnabas went to Jerusalem to settle this matter with the leaders of the assembly in Jerusalem. After much dispute, James concluded that those taken out from among the nations to be a people for His name should not be troubled; rather, what was taking place was prophetic fulfillment — the tabernacle of David which was divided at the "breach of Jeroboam" was being restored.

The rebuilding of the "United Kingdom of David" would include those who had been "scattered among the nations." The conclusion of this council in Jerusalem determined "putting a yoke on the neck of the disciples" by adding the "customs of Moses" was contrary to "the grace of the Lord Jesus Christ." God's goal was to rebuild the kingdom of David to include all His chosen, both Jews and Gentiles, coming together in ONE.

One would think after such a momentous decision by the leading apostles, and elders representing Jewish believers, everything should have been settled. The next story highlights the entrenched divide between Jew and Gentile.

In Antioch, Peter, with a number of Jewish believers, was eating together with Gentile believers. They were one in fellowship. At that moment, some Jewish Christians came from James, the presider of the conference in Acts 15. The unimaginable happened: Peter who was told by God he could eat all things; Peter, the one who opened the door to the kingdom for the Gentiles; the Apostle who defended the Gentiles from having to follow the "customs of Moses" in Acts 15 — withdrew from eating with those being called out from among the nations. He separated himself, split, and divided himself from these Gentile believers. Not only him, but all the other Jewish believers followed his lead.

Due to this public action of division, Paul had to condemn and rebuke Peter openly for corrupting the "truth of the gospel." The gospel is not just about one's salvation. The gospel has everything to do with the oneness of the Lord's Body for which He died. Jesus Christ's death was not just for the forgiveness of sins, but to bring divided people into ONE.

Just as there is zeal for preaching the gospel to people who are predisposed in turning away from God, there needs to be the same zeal for the gospel toward all believers who are inclined to division. There needs to be a recognition of the "breach" between Jews and Gentiles to appreciate

God's heart in terminating the enmity, the hatred, created by ordinances in order to bring these two people into One New Man. God's eternal purpose cannot be fulfilled without the oneness of His people — that includes both Jews and Gentiles.

Almost all Christian missions today are focused on the gospel for bringing humanity to salvation in Christ. Who will arise to preach and fight for the truth of the gospel: the unity of God's people for His One New Man, the Lord's assembly, the one ekklesia!

The point here is this: Since God, through the cross, has solved the problem between Judah and those *"swallowed up — now among the Gentiles"* (Hosea 8:7-8) by gathering them together in ONE (Hosea 8:10, Romans 9:24-26), then all other divisions are easily solved — all separation due to any other factors has been vanquished. Once the "United Kingdom of David" is realized (aka, "the Tabernacle of David"), the *"**the rest of mankind** may seek the LORD, even all the Gentiles who are called by My name, says the LORD who does all these things"* (Acts 15:16-17; Amos 9:11-12).

Romans Is the Gospel to Bring Divided People into ONE

Having the same purpose as God for the one ekklesia and understanding the natural inclination for people to be divided desiring to stay within their own kind, Paul wrote a letter to the saints in Rome — the epistle of Romans. To have the complete understanding of this letter, all 16 chapters of Romans are needed.

Romans 16, the last chapter, is not considered to have much theological enlightenment written by Paul. It is a chapter with twenty-three verses filled with greetings toward some thirty-six people with many names hard to pronounce. Even among commentators of the Bible, it is mostly relegated to Paul's personal salutations to assorted believers in Rome, showing Paul's heart and care for the saints. Most students of Romans consider they would not have missed much if Paul's letter to the Romans ended with Romans 15.

It is like not missing much of a book if you don't read the appendix in the back, or much of a movie if you don't catch the credits at the end.

Hopefully, by the time you finish reading this chapter concerning Romans 16 you will agree it is actually crucial in fulfilling God's eternal plan. Without this chapter, the critical reason for Paul writing this letter would be gutted. You will see how this chapter is a key to bringing divided believers together and expanding the fellowship of Jesus Christ. Without understanding and practicing what is commanded in this chapter, God's purpose would not be accomplished.

First, let's consider the background. When Paul wrote this letter to the Romans, he had not been to Rome, nor was there a record of any other apostle going there. Since he had not visited Rome, it is logical to assume he did not know all believers there. Some of them he had met during his missionary journeys (such as Aquila and Priscilla while they were in Corinth). It can be assumed some of the other names mentioned are names Paul heard from others, such as the two groups of believers he mentioned in Romans 16:14–15.

History confirms the territory under the administration of the Roman Empire, unrestricted and relatively safe travel throughout the empire existed, thus rapidly expanding commerce. Citizens and freemen of the Empire took advantage of this and were able to travel locating freely within this territory. Many residing in Rome traveled outside of Rome to Greece or Israel. Rome (being the capital) also attracted people from other regions, who relocated there. This is clearly affirmed by the backgrounds of the twenty-six people named in Romans 16, plus the five *groups* of people Paul mentioned.

Although Paul personally brought some in Rome to faith in Christ, and at least a couple became his fellow workers such as Prisca (Priscilla) and Aquila; it is also reasonable to assume many were brought to faith by other apostles and preachers who were active during Paul's time. Certainly, some could have come to Christ in Judea. Perhaps when they went to Jerusalem for the feasts, they heard the gospel through the ministry of the twelve apostles, or through Philip in Samaria, or from one of the many scattered believers who went throughout the territories preaching the gospel (Acts 11:19).

Here in Rome, they had become a collection of believers meeting in different homes who had come to faith in Christ through various preachers; they were as diverse as the population of Rome. There were well-to-do believers with large households, as well as slaves, Jews, Greeks, Roman citizens, and freemen from throughout the empire. In such a situation, it certainly would have been easy for the Christian community to segregate and separate themselves from each other. Naturally, those with similar cultural backgrounds, socioeconomic statuses, ethnic upbringing, apostolic preferences, and especially those with a kosher diet would prefer to gather together.

Even an assembly such as Corinth, which was raised up by the apostle Paul, experienced division. One can imagine believers in Rome would have had even more of a propensity for division because of the diversity in practices and doctrines resulting from their various cultural backgrounds, social status, and preference of ministers who brought them to faith in Christ.

As expected from the deep-seated divisions between Jewish and Gentile believers, Paul's main challenge was bringing these two groups of believers together in Rome. That was his focus since all the other divisions were simple compared to this. The building up of the Lord's One Body depended upon the "wall of separation" being broken down. Therefore, let's review the book of Romans with that in view.

Commonality between divided people

> "With all lowliness and gentleness, with longsuffering, bearing with one another in love, endeavoring to keep the unity of the Spirit in the bond of peace. There is One Body and one Spirit, just as you were called in one hope of your calling: one Lord, one faith, one baptism; one God and Father of all, who is above all, and through all, and in you all"
>
> (Eph. 4:2-6)

Since the challenge for Paul was to build up the saints in Rome into One Body, Paul wanted to show them every believer has a common inheritance. He first focused on the commonality of their condemnation and salvation. In Romans 1-3, Paul made a strong case that whether Jews or Gentiles, whether you were the "chosen" with God's law or one without law, both were sinners, fallen short of God's glory, and are condemned. There is no advantage of the Jews over the Gentiles or vise-versa. As people that are condemned equally, both need the common redemption through the death of Jesus Christ (Rom. 3:24). Without exception the only common way to justification available before God is through faith (Rom. 4-5). In Romans 4, while the Jews considered Abraham to be their forefather, it made clear Abraham is the father of faith for both Jews and Gentiles. Romans 6 unveils both Jews and Gentiles have been terminated through Christ's death and burial. Now both are sanctified the same way. . . by their identity in Christ. Romans 7 reveals that whether a Jew under the law or a Gentile without law, both have the common struggle with the same indwelling sin, and both need the indwelling Spirit in Romans 8. It is this Spirit Who brings both once divided people into the glory of the sons of God.

From a salvation perspective, Romans 8 ending with glorification should have been the completion of theology. Glorification is the end goal of everyone's salvation's journey. Through Romans 1-8 salvation was made complete starting with justification through faith, sanctification by identification in Christ, transformation through the indwelling and leading of the Spirit, and finally glorification of mature sons of God to bring in the new heaven and earth. Yet, that is only half the book of Romans. Why is there a need for another 8 chapters?

The reason is that God's goal is not just individual salvation. God's goal is to have One Body who would defeat His enemy. Without the One Body, God's eternal purpose is still not fulfilled. Therefore, Paul continued to focus on bringing together the most divided people: Jews and Gentiles. Romans 9 through 11 were written specifically focusing on the issues of Jews and Gentiles. Each chapter was to show from various angles using different arguments that in God's economy and purpose, the separation and partition between the two have been terminated. It is over. Three chapters were needed to make this case because of the natural innate division between them.

Finally, in Romans 12, Paul brought up the One Body of Christ. Do not be conformed to this world of having the pride of group association alongside class envy and warfare. Rather, members should not think of themselves more highly (or too lowly) than they ought, but they are all individual members, each belonging to one another. There are many members, whether Jews, Gentiles, rich, poor, male, or female, but One Body. They are all in a common Body.

The Body of Christ, though spiritual and heavenly, exists on earth today. Through the ekklesia, the assembly has authority to bind and to loose, its authority is over the spiritual realm and not the kingdom of this world. Therefore, Romans 13 tells the saints to subject to governmental authority. This is also a word to help the Jewish brethren not to expect an overturning of the Roman Empire for the return of the Jewish nation. For the Jewish believer, their lot is now the Body of Christ together with the Gentile believers. Both Jews and Gentiles now are in their common kingdom of God.

There are diverse individuals from contrary backgrounds together in the common Body; therefore, we need to receive and embrace one another. Romans 14 and 15 strongly charged the saints in Rome to receive one another without passing judgement. The differences Paul cited were clearly issues of conflict between Jews and Gentiles: diet (whether to eat meat or vegetable) and keeping of days (Sabbath or not). In these two chapters, there was no indication one should adopt the conviction and lifestyle of the other when there is a conflict. No, rather, each can continue with his or her own conviction; yet, fully receive and embrace another that might have a contrary conviction. Everyone has the freedom to live to God according to their own conscience.

Although believers are no longer under God's judgment due to sin, they will still face the judgment seat of Christ. They will have to give an answer to God concerning whether they have received the brethren or have judged and excluded them. (Rom. 14:10-13). It is a sobering matter to consider whether we receive those contrary to us in the Body is how the Lord will judge each one of His members at His coming. This is the seriousness of causing division in His Body. The Lord does not take this matter lightly. He will judge and each will have to give an account concerning His relationship with other members in His Body.

However, when believers live and act according to this admonition of receiving one another . . . What freedom in the Body! What an expression of love! One accord based on Romans 15:5-7 is not because all the members of the Body are the same, uniformed; rather, it is because they receive and love one another though conflictingly different. The commonality here is not they are alike, but God has received all of them just as they are in their individual differences. It is the love and oneness among people of diversity who give glory to God (Rom. 15:7).

Greetings Is the Essential Conclusion

> Greet Priscilla and Aquila, my fellow workers in Christ Jesus, who risked their own necks for my life, to whom not only I give thanks, but also all the churches of the Gentiles. Likewise [greet] the church that is in their house. Greet my beloved Epaenetus, who is the firstfruits of Achaia to Christ. Greet

> Mary, who labored much for us . . . Greet Apelles, approved in Christ. Greet those who are of the [household] of Aristobulus. Greet Herodion, my countryman. Greet those who are of the [household] of Narcissus who are in the Lord. Greet Tryphena and Tryphosa, who have labored in the Lord. Greet the beloved Persis, who labored much in the Lord. Greet Rufus, chosen in the Lord, and his mother and mine. Greet Asyncritus, Phlegon, Hermas, Patrobas, Hermes, and the brethren who are with them. Greet Philologus and Julia, Nereus and his sister, and Olympas, and all the saints who are with them.
>
> (Rom. 16:3-6, 10-16)

The epistle to the Romans may be considered Paul's complete theology, covering the entirety of the gospel of God with the revealed mystery (Rom. 16:25). After expounding on God's complete salvation, from man's condemnation to glorification (Romans 1 through 8), Paul continues in Chapter 12 to unveil the mystery of the One Body of Christ with many members. Each individual member is a gift that needs to function in the One Body. Since there were such a variety of people with an assortment of cultural and religious backgrounds, there naturally would have been a tendency to segregate and judge one another among the various groups. Because of this, Romans 14 and 15 was needed. Paul presented a strong case along with a warning believers needed to receive one another. Though all were believers and had been received in One Body by Christ, it was natural for them to settle in their comfort zone and group together with others who were similar to them.

Considering this generation of believers — with groups segregated by non-essential doctrines, practices, preference of ministers, politics and ethnicity, among other things — the situation in Rome may be considered a microcosm of today's Christian environment. No wonder Paul declared in Romans 15 believers would glorify God if they received one another. Though diverse in practices, they would be in one accord and with one mouth. Due to a thorough mixture of people and backgrounds, both cultural and spiritual, Rome was the ideal environment to show the oneness of believers, according to John 17, through the gifts of eternal life, the truth, and the Lord's glory.

"Receiving" in Romans 14 may be considered passive, in the sense that if believers come to a gathering or to a home assembly, the one hosting with all the saints needs to receive them for fellowship without passing judgment. But in Chapter 16, Paul charged the believers in Rome to go and greet other believers. Greeting in this sense is proactive.

As pointed out previously, just about all teachers of the Bible have considered this chapter to be Paul's own salutation or greeting of the various saints in Rome. It is understood to be: greet so-and-so for me. As such, the application of this portion is relegated to trying to remember all the saints if you are going to write a letter and don't leave anyone out. However, upon further consideration with the enlightening of the Spirit, it was not Paul who was greeting, it was Paul commanding the saints to go and greet all the various people listed in that chapter. They are to go and greet numerous believers who found themselves segregated from others in Rome. In fact, he emphatically told them to do this greeting seventeen times.

The word "greet" is not just saying "hi" when walking past someone. The word for "greet" in the Greek means: *to embrace, to be joined, a union, to visit or joyfully welcome a person* (Strong's and Thayer's).

It was customary for greetings to take place by entering a house with the occupant welcoming that person to stay for a while (Matt. 10:12; Acts 21:7). Greetings included intimate dialogues with another person (Luke 1:40-55; Acts 21:19). Additionally, the Greek verb form for "greet" as found in Romans 16 is *aorist middle deponent imperative*; which means Paul was commanding whoever was reading his letter to take continual action to go and greet those listed. This greeting is the initiation of fellowship. They need to continue doing this greeting whether they have done so in the past or not.

It is consistent through all the epistles the verb form for "greet" is different whether the greeting is done by someone remotely in another locality or done face to face in the same locality. For example, in Romans 16:16: *"Greet one another with a holy kiss. The assemblies* [ekklesia] *of Christ greet you."* In this verse, there are two "greets." The first one obviously is in-person, face-to-face greeting. The second "greet" is from all the assemblies. Obviously, the saints in those assemblies are not in Rome. Therefore, the verb form is different. Specifically, it was not imperative, a command; rather, it was indicative, a simple statement of fact. Over 37 times greetings were used in all the epistles. In every single instance, when it was face to face, it was imperative, a command; however, when it was remotely, it was indicative. Without a doubt, all the greetings in Romans 16:3-15 were Paul commanding the recipient of his letter, which was all the saints in Rome, to go greet all the saints in those verses. It was not Paul doing the greeting from afar. He was literally commanding, charging, the saints to intentionally, proactively and continually go and greet all the various saints in Rome. They needed to do it in-person, face-to-face, and intimately with a kiss.

Why is that important? It is important because the believer's situation and relationship with each other in Rome is the closest example of what it is today. Presently, there are a variety of factions and groupings of believers. The groupings are generally a result of comfort and familiarity due to similarity in ethnicity, doctrinally, worship tradition, and so on. Additionally, none of the first-century apostles founded any of the groups today. The one fellowship of Jesus Christ is fractured and limited. Therefore, today is precisely why the book of Romans is needed and specifically the last chapter with the command to go greet is as critical as it was 2000 years ago in Rome.

Believers today are to obey the Scriptures just as those in the First Century. God's people should take similar action to go and greet brothers and sisters individually, as well as those associated with other groups. They should continue to do this regardless of whether they have done so in the past.

Therefore, greeting was not Paul's casual addendum to his otherwise intensely theological discourse. No, it was Paul's way of engineering a mixing of normally segregated people and the expanding of the one fellowship among all the saints in Rome. If they did not proactively go and greet the believers who were normally not associated with their grouping, then segregation and division would persist, becoming systematized and institutionalized after a period of time.

By enjoining those who would obey Paul's injunction to go and greet all the various followers of Jesus in Rome, whether they be Jews or Gentiles, slave or free, it would initiate fellowship among all the Lord's followers in Rome. Such vibrant fellowship is the reality of the one ekklesia. This is what is upon the Lord's heart.

Without this ongoing greeting in Romans 16, Paul's theology concerning salvation, justification, sanctification, resulting in the One Body of Christ, would be utterly deficient. Without purposeful outreach to have vibrant fellowship with all those of the same faith, but not in the same grouping, the saints would succumb to gravitational separation, finding themselves with their "own kind" — whether ethnically, doctrinally, politically, socio-economically, or personality-wise. The result: division and sectarianism.

Crushing Satan Is a Fitting Finale

> The God of peace will soon crush Satan under your feet. The grace of our Lord Jesus Christ be with you.
> (Rom. 16:20, ESV)

This declaration of crushing Satan didn't show up in Chapter 15, but at the end of Romans 16. Satan being crushed revealed at the end is an answer to the Lord's promise in Matthew 16:18 that His ekklesia, assembly, will crush the gates of Hades, the stronghold of Satan. This shows that all 16 chapters of Romans are needed by the saints in Rome to crush Satan under their feet. Romans 16 is not "the credit to the movie," it is the conclusion of the movie itself. Stopping at Romans 15 would have missed the ending of the entire Roman movie.

This should not be easily dismissed. In Paul's presentation of his complete theological framework, we have to recognize that the entire letter to Rome was divinely inspired from Chapter 1 to 16 and each and every chapter was designed to be exactly where they need to be with their content. To proclaim Satan being crushed at the end of Romans 16 shows us Satan cannot be crushed by the God of peace under the saints' feet until the practice of greeting is accomplished. Only then is the Lord's assembly built up.

Remember the difficulties for Jews and Gentiles to even eat together? What a beautiful sight of fellowship and oneness as the city witnessed Jews going into Gentile homes to greet them and have a meal together, and vice-versa. The rich or freeman would greet believing slaves by welcoming them into their homes for a meal. Throughout the city, unlikely people would be greeting and fellowshipping together with each other at market, "coffee shops" and in their homes, from house to house.

As the number of believers in Rome who read Paul's letter increased, the greetings and thus the fellowship among the saints grew exponentially. What a testimony to the oneness of believers as they go from house to house greeting each other! Paul ended this section instructing readers to greet one another with a holy kiss. This kind of greeting expressed pure love and intimate fellowship among the believers. None would be isolated in their own home group, seeing the same believers year after year, but instead would be part of a growing network of homes in one fellowship with much traffic and support between them, because they were indeed one assembly. Today, most believers are segregated and isolated in their church or in their home. If believers accept Paul's directive to seek out other believers and greet them, the Lord will have a way to build up the assembly, His body.

There are so many churches and Christian groups today with believers isolated from each other. It is essential for God's purpose that believers heed Paul's command to go and greet fellow believers not in their own grouping. In God's eyes all of His children are in one family — in the One Body of Christ. As such, believers should not acknowledge any division, no matter what church or denomination may be segregating Christians. Greetings to a believer's meeting in the Catholic Church should be the same fervent greeting given to a believer in the Baptist Church, a Pentecostal Church, a non-denominational church, or even a believer not attending any church. For the purpose of mutual greetings among believers, no recognition should be given to which church a person belongs (since churches are artificially organized by men). No matter which church one belongs to or if a believer is completely outside the institutional church, each needs to proactively greet and receive other believers.

What if believers with an emphasis on Pentecostal experiences greeted those who disparage tongue-speaking? What would happen if those with a preference for reformed theology greeted those who preach salvation is a choice? Believers would automatically become one in the reality of the Body of Christ, and non-essential doctrines and pet practices would fade in priority and cease being an issue between believers. The intimate fellowship in Jesus Christ alone will cause the assembly to bloom from house to house. This will take place outside of and in spite of almost 2,000 years of separation within institutional Christianity.

How can believers testify to the God of Peace if they are divided? However, the God of Peace is in action and magnified among all the greetings of disparate believers. Therefore, Satan being crushed is an appropriate ending for this chapter and not before. In Matthew, Jesus was giving the promise, or a prophecy; here, however, Paul and the early believers are living out the reality of the practical building up which will crush Satan. When believers are in oneness in the one fellowship, built on the one foundation — Jesus Christ, with all the members functioning and active, Satan is crushed. It is the oneness of believers that defeats the enemy and satisfies the Lord's desire in His prayer in John 17.

Greeting Exposes Selfish Ministers

> I appeal to you, brothers, to watch out for those who cause divisions and create obstacles contrary to the doctrine that you have been taught; avoid them. For such persons do not serve our Lord Christ, but their own appetites, and by smooth talk and flattery they deceive the hearts of the naive.
> (Rom. 16:17-18, ESV)

These verses have been taken out of context and have been used to abuse believers in churches or Christian groups who are "trouble makers." Typically, those who are contrary or have conflicting ideas with the church they are attending, and especially if they start voicing their objections, will be told they are causing a division. Therefore, if they do not refrain from their criticism of the church or leadership, then these verses will be cited.

Not only so, but if these "divisive" members depart from that church or group then there is a likelihood the rest of the members will be told to avoid them for being rebellious and divisive. It is the threat of being ostracized from a community of believers which helps to maintain order within a church. Using these verses in such a way is appalling and just plain wrong.

Now let's consider these verses in context. Since believers were to go about visiting and greeting all other believers in the One Body in Rome, Paul also warned they would run into some who would not receive or give such greetings, believers who had decided to stand apart from the common fellowship of the Body of Christ. There were Christian teachers who taught things contrary to the apostle's teaching of Jesus Christ and His One Body with an intention of causing a faction — a standing apart — between those under their teachings and the rest of believers in Rome. While greetings among all believers were going on, these sectarian teachers deceived the hearts of the naïve to corral them into their own separate groups. If this were today, they might say their group is different because they have the "real baptism," and other believers are not baptized in the proper way. Another might say they have a special and higher revelation, so their group is not like other believers because they receive their teachings from minister so-and-so.

Paul appealed to believers to watch out for such teachers and avoid them. This should not be extended to the naïve or simple believers who are deceived by these teachers with their smooth-talk; it is not their fault they were misled into a sectarian group. Those who teach differently with the goal of recruiting their own followers are not serving the Lord; they are serving their own appetite for either material gain or power to control those who they have corralled into their sect. This is a serious matter, which can only be exposed through indiscriminate greetings among believers. If greetings do not occur between believers in these segregated groups, the self-serving teachers and their groups will be able to stay hidden. But once greetings transpire from house to house, those "standing apart" will be exposed; teachers and leaders of these stand-apart groups should be noted and avoided.

This division in Romans 16:17–18 is much more serious than the "division" identified in 1 Corinthians 1:10 — (i.e., the division among those in the assembly in Corinth). The division there is "schism," a rent or a discord. The "division" in Romans 16 is translated by King James and some older translations as "heresy" which in most Christian minds conjures up a teaching which finds one horribly departed from the truth.

Schism is like a division fomented by a family quarrel which is never good. At times it results in devastating rifts; however, family members still acknowledge they are in the same family, despite the rift. They just need to grow out of such childish arguments. However, the "division" in Romans 16:17-18 is literally a "faction" — a standing apart. It is like saying: "I am not part of that family. We are our *own* family." This type of division is deliberate separation, and those promoting such separations need to be marked and avoided.

While there are many ministers today who have a pure motive to serve God alone for His ekklesia and not their own "belly," there are other ministers whose motives are to draw people to themselves. By putting Romans 16 into practice when believers get out of their "comfort zone" and greet all kinds of believers, then the true ministers of God will shine forth for the building up of His One Body. Moreover, those intentionally dividing the Body will be recognized for their delimiting purposes contrary to building up of the Body of Christ.

Those serving the Lord Jesus Christ for His purpose should teach those under their leadership to follow Paul's command to go, visit, and greet all believers around them, even though they are not in their church or assembly. Those who serve their own appetite to build their own sect do their best to isolate those under their leadership; they do not want their members to be open in greeting and receiving others or be intimate with believers who are not part of their group.

While selfish ministers are exposed for what they are, the proper ministers of the gospel of Jesus Christ will find themselves more useful and their function extending beyond their immediate church confines. Those ministers with a heart for the oneness of the Body will thrive in their ministry to all the saints.

A couple of final observations are in order. The charge to go greet by Paul is to go out to many individuals he listed in Rome. It was not a charge to go greet any organization. Organizations are impersonal. Churches and ministries as organizations are not a living being. Fellowship is not possible at an organizational level; therefore, greetings can only be directed to individuals.

For example, it is impossible to greet the Roman Catholic Church or the Baptist Church, but you can greet a believer who is a member of the Catholic Church; you can even greet a pastor of a Baptist Church; you can also greet the minister who has an organized ministry. This greeting has nothing to do with the so-called ecumenical movement with a goal to unify Christian churches and organizations. Romans 16 involves individual believers obeying the Lord to go and greet other individual believers because they are in the same ekklesia, the One Body of Christ.

Reading through that list of people in Romans 16, in many cases, Paul attached something of interest to a person's name such as: Greet my beloved Epaenetus, who is the first fruits of Achaia (v.5); Greet Mary, who labored much for us (v.6); Greet the beloved Persis, who labored much in the Lord (v. 12). It could be Paul's way to entice believers to go greet them and find out more about their story. The fact is every believer has an interesting story. Each one has a testimony of how God has changed them or used them. Let's go and find out all the marvelous ways He has worked in each of His people – you will not know unless you go and greet them.

Greeting Is the Way to Expand Fellowship

> Greet Priscilla and Aquila, my fellow workers in Christ Jesus, who risked their own necks for my life, to whom not only I give thanks, but also all the churches [ekklesia] of the Gentiles. Likewise [greet] the church [ekklesia] that is in their house.
>
> (Rom. 16:3-4)

As was discussed in the last chapter, Romans 16 describes an environment where believers were segregated into various groups. That description can be analogous to today's Christianity where the churches are now systematically divided. Nevertheless, the greeting commanded by Paul is the solution in bringing once divided believers into one fellowship in Jesus Christ. Just as without Romans 16 one ekklesia would not have been built in Rome; likewise, today, without intentionally greeting diverse believers, Christians will remain highly segregated and divided and the Lord's ekklesia remains *un-built*.

Many Bible teachers have described this letter by Paul as "the Roman Road." It describes the different stages and experiences of the followers of Jesus from beginning to end. Various Christian groups and denominations have defined themselves based on what the founders of those groups have come to emphasize along this "road" of God's full salvation. For example, churches founded by the Reformers can be traced to the major discovery of Justification by Faith in Romans 3 through 5.

Other ministers have founded churches based on the need to live a sanctified life, one of holiness, in their understanding of Romans 6. Some have progressed along this spiritual "road" to emphasize the indwelling Spirit and the leading of the Spirit in Romans 8. In the last 150 years or so, some prominent ministers have taught and focused on the One Body of Christ, forming churches focused around Romans 12.

To enter into the experience of Romans 12 concerning the One Body of Christ, teachers over the last century or so have also highlighted Chapters 14 and 15 concerning the need to receive one another no matter what differences appear in doctrinal beliefs and practices. A group of believers, whose teachings and practices are based on Chapters 1 through 15, definitely would qualify to be called an ekklesia of the Lord. But without Chapter 16, this group of believers who have progressed through the book of Romans to become a genuine assembly, risk becoming sectarian due to the default tendency for believers to become passive when they contemplate they have arrived at God's goal.

If Romans 16 is not put into practice, then the assembly which arrived at Romans 15 with proper doctrinal understanding regarding justification, sanctification, identity in Christ, the indwelling and leading of the Spirit, the vision of the One Body, and the practice of receiving all believers into the One Body, would develop over time their own defined culture related to doctrinal applications and practices which in turn would segregate themselves from other believers. They would not be in a position to receive a diversity of God's people since those outside their defined culture would find it difficult to join with them. If that were to happen, then what started out as an ekklesia would degenerate into another defined group of believers segregated and divided from the rest of the Body in fellowship. They would then lose their standing as the Lord's ekklesia.

In Chapter 16, the first ones to greet were Priscilla and Aquila, and the ekklesia (assembly) that was in their house. Priscilla and Aquila were under Paul's tutelage and worked closely with him in Ephesus before moving back to Rome; therefore, Paul should have had confidence that they had the same understanding of Romans 1-15 and the heart for God's purpose concerning the One Body as he. Although there were other Christian groups in Rome (at least four others mentioned in Romans 16), it may have been because of Paul's assurance that Priscilla and Aquila would be practicing according to his vision of the Body of Christ; therefore, Paul only acknowledged the assembly is their home. Since the saints who gathered in their house were the assembly, Paul directed any who received his letter to go and greet them first. As the assembly, they had the reality of the One Body and were the pattern of building on Jesus Christ as their unique foundation. Likewise, every believer has the freedom to function in their capacity; and they also received all believers into one fellowship. With believers in Rome greeting them first, Paul could be assured anyone who went to greet them would be received into fellowship. By experiencing the assembly as a pattern, more and more believers would also learn the proper standing and functioning of an assembly.

At the same time, as the first recipients of Paul's letter, Priscilla, Aquila, and the assembly in their house had the foremost responsibility of proactively going to greet everyone on Paul's list. They were not to wait for believers in Rome to come to their house to greet them — they were to venture out and greet all the other believers in Rome. They were to go and embrace in fellowship believers in other households and groups. Through this greeting of one another, all believers in Rome would blend into one; and the assembly would spread from house to house. It would no longer be only in Priscilla and Aquila's house because the nature and expression of the universal assembly grew and spread from house to house just like in the earlier days with the assembly in Jerusalem.

When Aquila and Priscilla were in Ephesus, they were instrumental to bring Apollos into a clearer understanding of Jesus Christ (Acts 18). While in Rome, through their obedience to go greet, they would help believers see and practice assembly life, the One Body of Christ, without any divisions among believers. This greeting would naturally and continually expand the one fellowship of the Holy Spirit.

Let's consider the following diagram which is a continuation of the previous diagram. The few solid dots which are not in any of the circles represent the ekklesia in Priscilla and Aquila's house (Rom. 16:5).

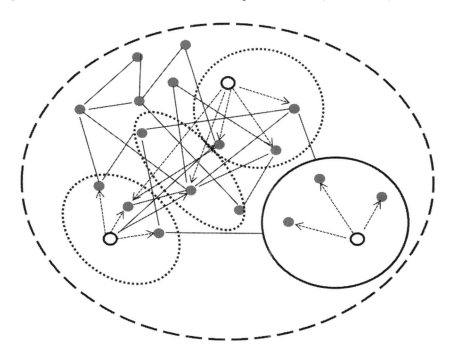

Figure 4–Greeting All the Saints in Rome

The bottom right circle comprises those who do not greet or receive greetings (Rom. 16:17-18). The solid lines show the greetings which are taking place among all believers in Rome and fellowship they would have initiated. In such greetings, those who are more gifted as ministers can now function beyond a group of believers they originally equipped.

Their actions would be expanded to reach more of God's people. A genuine gift in the Body of Christ should not be relegated to just one subgroup of believers. By greeting as commanded by Paul, those who are gifted ministers would now be able to equip more of the saints to operate as His One Body.

Building Up One Body

If the saints in Rome would continually go and greet as Paul commanded them, then over time those naturally segregating lines between the saints would fade, even disappear. The one fellowship of the ekklesia would spread throughout all of Rome. All believers would be in one fellowship without any demarcations.

Imagine all the greetings taking place throughout Rome. There would have been twos, threes, and small groups of believers gathering in homes all over Rome and her environs. Jewish believers would be visiting non-Jewish homes and vice-versa.

Believers who are free would have meals with believers who are slaves. From house to house, greetings would expand and increase. What originally took place in Jerusalem's ekklesia would now be taking place in Rome — this is how the apostles envisioned the ekklesia as expressed in Paul's letter to the Romans.

The diversity of God's people would now enjoy one fellowship and One Body. Through this fellowship and diversity, the ekklesia-assembly would spread from Priscilla and Aquila's house to scores of homes. There would be one ekklesia in Rome.

They would be seen together in a growing number of homes just like the beginning of the Lord's ekklesia in Jerusalem. The exceptions to this ever-growing celebration of the true ekklesia would be those still deceived by unscrupulous ministers who would have no intention of building up the One Body, but instead, they would be practicing *"whose god is their own belly."*

The next diagram illustrates how one fellowship takes place in One Body which stems from continuous meeting and greeting among all the saints.

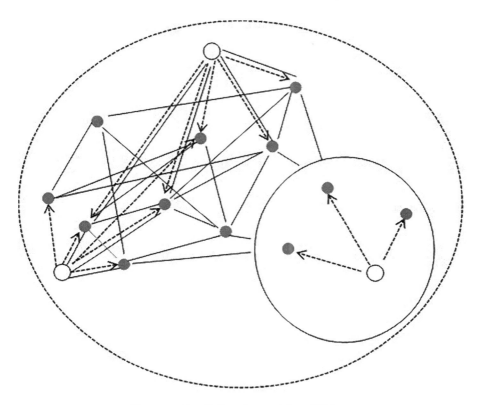

Figure 5–One Fellowship and One Ekklesia

9.
From Factions to Oneness

Ekklesia Starts with factions, but Arrives at Oneness

Although at the end of Acts 2 there are six verses which describe the practice of the Lord's ekklesia at inception, there is only one other description of an actual practice of an ekklesia of the Lord in the New Testament. It was illustrated in more than three chapters from 1 Corinthians 11:18 through Chapter 14. Since this narrative uniquely describes how an ekklesia operates, it sets the pattern for all assemblies of the Lord.

There can be many ways and methods concerning ministries, but there is only one pattern for the assembly. Just as there are a multitude of ministers in the Body, there can be just as many ways to minister. No matter how many ministers are serving, there is but one pattern given to building the assembly. It is essential we delve into these Scriptures with scrutiny and with a deep yearning for the full manifestation of His assembly.

What is shown in this pattern is a combination of the Last Supper the Lord had with His disciples prior to crucifixion and the actual practice of a secular ekklesia. Here are the key elements described in John 14 through John 17, the night of the Last Supper:

1. They had a meal together
2. The Lord Jesus introduced the bread and the cup symbolizing His broken body and His shed blood inaugurating the New Covenant.
3. The "new commandment" to love one another as He loved us was shown by the Lord's example of washing the disciples' feet.
4. There was revelation upon revelation spoken by the Lord concerning the Trinity and the Spirit to be given through His death

and resurrection (John 14, 16). There was also the revelation of the body of believers as the universal vine in John 15.
5. Finally, the Lord's priestly prayer for the oneness of His followers so the world would believe in Him.

Here are the key elements of a secular ekklesia, assembly:

1. Every diverse member of a community is called together for an assembly
2. Everyone in the assembly can freely speak and voice their opinions

> For to begin with, I hear that when you come together as a church [ekklesia] there are divisions among you, and in part I believe it. Indeed, it is necessary that there be factions among you, so that those who are approved may be recognized among you.
> (1 Cor. 11:18-19 CSB)

> For as often as you eat this bread and drink the cup, you proclaim the Lord's death until he comes. So then, whoever eats the bread or drinks the cup of the Lord in an unworthy manner will be guilty of sin against the body and blood of the Lord. Let a person examine [approve] himself; in this way let him eat the bread and drink from the cup. For whoever eats and drinks without recognizing the body, eats and drinks judgment on himself. This is why many are sick and ill among you, and many have fallen asleep.
> (1 Cor. 11:26-30 CSB)

Let us consider this portion of Scripture in 1 Corinthians. The Lord's ekklesia started with a meal together. It was like a potluck where believers brought dishes to dine together. In Corinth, there was a division in the assembly because rich believers ate their own food first to the point of being drunk while poor believers lacked food.

Paul used this division to point out it ***was necessary*** for the ekklesia to have factions. This word from Paul can be very troubling. What, is there a need for factions in the ekklesia? He continued to say it was due to these very factions, opportunity would manifest itself enabling those who were "approved" or "genuine" to stand forth.

Let's consider again the nature of the ekklesia: An assembly of individuals called out from every quarter of a community. By definition and practice, assemblies should include factions of every kind, and often with conflicting interests. The Lord's ekklesia is no different. Although believers have been regenerated, becoming members of the community of faith, there are Jews and Gentiles, rich and poor, politically inclined to the left and to the right. Additionally, there are conflicting doctrines between Reform and Pentecostals, immersion and sprinkling, pre or post tribulation raptures, young earth or the gap theory of creation.

Then there are preferences of teachers and ministers — conflict of personalities and styles. Although there is a wide diversity of individuals, nevertheless, God has called them to assemble. That is why it is necessary an ekklesia starts with factions. In a way, if there are no factions, it would not be an ekklesia. A ministry cannot initiate nor continue with factions; however, it is inevitable that an ekklesia starts with factions. Churches are typically homogeneous, based on teachings, practices, and emphasis of respective ministers; whereas, the ekklesia-assembly is widely diverse. Therefore, she can only survive and thrive with Christ being the unique foundation and cornerstone.

How do we recognize the "approved" or "genuine" in the midst of factions? They are approved and recognized specifically because they are among factions. The word "approved" in Greek means tried and accepted or certified genuine. These individuals are approved because they are not in a faction. A faction means those in any given faction consider themselves different and separate from those not in their faction.

So, within a faction, they have more love, care, understanding, and communication among themselves than those outside of their faction. Members of a faction may become critical, denigrate those outside their faction, and most likely avoid those not in their faction. Whereas, the "approved" are those not in a faction.

These approved treat every believer the same. They can easily fellowship with members of any faction; moreover, they are those who reconcile members of opposing factions. They are peacemakers. According to Paul's words there are factions in the ekklesia; however, there are those in a given assembly who are not in a faction. They receive and fellowship with all believers. They are approved and are manifested in an assembly. If there is no one approved in the assembly, then there will only be factions with true fellowship missing.

The next diagram depicts an ekklesia, an assembly of called out ones. Continuing previous diagrams, the factions are in the enclosures, with those among them who are influencers as open dots. Those approved are black/gray dots where they are not in a faction but rather are able to fellowship with all believers no matter what factions in which they find themselves.

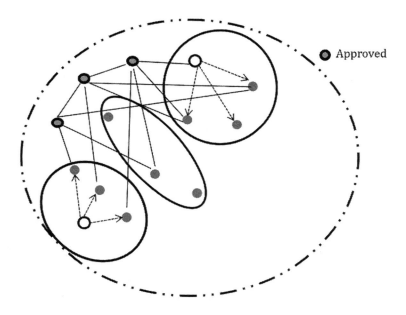

Figure 6- Overcoming Factions in the Assembly

Examine Yourself So Not to Bring Judgment

As with the Last Supper, the Lord's ekklesia practiced breaking of bread, having the symbol of the bread and cup after their meal. Consequently, Paul pointed out when each person partook of the bread and the cup, they would not do so in an unworthy manner; they would examine themselves and discern or recognize the symbol represented the One Body of Christ. If a person did not recognize the One Body — which is to partake unworthily — then this person would be found eating and drinking judgment instead of blessing. A most serious warning!

This symbol of the bread and cup is one of blessing. The cup is a cup of blessing (1 Cor. 10:16). He took the wrath of God on the cross for the sins of humanity so they could partake of the cup of the New Covenant in His blood with all its blessings. Jesus Christ accomplished everything for believers to simply drink of the Spirit (1 Cor. 12:13).

The bread signifies the Lord's Body broken for humanity on the cross whereby they may partake of Him. In so doing, all of God's people become the corporate Body of Christ (1 Cor. 10:17). Therefore, when believers partake of the bread, there should be a recognition they are partaking in the entire Body of Christ . . . not just Jesus Himself. The entire Body is seen as one bread. This bread does not represent any denominational church or any special Christian group. There is not one bread for Baptists and another for Pentecostals. No, there is only one bread, One Body of the Lord, where every believer may partake.

To eat and drink unworthily has to do with recognizing there is only One Body of Christ. If a person eats and drinks this symbol in recognition there is only One Body, and yet is still aligned with factions, then that person is guilty of a crime against the body and blood of Christ. Due to this guilty verdict, judgment will come in the form of weakness, sickness — even death.

Since this is such a serious matter, Paul charged believers to examine themselves when partaking of these symbols seen in the bread and cup. This word for "examine" in the Greek is the same word for "approved" found in 1 Corinthians 11:19 where it says those who are approved might be recognized. In other words, everyone partaking of these symbols needs to come out of any faction so they may be inclusive of all members of His One Body, accepting in fellowship all other believers as members of the Body of Christ.

Yes, in the beginning of any ekklesia, when the saints are called to assemble, there will be factions — this is mandatory! However, by the time of the breaking of bread and the drinking of the cup, every member must recognize and accept the reality they cannot stay in any isolated faction. Every believer needs to drop their factious identity and identify themselves simply as members of the Body connected to all other members of His One Body.

A believer in a faction does not fellowship with those in an opposing faction. Such a contrary posture cannot continue in the Body of Christ. Every believer needs to examine themselves and become *approved* as one who accepts into fellowship all other members of His Body, no matter how different they are.

The matter of judgment in this portion of Scripture is in direct opposition to the blessings of unity as portrayed in Psalm 133. Psalm 133 provides an environment of oneness and unity. It is here the outpouring of the Anointing, the Holy Spirit, the fresh experiences of Christ as the dew, and the commanded blessing of eternal life are realized.

These are the blessings of assembling as the Lord's ekklesia. In contrast to this blessing, there is a warning: a person who persists in a factious state within an ekklesia may receive judgment. It seems Paul is referring to a judgment related to physical sicknesses, weaknesses, and even death. Nevertheless, even if it is only referring to sicknesses, weaknesses, and spiritual deadness, that is still a terrible verdict.

If this judgment is from God, then no amount of prayer, fasting or laying on of hands can counteract these maladies. The only way to recover is through repentance by forgiveness, humility, acceptance, and fellowship with other believers who may have been marginalized or severed from fellowship.

Is this the reason why there is so little power and effectiveness among Christians in general? If the people of God are divided and segregated, how can there be blessings and a living witness to the world? Certainly, evangelism should continue throughout the whole earth, but, as was pointed out earlier, there are many countries today with more than 50% of the population already considering themselves to believe in Jesus Christ or who attend church; yet, the light of the Lord is dimly seen in societies.

If we believe these verses, then Satan's strategic warfare will be focused on dividing the followers of Jesus. Consider this: Satan might not be able stop us from spreading the gospel; but if God's people are divided, he wins by delaying his final demise. If God's people are divided, then it brings in God's judgment on His own people. What a strategy! In a cynical way, Satan stirs up division to cause God's judgment against His people; thereby, allowing Satan to continue to have a free reign on earth to prolong his inevitable demise.

Remember, it is the built-up assembly which will defeat Satan (Matt. 16:18). Therefore, the need today for believers to become one is a greater need than evangelism. At issue is *"that they may be perfected into one ... that the world may believe."* There are forms of evangelism which can cause more divisiveness, but the oneness of believers will cause the world to believe.

Oneness of God's people fulfills God's eternal purpose, defeats His enemy, and causes people to cry out for deliverance unto salvation.

The following diagram illustrates the transformation from the previous diagram when the ekklesia was called to overcome various factions. Now by participating in the bread and cup, those with factious conditions can become approved by receiving, accepting, and reaching out in fellowship with other saints whom they previously discounted. They now imitate those already manifested as approved in 1 Corinthians 11:19. Believers who continue in their factious isolation by not receiving and fellowshipping with other members contrary to them, will bring on judgment to themselves, according to Paul.

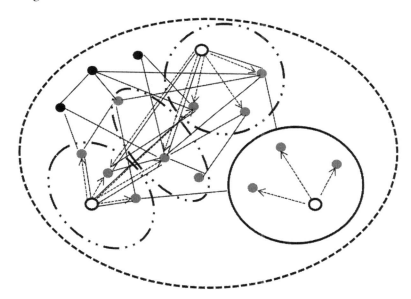

Figure 7- Believers Reaching Out to Fellowship

Many Diverse Members, but One Body

We find in 1 Corinthians 12-13 a continuing description of ekklesia and the functioning of all the members in the ekklesia (assembly). Many may read these two chapters out of context considering Chapter 12 as a chapter about the miraculous gifts in the Body and Chapter 13 about love. But these two chapters are embedded between Chapter 11 where Paul, on the one hand, clearly indicated in verse 18 the beginning of an ekklesia coming together and, on the other hand, Chapter 14 is a continuation of the same ekklesia in action (1 Cor. 14:4, 12, 19, 23, 28, 33). Let us consider some excerpts from 1 Corinthians 12.

> Now concerning spiritual [gifts], brethren, I do not want you to be ignorant: You know that you were Gentiles, carried away to these dumb idols, however you were led. Therefore I make known to you that no one speaking by the Spirit of God calls Jesus accursed, and no one can say that Jesus is Lord except by the Holy Spirit. There are diversities of gifts, but the same Spirit. There are differences of ministries, but the same Lord. And there are diversities of activities, but it is the same God who works all in all. But the manifestation of the Spirit is given to each one for the profit [of all]: . . . For as the body is one and has many members, but all the members of that One Body, being many, are One Body, so also [is] Christ. For by one Spirit we were all baptized into One Body—whether Jews or Greeks, whether slaves or free—and have all been made to drink into one Spirit. For in fact the body is not one member but many . . . And the eye cannot say to the hand, "I have no need of you"; nor again the head to the feet, "I have no need of you." No, much rather, those members of the body which seem to be weaker are necessary . . . that there should be no schism in the body, but [that] the members should have the same care for one another . . . Now you are the Body of Christ, and members individually.
>
> (1 Cor. 12:1-7, 12-14, 21-22, 25, 27)

In 1 Corinthians 12 it goes into detail explaining every member has his own unique gift, ministry, or activity; yet, there is only One Body. There is a vision for all to see: There are natural factions among Christians such as Jews and Gentiles, bond or free, male and female, but now they are all baptized by one Spirit into One Body and they've all been made to drink of the same one Spirit. Therefore, how can one stay in a faction within the Lord's ekklesia?

A faction is composed of individuals having the same affinity due to sharing similar experiences, backgrounds, understandings, or goals. Typically, there are conflicts between factions which are caused when a group of people view their faction to be superior, others can become envious of a faction, or individuals feel the pressure to adopt and conform to a specific faction.

So, 1 Corinthians 12 makes clear there is diversity in the Body. Each member has their own gift, ministry, or activity. There needs to be mutual respect and acceptance of all other members. Paul used the analogy of the human body where each member is needed for the entire body to function: the eyes need the hands; the head needs the feet; and each part needs all the other parts.

Among Christians, it seems it is so easy for factions to form around spiritual gifts or various Scriptural doctrines and practices. Those who speak in tongues can become a faction once they depreciate those who do not speak in tongues or try to convert non-tongue speakers. The non-tongue speaking faction can likewise avoid those who speak in tongues and look down on those as being swayed by emotion or, even worse, delusional, etc.

The enlightenment seen in 1 Corinthians 12 demonstrates varied members are needed. Believers called into ekklesia need to honor every member; more so, someone who is considered to be unnecessary or unattractive. Which member is unnecessary is not unanimous; rather, depending on whose estimation; in a diverse environment, one person's attractiveness to some can be unattractive to others. Whoever considers another member to be unnecessary, the person with such a consideration is charged to honor that "unnecessary" person as more necessary. How does one honor another person? By fellowshipping with that person. During ekklesia, especially during the meal period, honor can be given to ones considered unnecessary by intentionally extending oneself to fellowship with the "unnecessary" member.

All the members in the Body being one does not imply uniformity. In contrast with an ekklesia, a ministry or church is where members over time will conform to a similar doctrinal view or Christian tradition, making the members of a church uniform. However, in the assembly of the Lord, the diversity among individuals is accepted and honored. Therefore, when Paul speaks of the ekklesia being the Body of Christ, he made clear each member is still an individual. It takes maturity for a believer to be comfortable and confident of their identity in Christ, and simultaneously, honor and accept other believers who are different from themselves.

In any event, 1 Corinthians 12:3 sets forth the principle concerning gifts in the Body; no one can say *Jesus is Lord* unless by the Holy Spirit. Almost all gifts in the Body listed in 1 Corinthians 12 necessitates that a person be speaking. That is why there is a sharp contrast between those in the Body compared to those who are worshipping idols. Those who are led by idols are dumb or mute. Speaking is virtually nil in idol worship . . . aside, of course, from "vain repetitions."

How true even today: visit various idolatrous religious temples — all worshippers are predominantly silent. Many pagan temples are eerily quiet. Indeed, some Christian churches can come under this influence of worshipping idols resulting in those going to such churches to be mute with nothing to say concerning Jesus. But in the assembly, everyone confesses Jesus is Lord. It is by this uplifting of Jesus as Lord that the gifts of the Holy Spirit are manifested.

The principle here is this: When a believer speaks forth Jesus as Lord, it confirms that member is doing so by the Holy Spirit. Simultaneously, there are many other gifts of the Spirit, be they in ministry, or activities in which a believer may be exercised. If they are of the Holy Spirit, then Jesus Christ is uplifted as Lord.

Every manifestation of the various gifts in the Body of Christ exalts Jesus Christ as Lord. There may be diversity of gifts, ministries, or activities, seen as manifestations of the Holy Spirit; if so, then Jesus Christ becomes the focus — He is uplifted. He is Lord! If a gift, ministry, or activity uplifts another person, thing, teaching or practice other than Jesus Himself as Lord, then it damages the Body of Christ. If it does not uplift Jesus Christ as Lord, then this means something else is being uplifted; if it is something else other than uplifting Christ as Lord, then it is foreign to the Body of Christ. In the Body of Christ, only Jesus Christ is Lord, only He is the center — only He is elevated to the highest position.

Factions are formed when various believers identify themselves with an emphasis on a given teaching, experience, or doctrinal system. Those in a faction are prone to uplift a thing or a spiritual gift higher than Jesus Christ. That is why there is a depreciation of others who do not uplift the same emphasis of the faction. The result of this is competition or jockeying for superiority with those uplifting something else. A faction, no matter how good, is gathered around some other item. It is driven — purposefully or inadvertently — by lifting these "things" above Jesus Christ. Only if everyone uplifts Jesus Christ as Lord will such factions be eliminated.

Love Is Essential in the Lord's Assembly

> Though I speak with the tongues of men and of angels, but have not love, I have become sounding brass or a clanging cymbal. And though I have [the gift of] prophecy, and understand all mysteries and all knowledge, and though I have all faith, so that I could remove mountains, but have not love, I am nothing. And though I bestow all my goods to feed [the poor], and though I give my body to be burned, but have not love, it profits me nothing. Love suffers long [and] is kind; love does not envy; love does not parade itself, is not puffed up; does not behave rudely, does not seek its own, is not provoked, thinks no evil; does not rejoice in iniquity, but rejoices in the truth; bears all things, believes all things, hopes all things, endures all things. Love never fails. But whether [there are] prophecies, they will fail; whether [there are] tongues, they will cease; whether [there is] knowledge, it will vanish away . . . When I was a child, I spoke as a child, I understood as a child, I thought as a child; but when I became a man, I put away childish things. For now we see in a mirror, dimly, but then face to face. Now I know in part, but then I shall know just as I also am known. And now abide faith, hope, love, these three; but the greatest of these [is] love.
>
> (1 Cor. 13:1-8)

Verses from 1 Corinthians 13 are often quoted within the context of marriage. Some of these verses are frequently used during a wedding ceremony. But in context, this chapter is relating to the ekklesia, the assembly of the Lord. Clearly, the beginning of this chapter is contrasting some of the gifts manifested in Chapter 12; therefore, the content of Chapter 13 directly continues the thought in Chapter 12. This chapter on love can be an explicit development to define the Lord's New Commandment given during the Last Supper: Love one another as I have loved you (John 13:34). Again, the connection of the Lord's ekklesia (assembly) and the Last Supper is revealed.

It is evident: "New Commandment Love" is needed in an environment where there is such a wide disparity among believers in an ekklesia. It is this love which breaks down factious walls between believers. It is this love which causes believers to nurture and honor others dissimilar to themselves. Racially, politically, socio-economically, doctrinally, experientially, even with the gifting of the Spirit, believers abound with variations. All these are destined to result in factions unless they disappear in an atmosphere of love. "New Commandment Love" remains eternal. The greatest gift needed in the Body is love. Without love, as shown in I Corinthians 13, no matter how much a person may be gifted and absolute in their gifts, they are all for nothing; nor will they profit the Body of Christ.

It is within the environment of the ekklesia where people discover rich diversity. There is the need for love which suffers long and is kind; love does not envy; love does not parade itself; is not puffed up; does not behave rudely; does not seek its own; and is not provoked. The more conflicts we have in thinking, methods, doctrine, and so-called "spiritual experiences" within the ekklesia, the more "New Commandment Love" is needed to manifest the oneness of His Body.

Many pastors would apply this matter of love in their respective churches by telling their members to love one another, but this, as well, would be a misapplication. Overall, churches today are self-selecting in grouping people with similar-based goals, teachings, and practices of their respective ministers; therefore, loving one another within a church context is almost like loving yourself since it is easy to love another person like you. Whereas, loving one another in an ekklesia, as defined by 1 Corinthians 13, is sorely needed since one would need to literally love another person who may be their "enemy" — politically, racially, or doctrinally.

Many times, a Christian doctrine or practice can become so contentious it divides people within the same family. That is why real love is to love others who are dissimilar to one's self. This love can only come from the Lord, "... *as I have loved you*" in the New Commandment. This love is only achieved if the Lord Jesus Himself loves others within and through believers. This manifestation of oneness will cause the world to believe in Jesus Christ.

In this chapter of love, Paul used the metaphor of being a child and putting away childish things when one becomes mature. He also said followers of Jesus can only know in part, seeing things dimly, but one day everything will become clear. Many factions among Christians exist due to confidence in their correct doctrine or custom; if you don't see things their way, then you are in error. For example, one can be so certain regarding the doctrine of predestination. If another considers there is "free will," that person will be judged by the person who affirms predestination, to be in error.

Contrariwise, this goes in reverse if someone who is absolutely convinced people have a free choice in relation to salvation. Some Christians are adamant about "word of faith" preachers — they're nothing more than charlatans . . . those influenced by such teachings are deceived. If we apply this part of Chapter 13, then each side of every factious debate should be reflected in humility because we realize we only know in part . . . spiritual things are simply unclear. Various kinds of doctrinal understanding can be like a toy to a child. When a person is mature, they will no longer fight for toys, but will instead be a person who can love indiscriminately in Christ.

Dropping childish things does not mean a person no longer speaks in tongues, if that is his or her gift. Neither does it mean a person can no longer believe in God's predestination if that is her conviction. It does mean he or she can be comfortable in what the Lord has given to them without arguing and fighting over it. It is one thing to share a given understanding or experience as a member in the Body, but it is another thing to always argue or try to convert others to your way of thinking.

When something is contrary to your own understanding, it is important to listen to "opposing views" — learn to listen to other points of view without being envious or threatened. Even when a person clearly says something not in accordance with the truth in the Word, it is still important to correct members in meekness and in love.

When believers in the Lord's assembly drop their factions and become members in the universal Body of Christ, they will enjoy the freedom of fellowship, sharing, and ministering to anyone and everyone in the assembly. Each believer is a distinct individual; yet, completely one in fellowship with all individuals within the One Body of Christ. The following diagram displays a "reset to one." Within one ekklesia gathering, believers become transformed from being factious to true oneness. This process doesn't have to take days, months, or years. This oneness can happen immediately because all believers are already baptized into One Body and all drink of the same Spirit. They are already one to begin with at birth. Oneness is in the DNA of the Trinity which abides in every believer in Jesus Christ. The diagram below shows one fellowship within one ekklesia, assembly.

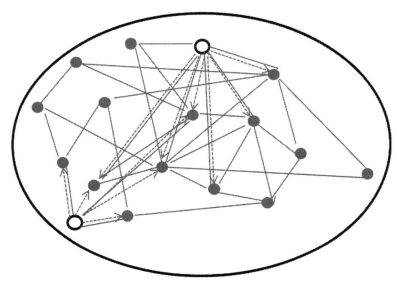

Figure 8 - One Fellowship, One Ekklesia

The Manifestation of Oneness answers the Lord's Prayer

> Therefore, if the whole church comes together in one place, and all speak with tongues, and there come in [those who are] uninformed or unbelievers, will they not say that you are out of your mind? But if all prophesy, and an unbeliever or an uninformed person comes in, he is convinced by all, he is convicted by all. And thus the secrets of his heart are revealed; and so, falling down on [his] face, he will worship God and report that God is truly among you. How is it then, brethren? Whenever you come together, each of you has a psalm, has a teaching, has a tongue, has a revelation, has an interpretation. Let all things be done for edification.
>
> (1 Cor. 14:23-26)

In 1 Corinthians 14, the last chapter illuminating how the assembly is to function, Paul states all can prophesy one by one (1 Cor. 14:31). First, let's define *prophecy*. According to *Vine's Expository Dictionary*, prophecy is "to speak forth the counsel of God, His message." The etymology of the Greek word includes enlightening and explaining by bringing a hidden thought into light for our understanding. Certainly, the ability to predict the future can be a prophecy, but that is not the primary meaning here.

Consequently, prophecy is any utterance which brings light and understanding to the hidden mysteries of Christ and His Body, the assembly. Not everyone can be a prophet to predict the future or to bring out what is hidden in a person's heart like the special prophets in 1 Corinthians 12:28-29. In this chapter, Paul says everyone in the ekklesia can prophesy one by one. Based on such a charge from Paul, it is necessary to come back to this portion of Scripture to apply the meaning of this word in Greek, bringing to light what is hidden.

So, what is hidden in God which needs to enlighten our understanding? In Colossians 2:2 it says the mystery (or "hidden truth") of God is Christ. The only way to know and understand God is to know Christ. Jesus Christ unlocks the mystery of God. Those who do not know Jesus Christ will find God an unsolvable mystery, but when Christ is revealed and enjoyed, God is realized and experienced.

In Ephesians 3:3-6 it says the mystery of Christ has to do with the Jews and the nations becoming joint heirs, joint members of One Body, and joint partakers. Even Jesus Christ today is a mystery. It is the One Body of Christ, the assembly, that manifests Jesus Christ to the entire universe. When the people of this world witness the oneness of God's people, they will know and believe the person and work of Jesus Christ.

Therefore, Ephesians 5:32 says Christ together with His assembly, is a great mystery. Two mysteries combined become a great mystery. Prophets are then needed to bring to light and reveal both Christ and His Body, the assembly. The mystery of Christ revealed is His One Body, the ekklesia.

Additionally, Ephesians 3:9 says Paul was charged to bring to light the economy (i.e., "stewardship" or "dispensation") of the mystery hidden in God. In short, the economy of God is completely related to Jesus Christ and His corporate body, the assembly (see chapter 11 in the book *ONE*). Today, even God's economy is a mystery which needs to be brought to light. Therefore, any speaking which unveils, teaches, brings to light, and causes people to understand and appreciate varied aspects of Christ, His One Body of believers, and His economy is prophesying.

In the New Testament, almost all the verses referring to the speaking of prophets were related to Jesus Christ or the Holy Spirit. Only a few instances refer to a prediction concerning the future. Therefore, every believer is qualified to give New Testament prophecies by unveiling the things of Christ at the appropriate time. This prophesying can be in the form of a song, a prayer, a teaching, a revelation, or a tongue with interpretation. "Five words" spoken at the appropriate time to unveil Christ is good enough for building up the assembly (1 Cor. 14:19). This aspect of everyone having opportunity to speak out is the environment of an ekklesia. Remember, a secular ekklesia is where diverse residents of a community are called together. They can all voice their opinions which frequently causes confusion (Acts 19:32). Similarly, in the Lord's ekklesia, everyone can speak one by one to unveil Christ and His Body, but without confusion (1 Cor. 14:31-33).

Since everyone in the assembly can speak, everyone also needs to exercise discernment to either question, receive or reject the various speakings which take place in an assembly. This will cause each one to look to the Lord and check Scripture to consider whether a given "speaking" is healthy to receive as from the Lord. This exercise of discernment will help each participant of the assembly to grow and know the speaking of the Lord in the Body.

In contrast to a minister speaking in a church, the minister cannot be interrupted; however, in the ekklesia, any speaking prophet can be interrupted when the Spirit moves to enlighten another member in the assembly. The one speaking should yield and let the one interrupting speak.

By 1 Corinthians 14, the assembly is expressing Christ in the oneness of the Body. Each can speak what the Lord has shown him/her to uplift Jesus Christ as Lord. The diversity of speaking, manifesting Jesus as His One Body causes an unbeliever to fall down and worship God because God is manifested in the assembly while the saints are prophesying in this manner. How awesome is this!

In one assembly, called together by God, believers start off in factions, but through the maturing of the assembly, they become truly one. Individually, they are still found in Christ with their distinct gifts, understanding, and experience, but now they are no longer divided by any factious walls. They are now accepting others who are different from them — having genuine fellowship together. They speak one to another regarding their experiences with Christ which they have gained and seen for the building up of all the members in the assembly.

Instead of fighting and arguing between factions, we find loving one another and nourishing one another for growth of the assembly. Again, this does not have to take years, months, or even weeks to accomplish; it can happen over the course of one gathering of an ekklesia. This is the Lord's assembly.

In such an assembly, believers are built up, and the unbelieving become believers. They are convicted, and convinced God is real and living among believers of this ekklesia. They are so convicted they fall before God in worship. This is the power of oneness; this is the moving of the Spirit in the atmosphere of oneness. This is what happens when diverse believers enter true oneness.

When true ekklesia is manifested, His prayer in John 17 is answered. Jesus prayed the world will know and believe Him when His followers are one as the Father and Son are one. Here in 1 Corinthians 14 is the fulfillment of our Lord's Prayer. Wow! There was no gospel campaign; not a special revival meeting; and no uninterrupted preaching by a gifted evangelist. It was just a regular ekklesia of the Lord happening in someone's home. Yet, the Spirit was moving in accordance with the oneness of His Body; therefore, people were built up; others came to salvation. This is the manifestation of the Lord's ekklesia.

In the view of the New Testament, ekklesia-style fellowship should be happening in every locality and community, in homes, from house to house. The kingdom of God spreads in this manner. It is very practical, and in a very experiential way through a community enjoying fellowship from house to house.

God Is Moving in the Insignificant

Often when Christians think of God's move, the imagery in their minds is one of masses being converted. Naturally, Acts, where 3,000 people came into the faith, comes to mind. When a person reads about the Lord praying for His followers to be one, so the world would believe, the imagination is akin to a stadium full of Christians being one in worship to God which in turn leads to a large portion of the population of the city or county to believe in Jesus and be saved. But consider this verse:

> Do not despise these small beginnings [things], for the LORD rejoices to see the work begin, to see the plumb line in Zerubbabel's hand.
> – Zech. 4:10 NLT

The Lord's ekklesia manifested in a home appears insignificant. Think about how many unbelievers can be affected in a home assembly. It's so few compared to the whole world. It would be easy to despise such a small thing. Christians frequently dream about seeing a great movement: TV and radio campaigns, headline news, stadiums full of people, mass conversions, etc. In John 17 Jesus says that the "world will believe," – the assumption is somehow the world of seven billion people will believe when they see millions of Christians in some kind of expression of oneness.

It is this sort of reasoning which begets "ecumenism." This movement is purely organizational. It is the work of major Christian organizations attempting unity through negotiation and compromise. It may be considered as an endeavor akin to the United Nations of Christian Churches. One of the biggest proponents of ecumenism is the Roman Catholic Church (RC). The RC considers herself to be the one true church; they believe their responsibility is to bring unity to all churches.

There is also a similar concept among certain pastoral associations – not only in a given community, but throughout an entire region. No doubt it's commendable when pastors/ministers of various churches and denomination gather together for prayer and fellowship for the sake of oneness. It is truly an improvement for pastors who have contrary doctrines and views to gather together to pray.

Planning unity events where Christians from various churches come together to worship is commendable; however, even after decades of these types of gatherings, it is rare there are lasting effects among believers in the churches of these pastors. There remains a dearth of sound teaching instructing God's people to regularly greet other believers in their daily living who are in other churches. Believers simply are not being taught to open their homes to assemble with a diverse group of believers. Therefore, even after decades of successful gatherings of pastors' associations with unity events in a region, the effect on the community at large is minimal – with evangelistic crusades at great expense producing little viable follow-up with "church growth."

What if the "world" mentioned in John 17 refers to the world surrounding those gathering as the Lord's ekklesia? If there are twenty people gathering in a home as the Lord's "called out" ones, then the world in view could be the people directly associated with those twenty including friends, colleagues, neighbors, and relatives. This is the world these twenty will affect. Through these 20, the world around them will see their testimony of loving one another and the attraction of witnessing the fruit of the Spirit.

Once the saints begin to invite their "surrounding world" to a meal at the home of someone hosting the Lord's ekklesia, then the saints functioning as members of the Body in love and oneness will impact that world. The world of that assembly, as described in 1 Corinthians, will see God manifested. Convicted, they will fall down to worship God and believe in Jesus Christ.

An assembly of diverse believers bound together in the unity of the Spirit, manifesting Jesus Christ by their love for one another, and "prophesying" concerning their understanding and experience of Jesus Christ, will have an immediate effect on unbelievers and novices in that assembly.

It is not a matter of a grandiose movement where millions of believers are joined in oneness before the Lord's Prayer is answered. As soon as one home expresses His assembly according to His desire, its effect will result in building up — manifesting God's presence to such an extent unbelievers will desire to worship God. That's awesome! There is no need to wait for millions upon millions of Christians to be one before the world is impacted.

One assembly in a home will have an instant impact upon that small part of the world. Initially, in Acts, 3,000 men were baptized in the name of Jesus; after that, the Body of Christ exponentially grew through home gatherings — from house to house. People kept coming to Jesus as the brethren through the assembly's eating meals together, while rejoicing in one accord, spontaneously saw scores of souls saved and brought into fellowship (Acts 2:47). As one home affects their small part of the world, and another home affects another small part of the world, the effect of thousands upon thousands of homes throughout the earth will ultimately cause the world throughout the globe to believe.

At the end of Acts, the greatest apostle completed his narrative by preaching and teaching the kingdom of God in his humble rented dwelling. Where Paul ended his quest to spread the kingdom of God and preaching those things pertaining to Jesus Christ, even so, believers should continue his pattern of hosting the Lord's ekklesia in their homes.

In a community, an assembly may start in one home; *if that one home is effective and fruitful, the Lord will spread to another home, house after house*. Just as humanity dominates the earth through its fruitfulness — one family at a time, the Lord's kingdom will reign on earth through His ekklesia — one household at a time. Therefore, let's not despise a home assembly as a small thing. The Lord rejoices to see the work begin.

In conclusion, in keeping with the distinction between ministries and ekklesia, the vision and practice of house to house ekklesia does not negate the need for ministries. More gifted believers will rise up to do ministries — operating in different gifts of the Spirit. Some will be raised to take the lead for children's ministry, high school ministry, college ministry, prison ministry, ministry to those fighting addictions, working with the homeless and so on. Some will mature their gift into a teaching ministry — perhaps specializing on certain books of the Bible or the entire Scriptures! Some may teach others how to pray or practice spiritual gifts.

All these types of ministry are taking place today. They should continue to increase with effectiveness. Saints who want to support such ministries should commit themselves and serve for a certain duration. Without "time and space" commitment to accomplish a certain work for the Lord, it most likely will not be accomplished. In this vibrant paradigm of building ekklesia, all sorts of various ministries will produce people with a vision for God's eternal purpose and a heart to participate and function in the Lord's ekklesia as prescribed in the New Testament.

Every effective ministry has the capacity to gather people in support of their ministry, but the goal of any and all ministries is to produce the Lord's ekklesia as described in 1 Corinthians 11-14 in homes, house after house. It is there each member can speak to unveil and uplift Jesus Christ. Everyone will be built up and "their world" will believe. Glory to God!

10.
What about Pastors and Ministers?

This chapter addresses the concerns of pastors, ministers, and leaders of churches today. Let's assume you are a church elder or a formal member of the clergy, having made it thus far in the book — and have been attracted to the overall vision and premise as presented. You're seeing our Lord desires all His children to be one, while at the same time you're thinking about the practical steps which need to be implemented in order for individual believers to proactively go and greet other believers — opening their homes to be hosts to the Lord's ekklesia.

While the text makes clear ministries (churches) and the Lord's ekklesia, His assembly, do not have to be in conflict; notwithstanding, due to entrenched practices found in today's churches, it may be too daunting a task for those in full-time ministry to see how they can pivot toward this new paradigm. It is new in the sense it is different from church practices since Constantine in the 4th century. Actually, these concepts are quite ancient because they are rooted in the New Testament. This book is simply proposing God's people return to the way God ordained for the building up of His ekklesia, assembly — reset to ONE.

Generally, the problem is traditional "church practice" has been declining. Worse yet, this decline in church membership has accelerated.[12] Sure, there are some churches for a host of reasons which appear successful and growing, but the majority are struggling to increase adherents — even treading water to maintain. Moreover, sizeable Christian populations are "church hopping" to find the most *avant-garde* ministry in their area. The commitment to one denomination or church is waning. Christians find themselves much more mobile and will gravitate to what's the most exciting church in town.

---

12 http://www.churchleadership.org/apps/articles/default.asp?articleid=42346&columnid=4545

Consequently, when a church with a dynamic speaker brings about new excitement or generates effective programs, other churches in the area lose attendees. Instead of expanding the pie, churches are competing for a shrinking pie — aka, "sheep stealing."

Methods of having church are being exhausted. Ideas for different ways to have church have been well spent. Old liturgical styles used in the Roman Church or state churches, fiery preaching from pulpits, Bible teaching formats, "feel good" messages, creative worship styles from pipe organs, choirs, to full blown rock bands with lasers and smoke, integrating performing arts, Pentecostal excitement, "cell groups" and "home groups" — well, you name it; just about anything people can think of to grow churches and maintain membership have been tried; nevertheless, church membership in the West continues to decline while the general population is perpetually growing.

Since it is such a challenge to grow and maintain church membership, why not try something radical? Why not try something out of the ordinary, normally not attempted by church leaders? Why not come back to the Biblical way of building the Lord's ekklesia? This chapter will consider out-of-the-box opportunities and assess the risks from a church leadership prospective in pivoting toward practicing oneness and ekklesia.

Special Gifts for the Equipping of the Saints

Initially, let's consider the Scriptural backing for having pastors and specially-gifted ministers in the Body of Christ. In Ephesians 4:11 below is the most often quoted verse for having pastors and other ministry leaders.

> And he himself gave some to be apostles, some prophets, some evangelists, some pastors and teachers, equipping the saints for the work of ministry, to build up the Body of Christ, until we all reach unity in the faith and in the knowledge of God's Son, growing into maturity with a stature measured by Christ's fullness. Then we will no longer be little children, tossed by the waves and blown around by every wind of teaching, by human cunning with cleverness in the techniques of deceit. But speaking the truth in love, let us grow in every way into him who is the head — Christ. From him the whole body, fitted and knit together by every supporting ligament, promotes the growth of

> the body for building up itself in love by the proper working of each individual part.
>
> (Eph. 4:11-16 CSB)

In context, the verses preceding Ephesians 4:11 speak of Jesus Christ's death, resurrection, ascension, and subsequent outpouring of the Spirit. The Lord Jesus became the Head of the Body in His ascension and the pouring out of His Spirit — God anointed the entire Body by His Spirit. In doing so He gave some special gifts to the body: some apostles, prophets, evangelists, pastors (shepherds) and teachers.

Not all Bible teachers agree whether this is referring to five types of ministries or four. Those who say four combine the last two as pastors and teachers into one since they claim the way to pastor or shepherd is through sound teaching of Scriptures. In any case, whether there are four or five, it has little bearing; the point is the Head of the Body has given these specially gifted brethren a specific gift or service for the greater Body of Christ.

We cannot deny there are "gifted brethren" who equip God's people for a greater service to all. Without these gifted ones the Body will not be properly equipped.

Therefore, support and prayers for those in leadership as pastors, teachers, evangelists, prophets, and apostles are needed. It is critical that these special gifts function to their full potential.

These "equipping members" are motivated directly by the Lord to seek Him, to study His word, to care for God's people, to be sent by the Lord for His purpose, and to preach the gospel. Once they have received God's calling, their desire is to persist in their calling. They are destined to seek and serve the Lord no matter what challenges they face. These gifted brethren depend on the Lord alone for their motivation, livelihood, and methods used in fulfilling their charge from the Head of the Body.

Paul and the early apostles certainly met these qualifications. Although Paul considered himself "the least of all the saints" (Eph. 3:8), he became the pattern for all those gifted in the Lord's Body (1 Cor. 4:16).

Read the testimonies of the various men and women of God throughout history. There is a persistent pattern — an effort to remain faithful to the Lord in their calling no matter what the cost. They continue to trust the Lord, seek His encouragement, continue in the Lord's service, and minister Christ to people in various ways — even when they have no one else supporting them. These specially-gifted members endure in their visions and ministries by abiding in the Lord and drawing their validation from Him alone.

Without controversy, gifted members of the Body are needed — let's examine their specific functions. Apostles are those given by the Lord for establishing and building of the Lord's ekklesia in various locations through preaching, teaching, and prophesying; essentially, the apostles employ all the various speaking attributes to accomplish their mission.

Prophets bring to light the person and work of Jesus Christ to His assembly, opening the eyes of God's people from His Word. Gifted prophets reveal and apply various aspects of Christ in any given situation. Brethren, through the prophetically-gifted, can see how Christ, no matter the challenges, will strengthen and enable them to overcome and fulfill God's eternal purpose.

Evangelists bring the good news of Jesus Christ to people for their salvation. Pastors (shepherds) and teachers care for the saints for their growth — establishing them in the faith through healthy teachings and applications of Scripture in life's diverse environments. Nevertheless, according to these verses, although there are such gifted ones, they all have only one primary function.

Equipping Every Believer to Have a Ministry

Ephesians 4:12 states the primary function of these gifted brethren is to equip or perfect the saints enabling them to do the work of ministry for the building up of the Body of Christ. This means it does not matter if they are an apostle, prophet, evangelist, shepherd and teacher — their main function is to perfect the saints by equipping them for ministry. These gifted ones are not there to build up their own ministries but to equip believers, so God's people will do the work of ministry.

In other words, those bestowed as apostles will send out more apostles. Gifted prophets will equip more saints who in turn will unveil how to apply Christ in their speaking to directly build up the assembly. Surely, evangelists are not only called to preach the gospel; likewise, they inspire and guide all saints to whom they minister to preach the gospel wherever they go. Gifted pastors and teachers will not only shepherd and teach the sheep in the Lord's pasture, but also teach them to do the same to a few young believers around them.

As saints are equipped to do the work of the ministry, then the Body of Christ will be built up. If those gifted disregard their primary function by operating only for "gift sake," then no matter how impressive they are in utilizing their gifts, the Body of Christ will not be edified or built up. Ephesians 4 is not complete until ordinary believers are raised up to function — in whatever small capacity — whereby they themselves are enabled to build up the Body of Christ. Building up the Body does not depend on gifted ones, but upon common followers of Jesus Christ equipped to participate in ministering the Lord to others.

What is the result when ordinary believers are equipped or perfected? First, they begin to function in ministry, no matter how small that ministry may be. It can be as small as consistently ministering to just one other person. Members who are truly equipped do their part by directly contributing to the building up of the One Body. No, they may not, as Paul, initiate gospel preaching in a completely unevangelized region. Instead, they can visit someone's home or open their own home to teach the Bible like the Apostle Paul did at the end of Acts.

They may not have the gift of a prophet whose ministry unveils the mysteries hidden in God throughout Scriptures, but they can be prophets who unveil Christ and His purpose in the Scriptures at timely moments when someone needs encouragement. They may not be able to preach like Peter did and baptize thousands after one message, but they can bring the good news to at least their relatives and friends.

Finally, they may not be a pastor or a shepherd caring for hundreds of believers, but they can at least shepherd and teach one other person in a way of discipleship. The primary goal of these special gifts should inspire and equip ordinary believers to implement the ministry given by those who are gifted.

To accomplish this, those so gifted need to function as apostles, prophets, evangelists, shepherds, and teachers; while simultaneously equipping the saints and encouraging them do the work of the ministry themselves. Only when ordinary believers are equipped and directly activated to do their part of ministry will the Body of Christ be built up.

The apostle Paul was able to equip new believers in Thessalonica within a few months. After he equipped them, he was able to leave while they in turn practiced how Paul did things. Paul said the Thessalonians spread the gospel throughout their neighboring regions enabling Paul and the other apostles to go elsewhere (1 Thess. 1:6-8).

These Thessalonians became a pattern to other believers just as Paul was a pattern to them. What we see here is Paul equipping saints in order that they directly minister in the building up the Body of Christ. Paul did not endlessly equip saints in one place — no, he equipped them to do the work of the ministry and they in turn set about to do just that!

"Five-fold Ministry" Results in Building Up One Body

According to Ephesians 4:13, the result of building up the Body of Christ is expressed in unity. Arriving at *"the unity of the faith"* with all believers is the manifestation of the Body being built up. This unity is of the faith and of the knowledge of the Son of God. This faith is what people need for salvation. Faith in Jesus Christ affirms He is God Who became man. He died for our sins, resurrected, and ascended as Lord of all — now He has sent the Promise of the Spirit to indwell us. That is the concise definition of THE faith. All believers started with that faith. Can they all return and remain in this simple faith?

Divisions come when believers add something else to this saving faith as a requirement for salvation. Additional items are typically taken from the Bible; nevertheless, they are superfluous requirements. These add-ons complicate the saving faith which in turn can divide Christians. Therefore, unity is in the simplicity of the faith. Whoever comes back to the faith of Jesus Christ is in unity with all others with the same faith. To equip God's people is to help them understand and practice *"so great a salvation"* (Heb. 2:3) enabling them to accept and fellowship with all those with the same faith.

Also, unity is focused on the knowledge of the Son of God. Paul said in Philippians 3:8 he counted all his religious attainments to be dross, since they are nothing when compared to the excellency of the knowledge of Jesus Christ his Lord. Since Paul was from the sect of the Pharisees, he knew the Scriptures. He knew the law and lived by the law. Nevertheless, he counted all those things as a loss compared to the knowledge of Jesus Christ.

Most divisions among Christians are over things in the Bible — even over the Bible itself. What about the knowledge of the Son of God? Let's consider Him (Heb. 3:1). Let's discover through Scripture all what He accomplished at His crucifixion and resurrection. Let's dwell on His ascension whereby He is now Lord of All! Let's study those items of His grace through the Promise of His Indwelling Spirit Who comforts and nourishes His people. Let's fellowship with one another concerning the mystery of the ekklesia, His assembly, for which He earnestly prayed. Isn't the very increase of Himself His heart's desire? If believers would stay in the realm of the knowledge of the Son of God, only unity would remain. This is the truth God's people need to speak one to another in love (Eph 4;15). [Note: In the book **ONE**, Part 2, the matter of truth is discussed in depth.]

The spiritually immature will be blown about and easily deceived into a faction or sect, but those who are truly being equipped and speaking truth in love will grow up in all things into Jesus Christ who is the Head of the body. Factions and sects among Christians exist because of add-ons — no matter how essential they may appear. If it is Jesus Christ, plus something else, then we're missing the mark. If we're determined to emphasize an extraneous teaching, or practice beyond the "simplicity that is in Christ" (2 Cor. 11:3) — thinking it supports salvation, even enables a more spiritual life — again, that very "essential" can be nothing more than a distraction for believers . . . it has little to do with *"holding the Head"* (Col. 2:19: *"And not holding fast the Head, from whom all the body, nourishes and knit together by joints and ligaments, grows with the increase that is from God."*

The oneness of the body can only grow into maturity by holding the head, Jesus Christ. The Body comes about only through the Headship of Christ. By holding on to the faith and knowledge of the Son of God, believers grow into maturity in Christ. They can be one with all kinds of diverse believers, while exercising whatever gift God has given them. Together with extra-gifted members, which are the ligaments in the Body, all "ordinary believers" will do their part in the building up of the Body by themselves (Eph. 4:16).

Something is wrong when pastors and other specially gifted brethren draw people to their church; yes, seriously wrong, when ordinary church attendees never graduate; never can function in their own ministries. By not greeting other believers outside their own church or excluding fellowship in their own homes with other believers, then no matter how much these five-fold gifted ministers are functioning to increase their church membership, they have failed in their primary directive in equipping the saints to do the work of the ministry.

The outcome of saints being equipped for ministry is manifested in the oneness or unity of the faith and the full knowledge of the Son of God. They become mature in Christ. Oneness with other believers in the Body is a result of maturity compared to the Corinthians who were divided because they were babes in Christ. The sign of maturity is oneness in the Body with all kinds of diverse believers. Divisions are a sign of immaturity. Gifted members, such as pastors, function to equip God's people to the point where those in their churches "arrive at the unity of the faith" (Eph. 4:13) and the knowledge of the Son of God with other believers. This is serious business for all who aspire as "church leaders": Are the ordinary believers under your care able to be one with all kinds of diverse believers without being blown about by every wind of doctrine?

As a pastor and a leader, are you able to equip, to shepherd God's flock to a point where your church members can greet all kinds of other believers in the joy and confidence of the Holy Spirit? Alas! Are your sheep inhibited from ministry, ill-equipped, unable to visit other believers, closing off their homes for fellowship and assembly? If so, you seriously need to reconsider the purpose of your mission and the methods so employed. Pointing back to the earlier chapters in this book: Saints being shepherded should be able to practice *greeting* according to Romans 16 — willing and able to host an ekklesia in their homes according to 1 Corinthians 11-14. This should be the mission and practice of every gifted member in the Body of Christ.

What is exposed in these verses is opposite to what is normally practiced in the "pastoral system." The pastoral system today results in regular believers remaining spiritually needy and churches segregated from other churches. Instead of entering a work of ministry in serving Jesus Christ to people around them, believers remain silent in church and outside of church. Instead of being able to greet and fellowship with all kinds of other believers not in their own church, they become more critical and suspicious of believers in other church groups.

Coming to grips with this present condition within the churches, the Lord would call out those leaders to repent and change their ways. If you are a pastor, a leader, gifted by the Lord, then you are clearly needed; but consider whether your efforts are producing believers who are actively building up the One Body of Christ. Are the sheep of your flock malnourished — divided from the other members of His Body? Are they maturing, or do they remain as babes tossed into confusion by every new teaching that comes down the pike?

Leaving "Church" As Is

Scripture shows us gifted members given by the Lord work together for the building up of the One Body. These verses clearly demonstrate there are multiple, extraordinary members given by the Lord, all of whom have the goal of building the Body of Christ by equipping ordinary saints to do the work of ministry. This clearly supports Paul's view found in 1 Corinthians where he said three independent, specially gifted ministers: Paul, Peter, and Apollos, are all servants who build up His Body in Corinth.

Since the Reformation, the Lord has given many special gifts to the Body. No doubt, there are so many items of truth which have been restored to us like justification by faith and the indwelling Holy Spirit. Many evangelists have brought the gospel of Christ to just about every corner of the globe. Notwithstanding this proliferation of the gospel and restoration of many items of Biblical truth, the issue of the oneness of His Body has not been a high priority.

Practicing oneness demands immediate restoration and focus. Tragically, so many with special gifts have spawned scores of sects and divisions—some purposefully, some inadvertently. When a believer is specially gifted with one or more of the five-fold ministries, they can be used by God; but at the same time, it is easy for them to draw people around them. If gifted ones are not careful, they may veer away from the pattern of Paul and the other early apostles. Once believers flock around them, then they can become another sectarian group. Every denomination and church federation were started by men or women who were at one time a real gift to the Body. However, instead of building up the One Body, they or their followers ended up organizing another group.

Just consider how many gifted men of God there have been throughout history. Yes, they have overall contributed to spiritual advancement, but the body of believers is still a baby in Christ, dormant, and fragmented. It seems throughout history, since the Reformation, real men of God with pure motives have been given by the Lord for His body, but their ministries were hijacked by the enemy, which has resulted in passivity and more divisions as surveyed in today's Christianity. What exactly is missing which has consistently caused more divisions by gifted men? Why can't gifted men and women of God work together to produce the One Body, the ekklesia? These are penetrating questions which should lead to greater urgency for us to return to the Scriptures in examining what is missing so that we might make a major course correction!

God's way of making radical changes throughout history is always by starting with one person or a handful of people. God rarely, miraculously affects His people in a massive way. He always starts with just one person or a small number of people. Through something small and insignificant, the results can become monumental.

No doubt this is the principle in Biblical history. Examples abound: Noah, Abraham, Moses, David, Mary, the twelve disciples, Paul. Here we have just one person or a handful of people starting from an insignificant or even an undesirable position; yet, God calls them. They challenge the majority. They find themselves against the current of the age. They eventually change the history of their world according to God's purpose.

Let us not continue the current history of Christianity. Let's consider afresh God's calling, His eternal purpose, the way of the New Testament, and the examples the original apostles have spoken about and lived as patterns. Let us not consider the insurmountable, the many issues which arise.

Let's be pioneers who reverse the downward trend and reach for the beginning when revival was spread through the oneness of His Body. If true conviction wrought by the Living Word of God grips our hearts — confirmed by the witness of the Holy Spirit, then even if just one person is obedient, against all odds, God will be faithful to exceed our expectations.

Servants of the Lord only need to do their small part in cooperating with God — He'll do the rest!

Questions and Answers

The following inquiries are from concerned pastors and ministers as to how ekklesia would be realized in relation to their ministries — response follows:

Protecting "My Flock"

Question: As a pastor, I am responsible for believers under my care. It would be risky to encourage "my flock" to go and greet all kinds of Christians since they can meet a "wolf" and be misled.

Response: This is a legitimate and widespread concern. If the goal of pastors is to equip and perfect ordinary believers until they have a solid foundation in the faith and knowing Jesus as the Son of God, how long does that take? Should it take weeks, months, or years? The longest time Paul stayed in a locality was two years, which was at Ephesus. In Thessalonica, it took Paul only months to establish a strong community of believers. We can logically conclude Paul felt these believers were sufficiently established to avoid "wolves" whose teachings would have drawn them away from the faith; apparently, between a few months to two years. In Rome, Paul made a blanket command for all saints to go greet one another without any qualifications as to whether they were established in the faith or not. It's the "wolves" who would discourage those under their influence to avoid greeting or receive greeting.

Physical parents raise their children to become mature and independent — even so, pastors and ministers of the gospel should shepherd their sheep with a similar goal in which the saints become sufficiently independent to raise their own ministries. Far too often over-protective parents delay a child's development. Keeping a flock dependent upon the pastor in this manner will result in the immaturity of the flock. Providing freedom to explore the Christian faith by pastors who grasp the importance of bringing saints into maturity requires guidance, not control.

In any case, at a certain point, pastors should encourage those under their shepherding to follow the Lord's command to greet other believers; thereby the saints will do their own work of ministry for the building up of the Body. After all, pastors need reminding: God's people are one flock belonging to the Lord Jesus as the Chief Shepherd. None of the saints are a possession of any church or pastor; therefore, there needs to be the utmost trust in the Chief Shepherd who will not lose any. Pastors can become too possessive of those under their care. Far too often they forget there is One Who is the Chief Shepherd — He is always with every believer . . . He will keep them and guide them. Eventually, as with our own biological children, we have to "let them stand on their own" — always bearing them in love . . . but love knows how to release them into maturity.

No Time for This

Question: Members do not have time to do the things you mentioned in this book since most are not even serving in church-oriented ministries.

Response: The first point concerning greeting is this: It should be the first thing young believers should know how to do — and all can do it. It doesn't have to be a scheduled event. Generally, there are believers surrounding members at work, at school, and even while commuting on a bus or train. If pastors encourage saints to greet, undoubtedly, they will find other saints to greet nearby. In their own neighborhoods, if someone has a heart to greet, they'll find them at the grocery store, mall or meet and greet parents and kids at the same school who are believers. The point being, all these places within one's daily life are full of opportunities to meet and greet the people of God over the course of a day. There are break times and lunch times where believers can experience greeting. If one has a heart to greet, there is time and opportunity to do so.

During greeting, they will know each other's testimony of faith in Christ, which will lead to praying for each other's challenges. Once this kind of greeting during one's daily living starts, then it would be natural to have a deeper connection over a meal together, to know each other's family, or to visit each other's homes. Greetings which take place in one's neighborhood can quickly lead to more social and spiritual interaction in each other's homes.

This kind of greeting is different than making time commitments to serve in various church ministries. Pastors would say, "If members of my congregation do not have time to join one of our church ministries such as: music, children, young adult, prison, elderly, homeless, or any other programs that we have, then how can I charge them to go greet?"

Other pastors may say, "If our members have time to greet, they can join one of our ministries first." It is critical to recognize greeting as commanded by Paul in Romans 16 is part of every believer's responsibility — it is something they can initiate during their daily living.

Joining a ministry within church is under the pastor's program. Members typically need to make a real commitment of time with a schedule to be at a certain place to participate in a particular ministry of the church. A lot of members cannot or do not want to make such a commitment. Church members learning how to greet other believers in their daily living are not in conflict with the scheduled ministry time of the church's programs. Therefore, pastors should not mix these two things together as if one's gain is the other's loss — meeting and greeting is not a "zero sum game" — it is for the oneness of His Body!

Believers who practice greeting open an entirely new area of spirituality and service once neglected. Since believers generally only associate spiritual activities with church programs, they unconsciously shut out all fellowship activities throughout their daily living. They are so used to partaking in "church orchestrated services," that they have been robbed of an entire swath of time in their daily lives where they can be active. They have compartmentalized between spiritual time for service with church activities and secular time in their daily living.

Greeting is un-programmed. It is not based on a schedule and it encourages every believer to become spiritually active in their daily living. All it takes is an individual initiative to obey Paul's command to greet. The same goes for God's people opening their homes for meals and fellowship. This type of fellowship does not have to be a regular occurrence. It can happen as the Spirit leads. Each believer is motivated to have more fellowship in their daily living. Pastors should recognize that God's people who are motivated to seek the Lord in this manner of "ordinary ministry," will grow into maturity in their own congregations — shouldn't that be what every pastor desires for his flock?

Not Starting Another Group

Question: Is this book suggesting that members start another Parachurch group to compete with churches?

Response: No, the message of this book is not for believers to start another group. There are already plenty of churches and groups which believers can join. Neither is this book proposing God's people leave a church they already enjoy and are being helped there. The message is this: All believers are already one; they already are part of the Body of Christ. There may be many ministries, churches and Christian groups who have diverse goals and charters, but there is only One Body of Christ. All believers are in the same Body together. The message of this book is to recognize that fact and act upon it. The two main actions needed, which do not have to conflict with current church practices, are to go and greet other believers in one's daily life, and to open their homes to host an assembly of assorted believers they meet in their practice of greeting.

Since ekklesia is composed of believers from various "factions," it is not possible for ekklesia to happen within any given church faction. Ekklesia must take place in a neutral location without the oversight and control of any ministry or church. Once an assembly comes under the control of any one ministry, it is no longer an ekklesia, but an extension of that ministry. That is why the view in this book demands our fellowship remain fluid, while hosting is focused on strangers. It is not building up another church to compete with current churches.

Gaining or Losing Members

Question: If believers in my church become so active outside of my church, will I eventually lose them as members?

Response: This really depends on the pastors' own motives and goals. If the pastors' motive is to shepherd those under one's influence to become spiritually mature and independent, then they are real spiritual "fathers." A spiritual father cannot lose their children. Consider the relationship between physical parents and their children: children, when they grow up to become independent, will appreciate their parents. Such a child-parent relationship does not terminate once they become independent. Likewise, spiritual children of pastors will appreciate their "fathers" more when their children function in their God-given capacity and are able to have ministry and fellowship on their own.

If a pastor causes those under his influence to grow by greeting and opening congregant homes for fellowship, those who are encouraged in this way will stay in fellowship and seek further guidance. A life relationship is built up through fellowship which cannot be broken. Just because ordinary believers are able to serve the Lord on their own does not mean their connection with their mentors and pastors is somehow terminated — to the contrary, it is enriched!

On the other hand, if the pastors' concentration is on growing "church membership" — viewing believers as a "number," then their energies will focus on things which will attract and maintain membership. These things may include sermon styles and preparation, music ministry and rehearsals, or having a wide-variety of ministerial programs. No doubt God can use all these various ministries to reach people. However, for most churches, this structure to grow and maintain membership becomes more challenging when there is a need to compete with other local ministries and churches with a bigger budget and better facilities. This becomes an uphill battle regardless of whether their members are out greeting or not. If their members start to consider they are just a number, and are not growing spiritually, then those who are serious concerning their spiritual growth will eventually leave or suffer from spiritual atrophy. If members are staying because of programs and services provided, then yes, they may stay, but most will continue to be spiritually dependent year after year. The tendency is to keep "shopping" for better programs in other churches.

There's a built-in desire for pastors to maintain control over membership which has negative results. If pastors are not at a charismatic level to engender and sustain loyalty, then church members will sense manipulation and domination within such churches. If they do, then eventually it is counterproductive since they will leave church and pastor, while their "shopping spree continues." If pastors are at a charismatic level to develop and retain loyalty, then they can be in danger of growing a "personality cult" following. Their members can become very spiritually active under the influence of such personalities, but then the group can become sectarian where they feel they do not need to fellowship with anyone else outside of their own group of believers associated with such pastors.

Members Rarely Fellowship with Each Other in their Own Churches

Question: I can't get our members to fellowship amongst each other, let alone go out and greet others outside of our church?

Response: When believers are segregated into various churches, they acquire the notion they can only fellowship freely with those in their own church since their "church practice" and beliefs parallel with their own. By limiting their spiritual activity to those of their own church, they conjecture this will avoid arguments and conflicting interpretations. The problem is that once people have the mind-set to only fellowship with those who are like them and avoid others, the set of people they will "fellowship" with will shrink down further and further because they become highly selective. Eventually, there may only be a couple of people with whom they have spiritual interactions.

Another reason, if the circle of fellowship is with the same group of church people, then there can be a thought everyone already knows what the other will say. If people in your church are learning the same things and have the same perspective, then there is little need for further discourse. Whatever one person says, the other already knows. I'm not saying that "familiarity breeds contempt" but I am saying, "I heard that already."

Also, when it is the same group of people, it can be more difficult to share your problems and questions because there may be some fear others in the group will discover what is shared in confidence. To limit potential gossip or suspicion among a familiar group, individuals may withhold from sharing things potentially damaging about themselves.

That is why when believers are encouraged to fellowship with all other believers around them, whether they are Catholic or Protestants, Reformed or Pentecostal, whether Evangelicals or no church affiliation at all, they will recognize the only common denominator among them is Jesus Christ. Since faith in Jesus Christ is our single requirement for fellowship, the universe of believers for greeting each other is limitless. If the followers of Jesus start reaching out to greet other fellow believers, they may find there are believers all around them. It is here they experience the love of God and the grace of Jesus Christ being shared — this is our common attraction for fellowship between all Christians. Any other emphasis becomes marginal at best, and at worst leads to tension or disputes. Those with a heart to greet other believers are then compelled to focus on Jesus Christ, His person and work.

All believers can testify to the love of God with all of His kindness, goodness, and patience. They can all speak of the mystery of Jesus Christ being both God and Man. They can apply the work of Jesus' crucifixion, resurrection, and ascension in their daily experiences. They can testify of their salvation encounters.

They can share their challenges with one another for mutual support and prayers. What a wonderful time of greeting and fellowship between believers who may be unfamiliar with one another. No doubt this kind of fellowship will lead to further encounters in the future. Again, are pastors teaching such encounters or "spiritual extensions" for their members? Are these items essential for "normal Christian life" practice? Greeting celebrates our oneness in Christ with the greater Body of Christ in answer to our Lord's Prayer in John 17.

If believers obey Paul's command to go greet in this way, the Triune God will be part of their daily living — believers will be brought into the fellowship of the Father, Son and Holy Spirit. Imagine, Jesus Christ is no longer relegated to just church activities. He will be real and living in the daily life of every believer. The positive impact upon the church where believers now attend will create a new vibrancy of the Spirit in that congregation!

It will generate more fellowship in their own churches. In other words, if pastors encourage their saints to go and greet other believers, those saints will become equipped to fellowship and will positively affect their own churches. Conversely, if they isolate saints in their churches from other believers, those saints will become stunted and their churches weak and ineffective.

Financial Support

Question: What about financial support?

Response: It is clear from 1 Corinthians 9:9-14 those who preach the gospel and shepherd believers as pastors should be supported financially. Believers who are being equipped spiritually by those gifted ones mentioned in Ephesians 4 should materially share with those helping them. God's people should be taught to honor and support those who are feeding them and perfecting them in the Lord. It is healthy for all believers to learn to give and share in this manner. Additionally, even when God's people are not directly benefiting from a gifted minister, their financial support to a servant of the Lord expresses His grace and fellowship toward their ministry (2 Cor. 8:4). In other words, when the apostles go out to minister, those who support them financially are participating in the same grace and fellowship as the apostles. It is worthwhile to support true ministers of Christ.

On the other hand, even though the apostle Paul had a right to receive financial support from those he brought to the Lord — those he was spiritually perfecting — he didn't use this right. By preaching the good news willingly, his reward from the Lord was he could minister Christ to people without charge (1 Cor. 9:18). He did his best not to put a financial strain on believers to whom he ministered the gospel by working night and day through carrying on some sort of tent making business (1 Thess. 2:9, Acts 18:3). Paul was the greatest apostle whose life became a pattern to be emulated by all ministers: he financially supported himself — even his co-workers — so as not to be a burden to anyone (Acts 20:34).

This pattern of Paul exemplifies a beautiful relationship between the extra-gifted ministers and ordinary saints who they supply and equip. From the side of the saints, they should happily supply and share materially with those equipping them. Likewise, from the side of the pastors and ministers, they should not demand any support, rather, they should do their best not to be a burden. This is loving one another in the Lord.

This may come as a shock to some; however, "gifted ministry" in the New Testament was not looked upon as a job with a salary. Shopping around for compensation and fringe benefits was not on the radar. No, the servant of the Lord was to serve God and His people with joy and faithfulness, utterly dependent upon God for one's livelihood whether through a secular job or by receiving support from fellow believers, or from both sources.

No doubt God will supply all the needs of those serving Him. God will not allow His servants to starve or to die from poverty. As gifted ministers, there is a need to learn to be poor and to have plenty — to be *"abased and to abound"* (Phil. 4:12). They should not set any requirements on having a certain standard of living so when they are poor, they can be at peace and when they have plenty, they can share with others. It is a travesty for gifted ministers to abuse their right of financial support by using money from their donors to live at a standard of living much higher than those they serve; this is especially egregious given our propensity to display the "gospel of prosperity" as a sign of God's so-called blessing in one's ministry.

If pastors and ministers do not have to worry about supporting a physical church facility and the associated overhead, it is not too difficult to serve the Lord with their full time and be supported by those they shepherd and equip. Can a full-time minister shepherd and equip twenty believers or twenty families? That should be a reasonable task. Can believers who are being helped to spiritually grow to maturity share 5% of their income with someone equipping them? Tithing among Christians is considered to be 10%; therefore, 5% is half of that. This should be a reasonable burden of love to bear to support those equipping them. If on average 20 believers share 5% of their income with their equipping pastor, the pastor will have a similar living standard as those he serves.

This is not suggested as a rule nor does it establish a new requirement. This is merely showing how reasonable, without undue burden on anyone, believers who have this kind of heart can share material things with those who minister to their needs — then the Lord can call out many more ministers to serve Him full time. A gifted minister can also serve the Lord on a part-time basis by doing "tent-making." This kind of practice is healthy and would open the way for more gifted ministers to respond to the Lord's move and build His body. Such part-time work can also allow the gifted minister to meet other believers and most certainly contact with those in the world who so desperately need the Savior.

It is a whole different challenge when church buildings and various church programs are involved which demand financial support. The New

Testament didn't make any allowances or instructions on financing church buildings since believers didn't gather in churches in the New Testament period — it was only when they dropped the practice of meeting from "house to house" and with government encouragement started meeting in "houses of worship" (e.g., "basilicas").

Supporting "church buildings" is not the prevue of this book — the Lord's workers are. It is also because of this undue burden many pastors must spend an inordinate amount of energy doing fundraising in order to support all the peripherals which are not directly related to shepherding believers. We're not criticizing having church buildings. It is just not within the scope of this book. Those pastors who desire to serve God and people as outlined in the New Testament will be liberated from so many unnecessary burdens. They will be able to spend their time doing what is profitable and enjoyable, which is to care for God's people, teach the truth, equip saints to minister and build up the Body of Christ.

If pastors and ministers would take the New Testament way of perfecting believers and building up the ekklesia, they would be compelled to have their full trust in God to care for their physical needs.

Pastors and Ministers Are Still Needed

Question: If all the members of the Body are actively functioning in the work of ministry, wouldn't I as a pastor or a person with one or more of the five-fold ministries be redundant and not needed?

Response: No, all those gifted members are needed until the Lord's second coming for His Bride, the assembly. In fact, the more gifted ministers and pastors operate according to New Testament revelation, the more they are needed. Consider the following verses again:

> But speaking the truth in love, let us grow in every way into him who is the head — Christ. From him the whole body, fitted and knit together by every supporting ligament, promotes the growth of the body for building up itself in love by the proper working of each individual part.
>
> (Eph. 4:15-16 CSB)

Notice there are two groups of members identified in verse Ephesians 4:16. There are those *"supporting ligaments"* and *"each individual part."* These supporting ligaments refer to those gifted members such as *"apostles, prophets, evangelists, pastors and teachers"* in the previous verse. The individual parts are the "regulars" or ordinary members in the Body. This demonstrates those gifted members of the Body will always be needed to support all the other members. It also discloses every member needs to be working; they need to be functioning to their capacity. It is through each member working we witness both these specific descriptions (ligaments/joints and "functioning members") whereby the whole Body is built up in love. The supporting ligaments, though special in their supply, are essential parts of the Body, but so are all the individual parts. Every part functions for the Body's growth and maturity.

Pastors with their functions of shepherding and teaching believers will be all the more necessary as the saints under their care become more activated, more independent in their new-found ministries, fellowshipping from house to house.

The gifted members are not needed to control and regulate but to supply more spiritual nourishment — provide more guidance when believers run into challenges. When pastors merely give sermons and set-up programs for their congregants, believers will just choose what programs they desire; and, sure, it will run like clockwork. However, if pastors equip and motivate believers to independently minister and meet in homes without a program to follow — learning to follow the Holy Spirit — pastors will find they need to do a whole lot more follow-up and visitation in order to support all these activities.

Take note that the "supporting ligaments" are not for controlling or dominating the ministries of the "regulars." First, "support" in context is designed to supply the nourishment with faith and teaching in the knowledge of the Son of God. This primary truth where believers keep speaking in love must be our focus. Christ is the unique Head. The "ligaments" are not little heads controlling the regular members of the Body but are designed to supply these members with truth in love.

As pastors direct their mission toward equipping the saints, their own function will become increasingly necessary. Rather than being drained by administrative duties, they will enter a realm of freedom of shepherding with the Chief Shepherd, working together for the increase of just one flock.

In fact, the function of the extra-gifted ministers will be expanded. Previously, your gift was only utilized within the confines of one church. However, as you become conscious of the One Body wherein your labor was not just for your own church, the utilization of your gift expands to include more and more believers and extends into other places. Especially, if your gift is apostolic, prophetic or evangelistic, your ministry will be needed outside your church for the entire Body of Christ.

Ekklesia is different than "cell groups"

Question: We already have group meetings in homes, which are sometime called "cell groups," so isn't this the same as what your book is describing as home assemblies?

Response: No. The reason is home or cell groups under church sponsorship are an extension of that church's ministry. Those groups are under the auspices of the pastor or leadership of that church. Typically, the material used for discussion or lessons in such cell groups will be predetermined. You'll normally find embedded leadership designed to guide the home group so that it stays on course — based on the direction of the church. No doubt these types of home groups have been very effective in growing a church and giving church members an interactive venue; however, this kind of home or cell group is not what is described in 1 Corinthians 11-14.

Pastors and church leaders need to experience home assemblies themselves, if they are inspired to help those under their influence to open their homes for ekklesia. The difficulty for pastors to practice ekklesia with just people from their own church has everything to do with the fact that those meeting "with pastor" will see the pastor in a different light and extend more "honor" to him — it's inevitable. The pastor in such a home meeting automatically becomes the "default leader" in the group; indeed, the ordinary members most likely will not freely interrupt or disagree with "the pastor."

If pastors want to practice ekklesia, they'll initially have to go and greet other believers; not in their respective churches, but simply as another "regular," and not as a gifted pastor or teacher. They will then learn to fellowship with other believers with different viewpoints and become one who practices ekklesia as so described. It's both humbling but very refreshing!

In ministries, those who are gifted can have a strong leadership position. As pastors of churches, they have the right to do it their way and teach their doctrines as *the* authority. But in functioning within the context of the

Lord's ekklesia, everyone is at the same level: everyone can speak, everyone can be interrupted, and everyone will be discerned. No one can claim any special authority. It is the Lord's assembly. He is the Head and everyone else is a member. When pastors experience the Lord's ekklesia themselves, then they can readily equip believers under their shepherding to host the Lord's assembly. It is through equipping God's people that regular believers can practice having independent assemblies with diverse believers gathered by the Lord to manifest the oneness of His Body.

A "Missional Church"

Question: We already have a "missional church." How is this any different?

Response: When Christians have a "missional vision," what does that mean? It actually means Christians are mobilized to carry out a mission. Believers can carry out any variety of missional activity. All believers should involve themselves in a "mission" – be it helping the less fortunate, preaching the gospel, new church planting, Bible instruction, etc. But to be truly missional, we need to participate in the same mission accomplished by Jesus Christ.

Christ's mission was focused on building up His ekklesia, His Body – this was His central purpose. Today, His disciples and followers must enter the same mission of Christ. Far too often, Christian mission stops short of this destination – obscuring the goal of all missions. For example, if your mission is to evangelize, to preach the gospel for the salvation of the lost – that is still short of God's ultimate intention. Yes, we need all Christians to share the gospel message, heal the sick, care for the needy, visit those in prison – but all "mission activity" must be governed by the overall goal of accomplishing God's eternal purpose in the building up of His Body to express the Body's oneness. If this is not the supreme goal, no matter how noble the mission may be, it still falls short and can result in "mission superiority" where you become so enamored with your ministry you begin to see the deficiencies in other ministries and feel your ministry is much more on the mark and essential than that of others (i.e., pride and consequent sectarianism enters in).

Building up a proper functioning assembly (I did not say "church" in the context of a traditional meeting in a building designed for that purpose.) should be the final result of all missional work. Whether you're preaching the gospel, nurturing young or weak believers, discipling or being proactive in embracing in fellowship with other believers (e.g., *"where two or three are gathered into my name"*) — the ultimate purpose, once again, of all missional activity is gathering as the Lord's ekklesia to express the very mission of Jesus Christ in the building up of His One Body.

This universal fellowship is manifested in home assemblies as described in 1 Corinthians 11-14. It is here genuine love for one another is displayed and mutuality in function is witnessed through each member. This was the practice throughout the book of Acts. Its aim is one assembly testifying to the unsearchable riches of Jesus Christ from house to house.

Most Christians consider gospel preaching to be synonymous with the "great commission." Scarcely anyone would consider the "great commission" has anything to do with greeting other believers. Yet, greeting other believers in building up the One Body in one fellowship as enjoined by Paul in Romans 16 is just as missional as evangelism. Moreover, hosting an ekklesia comprised of diverse believers gathering as one in Christ is as much a demonstration of the "great commission" as embarking on foreign missions for the sake of the gospel. In fact, it can be argued that it is more "missional" since it is directly for and within the experience of the One Body, one assembly.

It is essential to understand being missional in this manner of greeting is within the reach of every believer — regardless of their environment, limitations, or inhibiting personality. It's wonderful that some can do foreign missionary work. It's admirable for some believers to missionize in another country because it displays extraordinary courage to launch out in faith to do such exploits for God. However, while waiting to launch, one can still be missional by taking "baby steps" in carrying out Christ's mission right where they are. When a believer catches this vision of God's eternal purpose, then your entire living is missional! When we come to grips with the vision of Christ's One Body as the goal of mission, then preaching the gospel becomes part of that ultimate vision. Seeking out unfamiliar believers for prayer and fellowship — whether on a commuter train, while at the grocery store, or at a local soccer game — all are part of the mission given to us by Christ to build up His One Body!

11.
SATANIC TACTICS

Categorizing the Brethren Day and Night

> So the great dragon was cast out, that serpent of old, called the Devil and Satan, who deceives the whole world; he was cast to the earth, and his angels were cast out with him. Then I heard a loud voice saying in heaven, "Now salvation, and strength, and the kingdom of our God, and the power of His Christ have come, for the accuser of our brethren, who accused them before our God day and night, has been cast down."
>
> (Rev 12:9-10 NKJV)

Satan is already defeated and judged by Jesus Christ's death and resurrection. It is finished. Satan has no more power over God's people. His most effective weapon, which is death, has lost its sting. His ability to put people in slavery through the fear of death has been terminated (Heb. 2:15). Today his only real weapon is deception: It's all smoke and mirrors . . . he is the best illusionist.

Since Satan has been defeated already, why is this world still under his rule? Why is the world still his kingdom and not yet the Lord's? The reason for Satan's lingering efforts has everything to do with the purpose found in the Lord's built-up ekklesia — the oneness of God's people will be the executioner of Satan's sentence. It is like Satan has already been found guilty and sentenced to the lake of fire, but the sentence has not yet been executed. He is now on "death row" waiting for his final exit. Nevertheless, if God's people are not brought together in oneness, Satan will continue his reign on earth as the supreme interloper. Therefore, Satan's highest priority and strategy is to disrupt the building up of the Lord's ekklesia, assembly, by keeping God's people divided. If they are divided, then his kingdom continues. God's people in division and faction are ignorantly prolonging Satan's kingdom on earth!

Based on that strategy, what is Satan doing before God day and night? (He is not afraid of being before God. He can even challenge God to His face according to Job Chapter 1.) According to Revelation 12:10, Satan is the *"accuser"* of the brethren" who accuses believers before God day and night. What is surprising, an "ah ha" moment, is that the Greek word for "accuse" is κατήγορος (*katēgoreō*), from whence the English word "category." What is Satan doing based on his devious strategy? He is literally categorizing the brethren, believers. He is the chief categorizer. As the categorizer, he is classifying and labeling believers into groups.

According to Strong's concordance, this Greek word κατήγορος (*katēgoreō*) is made up of two other words *"kata"* and *"agora."* Kata means against and *agora* means a group of people. So literally, κατήγορο (*katēgoreō*) is grouping people together and instigating something against each one. Satan's cunning strategy is clearly to formulate a plan whereby brethren are segregated into groups — he pits them one against another. That is what he is doing day and night. His full-time occupation is to make sure the followers of Jesus are grouped in factions, so they will stand apart and have something against each other.

Believers have fallen into Satan's trap, ignorantly and unknowingly. Believers have become aligned with Satan in this matter of categorizing to create factions. Just as Peter was called Satan when he told the Lord not to go to the cross, believers today can quickly become "Satan" by joining him in categorizing God's people. In the Lord's Body, all believers are members one of another and cannot be divided. Any categories or sub-groups in the Body of Christ are automatically divisive.

Believers have become so entrenched in Satan's scheme that when they meet each other, just about the first question asked: What church do you go to? Basically, what category of Christian are you by which you are labeled? Instead of looking at each other merely as believers with the same faith, believers quickly try to put a label on each other to gauge whether they are in the same faction or in opposing factions. How good it would be if believers only considered the Christ in one another when they meet so that they can immediately have fellowship with each other. However, believers naturally place each other into groups or categories before they will consider whether the person with whom they are speaking is someone with whom they can fellowship.

Before the "categorizer" Satan is cast out before the throne of God, today's faithful need to cast him and his categorizing nature out of their attitude, thinking, and consideration when they meet fellow believers. We need to be like Paul where he determined not to *"know anything among you except Christ and Him crucified"* (1 Cor. 2:2). Such an attitude toward one another will bring in God's ekklesia which shall soon crush Satan; otherwise, Satan's categorizing will continue to divide believers.

To most Christians, evangelism or bringing people to salvation is priority, but from Satan's view point, his life and death struggle is to keep God's people divided so his ultimate demise would be delayed.

Satan's Strategy: Cause Division

> Immature believers are susceptible to Satan's strategy.
>
> God is faithful, by whom you were called into the fellowship of His Son, Jesus Christ our Lord. Now I plead with you, brethren, by the name of our Lord Jesus Christ, that you all speak the same thing, and that there be no divisions among you, but that you be perfectly joined together in the same mind and in the same judgment. For it has been declared to me concerning you, my brethren, by those of Chloe's house-hold, that there are contentions among you. Now I say this, that each of you says, "I am of Paul," or "I am of Apollos," or "I am of Cephas," or "I am of Christ." Is Christ divided? Was Paul crucified for you? Or were you baptized in the name of Paul?
>
> (1 Corinthians 1:9–13)

All believers have been called into only one fellowship — that of Jesus Christ. Believers may mistakenly consider the group with whom they fellowship is a unique fellowship, and that every other group has its own separate fellowship. The truth is, all believers belong to only one fellowship. It is God Who called us into one fellowship. It is the work of Jesus Christ Who brought all believers into His fellowship. Thus, the only way all believers can speak the same thing and have the same mind and judgment is by staying in this unique faith of the Person and Work of Jesus Christ. This alone makes one a believer and brings that person into such a fellowship.

"That you all speak the same thing" is not related to having the same political views, or the same mind about education, child rearing, and careers.

Focusing on these topics will spawn divisions. Despite having different views and opinions on such things, believers can be one and continue enjoying fellowship in Christ. This kind of oneness will cause the world to believe: people in diversity, yet one in fellowship, loving one another.

All believers are in the Body of Christ; there should be no divisions in Christ. Notwithstanding, it is common for believers to associate themselves with a sub-group within the body. When some have received extended help from a minister or preacher of the Word, it is easy to say, "I am of so-and-so," to identify themselves according to the minister they genuinely appreciate. But according to Paul, any labeling or naming of oneself other than that of a common believer or Christian who is a member of His Body, it is considered a division. In fact, that is the satanic, devious method of categorizing.

The actual meaning of "denominating" is *naming* — being labeled by a name. "I am of Paul, I am of Apollos, I am a Lutheran, I am a Pentecostal, I am Baptist" . . . any designation divides the Body of Christ. Even a spiritual category such as, *"I am of Christ,"* as a way of excluding others, harms the Body of Christ. Those who say, *"I am of Christ,"* may feel more spiritual — even possess a judgmental attitude toward those who say, *"I am of Paul."* They can separate and group themselves only with those who say, *"I am of Christ."* To say that, *"I am of Christ"* is certainly more spiritual and could be a reaction to those who say, *"I am of Apollos,"* but when the "more spiritual" react to those "less spiritual," their reaction is also a cause of division.

Therefore, those who are genuinely more mature brethren will not react or be distracted by those saying or doing things which are not entirely scriptural. They will continue to stay in fellowship with Jesus Christ by bringing all those around them into this fellowship no matter what category believers put themselves into because of immaturity. Since all believers are domiciled in the One Body of Christ, all should refrain from denominating or labeling themselves and categorizing other believers.

> And I, brethren, could not speak to you as to spiritual people but as to carnal, as to babes in Christ . . . for you are still carnal. For where there are envy, strife, and divisions among you, are you not carnal and behaving like mere men? For when one says, "I am of Paul," and another, "I am of Apollos," are you not carnal? Who then is Paul, and who is Apollos, but ministers through whom you believed, as the Lord gave to each one?
>
> (1 Corinthians 3:1, 3–5)

Paul showed the Corinthians they were forming factions around various ministers — they were naught but babes in Christ. They were "carnal" or "of the flesh," just like people of the world. Immaturity in Christ causes believers to uplift various ministers, their teachings, and practices, thus forming a faction around such people or things. Even when ministers innocently preach the Word and bring people to Christ with pure intentions, factions can instantly form due to the immaturity of believers. It is incumbent upon every believer to help one another to become mature in Christ thereby building up of the assembly. True ministers of the gospel, like Paul, warn those under their influence of such counter-productive tendencies:

> And he has given [still giving] some apostles, and some prophets, and some evangelists, and some shepherds and teachers, for the perfecting [equipping] of the saints; with a view to the work of the ministry, with a view to the edifying [building up] of the Body of Christ . . .
>
> (Ephesians 4:11–12, DBY)

Grammatically, the verb form for "given" in Ephesians 4:11 in Greek means our Lord Jesus is *still actively giving* more gifted believers to be apostles, evangelists, prophets, shepherds, and teachers. Those who are extra-gifted may have a greater or more fervent heart, a clearer understanding of the Scriptures, and a stronger will for God's purpose. As gifts to the body, their job is to equip *all* saints under their ministry, so every follower of Jesus will be raised up to do the work of ministry; thus, the Body of Christ will be built up. When every believer is raised up to serve others and, consequently, functions according to their God-given capacity, then, the Body will be built up. The *more* gifted members cannot build up the body directly; even the apostle Paul himself could not do it!

Today's system of clergy and laity, where a few believers do all the teaching and preaching, while the majority stay passive year after year has not and does not equip believers to carry on the ministry. Instead of building up the Body of Christ, gifted pastors are creating mostly idle brethren unable to build up the Body of Christ. The "equipping norm" by more gifted ministers is to equip the saints to visit, meet, and greet other saints in fellowship rather than assigning the task to "visitation pastors" while the "pew sitters" await to be visited!

There are some "ministers" and "teachers" with an ulterior motive. They desire to build up their own group — their own following of believers, while maintaining a form of control over the member's communication with other saints. They teach something else — something different from *"arriving at the unity of the faith and the knowledge of the Son of God."* They may emphasize some other scriptural points or biblical practices to turn believers aside from the main focus. This is usually evidenced in the elevation of various non-essential doctrines or practices to the same level as Jesus Christ.

A believer who does not practice their doctrine will be deemed inferior. With their cunning speech and trickery, using Scripture to their benefit by emphasizing a certain doctrine, personality, or practice, they carry off babes in Christ into their group, their system of organization, and away from the building up of the One Body of Christ. Believers should not underestimate the shrewdness of those who present Scripture in a way convincing immature believers their way of practice or their special doctrine around which a new division is formed.

For example, only Paul spoke of women having their head covered in an assembly in just one chapter of an epistle; nevertheless, some Bible teachers highlight this in their teaching and form groups based on that emphasis. Speaking in an unknown tongue is used in the same way. Only Paul (and no other apostle in any other epistle) wrote concerning miraculous "speaking in tongues" in just two of his chapters. In one chapter it was spoken of with a caution. Yet, an entire denominational organization can be built around speaking in tongues.

Let's take baptism as another example. Factions have formed over whether baptism must be by water. Some teach it is nothing more than a spiritual experience — no physical water is involved. If water is involved, then more factions form like those around immersion or sprinkling. If immersion, even more factions have formed over whether the words spoken when a person is baptized should be *"in the name of the Father, the Son, and the Holy Spirit"* or only *"in the name of Jesus Christ."* Each of these doctrines can be used by Bible teachers (who quote Scripture) to deceive people into believing if a person does not adhere to the teaching or practice of the group, then their salvation or holiness may be in question. There are literally thousands of teachings that are blowing about immature believers into various factions, each dividing themselves from other believers who are not like them:

> "That we should no longer be children, tossed to and fro and carried about with every wind of doctrine, by the trickery of men, in the cunning craftiness of deceitful plotting."
>
> (Eph. 4:14)

There are certain brethren who are very keen on what the "kingdom of God" looks like — how it is manifested. If certain "signs and wonders" do not follow the manifestation of the "kingdom of God" — then they feel all the "talk" about the oneness of the Body of Christ is meaningless. If the kingdom of God does not manifest in demons being cast out, healings, prophetic signs, and wonders — then true oneness is only talk; and, talk is cheap!

Another believes the gospel is the foremost manifestation of the One Body. In other words, if believers are not motivated to "hit the streets" in some way, shape, or form — then all the preaching of One Body in Christ is meaningless!

Notwithstanding, such manifestations wrought within the kingdom of God — be they speaking in tongues, casting out of demons, divine deliverance, and all manner of the gifts of the Spirit are, nevertheless, absent in our Lord's prayer in John 17. Jesus' prayer regarding the oneness of His Body, His people, will result when saints enter the fellowship embedded within the Triune God. It is by God's people aligning in the uniting bond of peace with faith in the knowledge of the Son of God — this alone results in the world believing the Father sent the Son. By uniting with the fellowship of the Triune God, the world will believe — signs and wonders will FOLLOW, as will the preaching of the gospel. Pentecost is the prime example — the disciples prayed for ten days after His ascension; then came the outpouring of the Spirit confirming His One Body . . . then came the prevailing preaching of the gospel, with signs and wonders following.

Satan's incessant tactic is to divide the Body of Christ by attacking the assembly through a myriad of personalities, practices, even solid teaching. Solely focusing on these matters inhibits God's purpose in bringing together the oneness of His Body. Whether the assembly is described as the Household (temple) of God, the Bride of Christ, the Body of Christ, the One New Man, the Kingdom of God, or the New Jerusalem — oneness of believers stems from the oneness of the Triune God . . . this is paramount. While Satan is doing his best to cause division, believers need to do their best to mature by holding on to the *"unity of the Spirit"* until arriving at the built-up assembly according to the ultimate result of Christ's work. Again, therefore, understanding John 17 is critical for understanding God's purpose.

No Separation on Racial, Cultural, Political, Socio-Econ.

> ... and have put on the new *man* who is renewed in knowledge according to the image of Him who created him, where there is neither Greek nor Jew, circumcised nor uncircumcised, barbarian, Scythian, slave nor free, but Christ is all and in all.
> (Colossians 3:10–11)

> For you are all sons of God through faith in Christ Jesus. For as many of you as were baptized into Christ have put on Christ. There is neither Jew nor Greek, there is neither slave nor free, there is neither male nor female; for you are all one in Christ Jesus.
> (Galatians 3:26–28)

Believers in Jesus Christ have a new identity. Their identity is a new creation in Christ. When people enter the world through a physical birth, they are divided by all manner of differences listed in this above subheading. But once believers are born anew in their second birth, their first identity is terminated — buried with Jesus Christ. Their new identity is found in the risen Christ, *"Christ is all and in all."* In the assembly, those who are Jews should no longer consider themselves Jews; neither should Asians nor Caucasian, or people of color identify themselves as such. All believers should no longer view themselves or other believers according to their natural birth, but according to their new birth: We are now Sons and Daughters of the Living God — we are IN Christ!

It is natural and easy to be segregated, separated based on a myriad of differences. It is very difficult, even impossible, without the new birth and life in Christ, for people who are diametrically opposed to each other to become one. Worldly people have this ideal that diverse people can be one as memorialized by John Lennon's song: *Imagine*. It is abundantly clear the more the world talks about oneness, the more divided and segregated it becomes. But in the genuine assembly, divisions based on preferences of the old creation in our natural life cannot exist. In Christ, though believers are diverse and different, the acceptance of each other in fellowship unites us all.

Today's multitude of churches within Christendom is segregated by various doctrines, practices, personalities, politics, racial, or socio-economic demarcations. Although not scriptural, some claim it is necessary to care for various Christians within an environment in which they are comfortable. According to this reasoning, if Christians are not able to gather in a place in which they are at ease, then there's no sense having fellowship with other believers. This is an acceptable logic for a ministry catering to various demographics. Certainly, this method of ministry cannot be extended to the Body of Christ. Believers who are more mature and see the oneness of His Body will receive and treat believers in other church groups as equal members in the Body of Christ — they should be greeted and accepted without discrimination or judgment. Greeting believers extends to wherever they are, no matter what denominational church or Christian group they attend.

Some believers, due to their understanding of the Scriptures, have condemned denominational churches and groups. They group themselves as a unit for the oneness of the Body of Christ, against the system of denominations. However, if they don't proactively greet and extend themselves in fellowship with other believers in various "divided" groups, then they too can become segregated by their correct teaching. Their strong denunciation of institutional churches isolates them, segregates them, and makes them more divisive. This is like those who have become divisive by saying they are of Christ (1 Cor. 1:12). A group can fall into the same trap of divisiveness by declaring it is the group of the One Body!

Deceitful Teachings Damage the Assembly

Teachings which uplift something other than Christ or distract believers from Christ, damage the assembly. These deceitful teachings from Christian workers are aimed at carrying believers away from the simplicity of life in the Body of Christ into "systematized error."

> For I am jealous for you with godly jealousy. For I have betrothed you to one husband, that I may present you as a chaste virgin to Christ. But I fear, lest somehow, as the serpent deceived Eve by his craftiness, so your minds may be corrupted from the

> simplicity that is in Christ. For if he who comes preaches another Jesus whom we have not preached, or if you receive a different spirit which you have not received, or a different gospel which you have not accepted — you may well put up with it!
>
> For such are false apostles, deceitful workers, transforming themselves into apostles of Christ. And no wonder! For Satan himself transforms himself into an angel of light. Therefore, it is no great thing if his ministers also transform themselves into ministers of righteousness, whose end will be according to their works.
>
> (2 Corinthians 11:2-4, 13-15)

It is evident from Paul's writing: Satan is very deceptive and cunning. He is not easily recognizable, and his corrupting teachings cannot be easily discerned. The assembly is betrothed to only one husband: Jesus Christ. He, as the Bridegroom, deserves the Bride's complete attention, adoration, and focus. That is simplicity. It is just Jesus Christ, His person, and His work. Believers need to be alerted to Satan's strategy in corrupting this simplicity by adding on other items in addition to Jesus Christ. Take note: The attack starts in the mind, through appealing and seemingly Scriptural teachings ... the goal is always to add something else to Jesus Christ ... adding to *"the unity of the faith and the knowledge of the Son of God"* (Eph. 4:13).

These deceitful teachers corrupt believers' thoughts, side-tracking them by using many different appealing and eloquent methods — even pulling quotes from the Bible. Although their teachings may be law-centered, and culturally and politically relevant, the result is the same: the believer loses heart and love towards Jesus Christ and misses out on the enjoyment of the riches of Christ. Doubt creeps in by effectively deprecating the work of Christ. Believers begin to trust in human effort rather than in the work of the Spirit, which inevitably causes divisions.

Many times, those involved in the *"trickery of men"* or *"in the cunning craftiness of deceitful plotting"* (Eph. 4:14) do so with good intentions. They may be perfectly fine Christians without any conscious intent of misleading believers. It could be ignorance — they might be completely unaware Satan is using their teachings to mislead people. When Jesus called Peter *"Satan,"* Peter was only voicing his concern about Jesus' physical well-being — going to the cross was akin to a "death wish" as far as Peter was concerned. His intentions were good, but it was contrary to the Lord's purpose; therefore,

Jesus called him *Satan*. Similarly, Christian teachers may possess a good heart, with good intentions, but if they distract believers from Christ to something else, even if Scriptural, they are doing the work of Satan.

Teachings Sever Believers from Enjoying Christ

Philosophy, traditions, forms of living and worship, ordinances, being judged as not worthy, and asceticism — all these sever believers from the enjoyment of Christ and harm the Body.

> See to it that no one takes you captive by philosophy and empty deceit, according to human tradition, according to the elemental spirits of the world, and not according to Christ. For in him the whole fullness of deity dwells bodily, and you have been filled in him, who is the head of all rule and authority.
> (Colossians 2:8-10, ESV)

The enemy's goal is to take believers captive and enslave them by suppressive teachings which are not according to Jesus Christ. Through the ages men have held to various philosophies concerning life and living. They have their logic and reasoning about what is human life. Generally, a people's logic and philosophy govern how they live. The Chinese have their own philosophies; Muslims hold to their own traditions; and western culture has its own unique logic and ways of living. However, the assembly is *according to Christ alone* — it liberates people from the enslaving spirits of the world. The assembly's focus is only related to being filled with Christ, who is the fullness of all that God is; the Head of all rule and authority. Believers need to reject these various distractions in the assembly, since they are deceitful and not beneficial for building up the One Body with the *"knowledge of the Son of God."*

> Let no man therefore judge you in meat, or in drink, or in respect of a feast day or a new moon or a sabbath day: which are a shadow of the things to come; but the body is Christ's.
> (Colossians 2:16-17, ASV)

When teachings other than those which further God's stewardship or economy (see Chapter 11 in the book *ONE*) are preached to believers, obstacles to the true oneness of believers are generated. In Colossians 2:16–17, Paul addresses items relating to keeping dietary laws, or observing certain days and festivals of the Old Testament, which were being taught among believers. Believers were passing judgment on each other according to Jewish laws found in the Old Testament. Those influenced by these teachings of Jewish ceremonial laws were judging those being called out from among the nations who didn't abide by these laws.

These Old Testament ceremonial laws were all *shadows* being cast by the *reality* of the coming One. This is not unlike the sun shining and casting a shadow on the ground. The shadow is not real. The person or object that casts the shadow is real. Jesus Christ is the person Who came; therefore, in the assembly, believers have the Body or fullness, which is Jesus Christ, and not the shadow. In the assembly there is only reality — no shadows; therefore, there should be no judgment cast on each other according to the shadows of the Old Testament. By implication, this should also apply to all practices in the New Testament. For example, the practice of partaking of the bread and the cup is a symbol or "shadow" of the supply of our nourishment from Jesus, which is the reality. Therefore, no judgment or division should occur over how to practice such a symbol.

> Let no man rob you of your prize by a voluntary humility and worshipping of the angels, dwelling in the things which he hath seen, vainly puffed up by his fleshly mind, and not holding fast the Head, from whom all the body, being supplied and knit together through the joints and bands, increasing with the increase of God. If ye died with Christ from the rudiments of the world, why, as though living in the world, do ye subject yourselves to ordinances, handle not, nor taste, nor touch (all which things are to perish with the using), after the precepts and doctrines of men? Which things have indeed a show of wisdom in will-worship, and humility, and severity to the body; but are not of any value against the indulgence of the flesh.
> (Colossians 2:18–19, 20–23, ASV)

Paul addressed concepts influenced by Greek philosophy which say a man is too vile to worship God directly; it is the proud person who thinks they can approach God and have direct fellowship with Him. This philosophy says one needs to humbly approach angels instead (Col. 2:18); let angels be our mediator with God.

However, this concept leads to angel worship. Today, even among many Christians, people adore and uplift angels who are just their servants (Heb. 1:14), while losing sight of Christ, who should be their prize. Teachings which distract in this manner cause believers to let go of Christ as the unique Head; instead we begin to trust and adore angels. When believers do not hold on to Christ as the sole authority in His Body, there is neither growth of the Body nor increase of God; therefore, there is no knitting together for the building up of the assembly.

Finally, there is the issue of asceticism. This doctrine teaches us that man's body is lustful. It needs to be restricted and punished severely. Almost every religion of the world has this element and practice. According to man's wisdom (and most Christians will readily agree), since man is lustful by nature, it would be wise to develop a strong will to stay away from temptation and relentlessly control the urges of the body.

However, according to Paul, this type of practice has no value against the flesh. Rather, it is a distraction from what Christ has already done for all believers. All believers have already died with Christ and resurrected with Him. A strong will is needed to stay focused on Christ, enjoying Him, and ministering Him to others, rather than focusing on dealing with the negativity of the flesh.

These destructive teachings and concepts listed in Colossians 2 subtly appeal to religious minds; they sound spiritual and full of humility. It is hard to resist such teachings, especially when some can be backed by Scriptures, but in a twisted out-of-context kind of a way. It is difficult not to adore angels!

Knowing the natural instincts of the body [i.e., the "flesh"], readily prepares one for asceticism. Paul forcefully pointed out these teachings on asceticism, and how they distract believers from Jesus — causing divisions in the Body of Christ. Therefore, keen discernment is needed when listening to Christian teachers, identifying whether their teachings are profitable for bringing believers into enjoying our oneness in Christ, or whether such teachings will sidetrack them from Christ — diminishing the unity of the Body of Christ.

Differences between "Doctrine" and "Doctrine"

The matter of Biblical "doctrine" or "teaching" has also been a great source of division in the Body of Christ. These two words "doctrine" and "teaching" can be used interchangeably. It simply means "that which is taught" (Vine's).

The Bible is full of doctrines, unless you do not read the Bible, but if you do, it is unavoidable to pick up all sorts of doctrines. Believers are encouraged to study the Bible in order to be taught by various doctrines. Some have such a strong emphasis in learning doctrines with a desire to resolve all seemingly contradicting ideas in the Bible that they formulate and organize the various doctrines into a more uniformed and cohesive arrangement for easier understanding. That body of doctrine is what can be defined as "systematic theology."

The difficulty is this: There are literally thousands of teachings in the Bible ranging from the mysterious and heavenly concerning the person and nature of God . . . to the mundane and earthly such as what one should wear and eat. The more students of the Bible desire to teach and live according to the doctrines in the Scripture, the more conflict they discover — interpretations widely vary.

Therefore, Christians are inclined to simplify doctrine by asking: "Just tell me the right doctrine to believe and live by." Depending on personality and influence, some will emphasize one side of conflicting teachings while others will highlight the other side. For example, the Bible does not actually have a doctrine of the Trinity. Sometimes it refers to God in the singular and at other times it speaks of God in the plural, specifically: Father, Son and Holy Spirit. Some can then emphasize their teaching on the side of God being one, while others on the side of three persons of the "Godhead." This has caused great divisions in the past.

Salvation by faith or works can also have conflicting verses. Some will cite why believers are saved by grace, not by works (Eph. 2:8-9), while others will cite *"faith without works is dead"* (James 2:20). This is the same for whether salvation is eternally secure or whether a believer can lose their salvation. This has been a major divider among Christians for hundreds of years — right up to the present. Beyond these major theological doctrines, there are hundreds or thousands more concerning church practices, methods of prayer, end times, Christian blessings and even life-style doctrines such as marriage, diet, clothing, music, etc.

Due to the many doctrines throughout the Bible, many divisions and factions have been formed among Christians. Additionally, the misuse of Biblical doctrines has placed many people into bondage. They feel that if they don't follow and abide by the teachings in the Bible then they are breaking God's laws and are thereby susceptible to God's judgment.

Reacting to how Christians have used doctrines to divide and oppress God's people, numerous believers begin to devalue and even belittle doctrine. They may say something like: "We don't need doctrines, we just need the Spirit." Or, "Doctrines kill and divide." Or, "Studying the Bible is not necessary, it's the Spirit that gives life." They have pitted the experiences of the Spirit against the understanding of the Bible; yet, that is itself their doctrine. Ironically, Christians pushing-back on this "no-doctrine" teaching, respond by doubling-down emphasizing all controversies can be explained with intensive study and "cutting-straight" (e.g., "rightly dividing") Scriptures. It seems the constant arguments over doctrines in the Scripture are unavoidable and unending.

The English word for "doctrine" or "teaching" actually comes from two different Greek words. The two Greek words are used differently and have two distinct meanings, but since they are both translated as *"doctrine"* in English, the exact meaning of each is lost. It is a source of confusion for English readers when these two Greek words are not clearly delineated. It would be a great help for believers to understand the "doctrine" that they need to embrace as truth, and the doctrines that are flexible in application so as not to divide nor be oppressed by them.

The two Greek words translated to "doctrine" or "teaching" are: *Didachē* (Strong's #1322) and *Didaskalia* (Strong's #1319). According to Biblehub.com, *Didachē* means: established teaching, especially a "summarized" body of respected teaching (viewed as reliable, time-honored). However, *Didaskalia* means: applied-teaching; systematic theology; Christian doctrine (teaching) as it especially extends to its necessary *lifestyle* (applications).

Didachē is used 30 times in the New Testament and 25 out of the 30 times refer to the doctrine spoken by Jesus (Matt 7:28, Luke 4:32); the doctrine of Jesus Christ (2 John 1:9-10); and, the doctrine of the apostles (Acts 2:42, 5:28). The other five times are used negatively (Heb. 13:9) — specifically, doctrines of: the Pharisees (Matt. 16:12), Balaam (Rev. 2:14), Nicolaitans (Rev. 2:15), and Jezebel (Rev. 2:24). Both the positive doctrines relating to Jesus Christ or the damaging ones are consistently time-honored and reliable for acceptance or rejection. There are no situations where the doctrine of Jesus Christ should be rejected or the doctrine of Jezebel should be accepted.

The constant and eternally profitable ***doctrine*** (Didachē) represents the teaching concerning the person and work of Jesus Christ. It is the fundamental doctrine that is the truth of the New Testament. It teaches people to know God, Jesus Christ, the Holy Spirit, the entire work of Christ from incarnation, human living, death, resurrection, ascension, the outpouring of the Spirit, the regeneration of His believers to the building up of His ekklesia, the assembly, His Body unto His bodily return in glory. This is the doctrine that all believers should speak (1 Cor. 14:6); and from which Christian teachers should not deviate (Rom. 16:17). The above usages fit the definition of a "summarized body of respected teaching (viewed as reliable, time-honored)."

Didaskalia, on the other hand, is used 21 times. It refers to applied-teaching, application to Christian life-style with a view to systematizing theology. Therefore, this kind of doctrine instead of being "time-honored" is more contemporaneous. It seeks influence on the hearer's lifestyle. The effect on the hearer can be positive: leading them toward seeking and living a well-pleasing life before the Lord Jesus. However, it could also be negative: leading them away from the Lord toward self-efforts and bondages. Whether positive or negative, those influenced believe the source of this doctrine is divine or Scriptural — Biblical teachings.

On the positive side, we are told the teaching (*didaskalia*) of Scripture is for learning so that it would provide patience, comfort, and the giving of hope through difficulties with conflicting personalities (Rom. 15:4). The Scriptures also provide doctrine (*didaskalia*), corrections, and instructions in righteousness. When one comes to the Scripture for Spiritual breath (life-sustaining), he/she receives the proper "doctrine" to be instructed to live and work in an evil generation (2 Tim. 3:16). How we apply Scriptures becomes the doctrine which governs how we live and act as Christians from day to day (2 Tim. 3:10).

Therefore, ministers of the Word should do their best to apply Scriptures in a way that is healthy or sound. When it comes to applying Scripture to a lifestyle, one can imagine all the various approaches. Thus, Paul stressed it needs to be healthy (1 Tim. 1:10; 2 Tim. 4:3; Titus 1:9; 2:1). "Healthy" points to life and growth, not merely behavior. When applying Scriptures, it needs to be in a way leading people to grow in their spiritual life.

It is by this strengthening and growing through the indwelling life of Christ believers are transformed. It is through life-transformation the daily living of believers is truly affected. The Christian life should not be governed by a set of rules; rather, it should be by God's eternal life within each believer. Healthy doctrine (*didaskalia*) is applying Scripture in a way leading the hearer to turn to Jesus Christ, so that His life will cause the believer to grow and be transformed from within.

Nevertheless, applying Scriptures improperly can also have a very harmful effect.

> And in vain they worship Me, Teaching [as] doctrines [*didaskalia*] the commandments of men.
>
> (Matt. 15:9)
>
> In order that we may be no longer babes, tossed and carried about by every wind of that teaching [*didaskalia*] in the sleight of men, in unprincipled cunning with a view to systematized error . . .
>
> (Eph. 4:14 DBY)

In Matthew 15, when Jesus condemned the Pharisees, their teaching was about tithing. They were not teaching something sinful, such as lying or stealing. They were teaching something according to God's command: tithing—giving something to God. However, in their application of God's law concerning tithing, they negated another one which is to honor one's father and mother. This doctrine of "If anyone tells his father or his mother, 'what you would have gained from me is given to God'" became a commandment of men. It sounded so spiritual and Scriptural, but it was also in direct disobedience to another one of God's commands: *honor your father and mother*.

The Scriptures are full of seemingly competing and contrary ideas. When a person applies only one set of verses and negates conflicting verses, the doctrine derived by a one-sided application, no matter how Scriptural, is of man and not of God.

In Ephesians 4:14, the doctrines that were like a wind blowing young believers about can be assumed to be those doctrines from the Bible. It is the differing emphases in applying Scripture that became a wind to toss and carry immature believers from one side to another. Bible teachers can use their cunning ways of interpretation to come up with doctrines to support their sectarian systems. Babes are blown about, captured into such a system by doctrines (*didaskalia*) or "systematized error."

Even doctrine (*didaskalia*) of demons as described in 1 Tim. 4:1-3 were not related to idolatry or some other sinful act; rather, they can be traced to applying scriptural and spiritual references. Didn't Paul say it is better for a man not to marry, so he can be pleasing to the Lord (1 Cor. 7:1, 8, 32)? A doctrine to forbid marriage is just a codifying of a portion of Scripture to help believers to love the Lord without entanglement. As far as abstaining from foods, isn't that also Scriptural and spiritual? Jesus Himself spoke of fasting (Matt. 6:16); and the believers in Acts also fasted (Acts 13:2-3; 14:23). Demons merely formulated a doctrine by applying Scripture to regulate a Christian life-style.

Today, doctrines (*didaskalia*) which are causing arguments and divisions are mostly focused on how Scriptures are applied. It is not over the doctrine (*didache*) of Jesus Christ. Understanding and appreciating the doctrine of Jesus Christ as the truth brings believers into oneness. Attempting to systematize the Bible correctly among certain Christian life-styles continues to segregate and divide believers. One desiring to serve the Lord needs to be grounded on and enriched by the doctrine of Jesus Christ with all His unsearchable riches, and simultaneously, be able to apply the appropriate Scriptures to a person in need with a particular condition.

For example, if a person's doctrine (*didaskalia*) is "once saved, always saved" and "saved by grace" then that person cannot apply verses such as Philippians 2:12 *"work out your own salvation with fear and trembling"* to help a believer who is lackadaisical in his pursuit of the Lord. Likewise, if a person's doctrine is "you can lose your salvation," there will be another list of verses concerning the security of the believer's salvation which will not be used for comforting one who is under condemnation due to sinning willfully. Rather, a person who is fortified with the doctrine (*didache*) of Jesus Christ will be able to apply all verses without negating any. A healthy word can be spoken based on the need of the person at any specific time. This healthy word will turn the hearer to Jesus, strengthen his or her faith to pursue and serve the Lord.

Therefore, it is crucial for those desiring to answer the Lord's Prayer for the oneness of His people to understand the two different kinds of doctrine. On the one hand, we need to be those who keep mining the unsearchable riches of Jesus Christ so that the doctrine (*didache*) of Jesus Christ becomes fuller and deeper for our enjoyment and our ministry to people. This is part of Satan's strategy: distract believers from focusing on and knowing Jesus Christ.

On the other hand, we need to be wary of Satan's other tactic: motivating ministers to emphasize Biblical doctrines (*didaskalia*) to the point of divisiveness. Instead of teachers divisively tossing believers around by every wind of doctrine, what is needed are teachers who can apply Scriptures to a person in need at the right moment to bring that person back into fellowship with Jesus for the building up of the One Body of Christ. *"Sound doctrine builds up the Body of Christ."* Know this: the doctrine (*didache*) of Jesus Christ is always beneficial for building up; whereas caution is needed when applying doctrine (*didaskalia*) to a person's lifestyle. Ministers are needed to equip the saints, so all believers can speak the doctrine of Jesus Christ which is the knowledge of the Son of God. This will build up the Body of Christ into one ekklesia.

Division Is a Result of Idolatry

> And Jeroboam said in his heart, "Now the kingdom may return to the house of David; if these go up to offer sacrifices in the house of the LORD at Jerusalem, then the heart of this people will turn back to their lord, Rehoboam king of Judah, and they will kill me and go back to Rehoboam king of Judah." Therefore, the king asked advice, made two calves of gold, and said to the people, "It is too much for you to go up to Jerusalem. Here are your gods, O Israel, which brought you up from the land of Egypt!" And he set up one in Bethel, and the other he put in Dan. Now this thing became a sin, for the people went [to worship] before the one as far as Dan. He made shrines on the high places, and made priests from every class of people, who were not of the sons of Levi.
> (1 Kings 12:26-31 NKJV)
>
> For the weapons of our warfare [are] not carnal but mighty in God for pulling down strongholds, casting down arguments and every high thing that exalts itself against the knowledge of God, bringing every thought into captivity to the obedience of Christ.
> (2 Cor. 10:4-5 NKJV)

In the previous chapter it was pointed out how idolatry was the cause of division between Judah and Israel, resulting in the loss of the glory of God. Certainly, idolatry started with King Solomon; however, it was King

Jeroboam of Israel's Ten Northern Tribes who devised a system which codified the division between Judah and Israel through idolatry. Indeed, King Jeroboam institutionalized idolatry and division. Consequently, throughout the rest of the Old Testament, this became known as the "sin of Jeroboam" which God remembered. This "sin" or "sins" were referred to at least fifteen times as judgment befalling Israel's Ten Northern Tribes. Let's examine more closely what Jeroboam did which caused God's condemnation.

Based on King Solomon's idolatry, God told Jeroboam he would become king over the Ten Northern Tribes (1 Kings 11:31). The house of David would retain only two tribes: Judah and Benjamin. Yes, Jeroboam was chosen by God to be King of Israel's Ten Northern Tribes (also known, as Israel, Ephraim, Jezreel and Samaria). In this sense Jeroboam was not a usurper of the once United Kingdom of David nor was he an upstart with wild ambition whose design was to steal the Ten Northern Tribes from King Rehoboam. The prophet of the Lord, Abijah, authorized this *"mighty man of valor"* who was *"industrious"* who King Solomon had *"made him the officer over all the labor force of the house of Joseph"* (1 Kings 11:26-28), to divide the United Kingdom of David by taking *"hold of the new garment that was on him, and tore it into twelve pieces ... and Abijah said to Jeroboam, 'Take for yourself ten pieces, for thus says the LORD, the God of Israel: 'Behold, I will tear the kingdom out of the hand of Solomon and will give ten tribes to you"* (2 Kings 11:29-31).

King Jeroboam became God's man for the hour. In New Testament terms, he would be considered a Christian, someone of the faith of Jesus Christ. He would be someone who started out under the authority of the Lord, doing God's service.

According to God's word, Jeroboam was made king of Israel (1 Kings 12:20). Imagine, used by God — given a kingdom to rule for God. Notwithstanding, King Jeroboam did not trust God's promise in giving him this kingship over the Ten Northern Tribes. King Jeroboam, knowing full-well Jerusalem was Israel's center of worship, purposefully went about to establish multiple centers of worship within the territory of the Ten Northern Tribes. King Jeroboam's insecurity and ambition caused him to establish a plan whereby he could keep his kingdom in case the Ten Northern Tribes would unite together in worship in Jerusalem, thereby losing their affection for him.

Thus, he diverted the Ten Northern Tribes from the place of true oneness, from the temple on Zion in Jerusalem. The two golden calves were replicas of the golden calf in the wilderness after coming out from Egypt and worshiped by the children of Israel where they were subsequently judged by the Almighty for doing so. These false idols represented a false salvation — King Jeroboam replaced the invisible God with two idols. These idols were uplifted in a way whereby the true story of salvation was marred, destroyed.

King Jeroboam then went about by establishing two alternative worship centers called "high places." A "high place" is where an idol is uplifted so God's people would gather there instead of going to Zion's "holy hill" to worship. This made the division permanent and systematic.

In the same way, a Christian minister, doing God's work can still speak of the way of salvation through Christ as Savior — bringing men and women to worship the One True God; however, they can also uplift a Christian doctrine or practice to a point where those under their care and teaching consider this emphasis as an "uplifted idol" able to deliver them. Uplifting these Biblical things can become idolatrous and divide the brethren from each other.

In Paul's days, he was contending with those who were uplifting the Law of God contained in various ordinances. Some were teaching they would receive more of the Spirit if Christians would come back under these laws of ordinances (Gal. 3:5). There are numerous good teachings and practices in the Bible which can become uplifted idols . . . "golden calves."

Throughout Christian history some have claimed if people pray in a certain way, live according to certain Biblical principles, and follow certain ministries, then they will be delivered. More than likely, these things being taught have been helpful to those initially receiving these teachings. However, now the very thing that God used to help them has itself been uplifted to the point where that practice, that teaching, that doctrine has become more essential than simple faith in Jesus Christ.

"The sins of Jeroboam" are manifested when teachers uplift their favorite teachings to gather people around themselves with the result being division among believers. Throughout the history of Christianity — from the sins of King Jeroboam — we witness how certain doctrines and practices gather the unsuspecting around these "idols" with the tragic result being division after division within the Body of Christ.

It is a very serious matter to follow the "way of Jeroboam." God's judgment is upon this way — He is against the "sins of Jeroboam." All followers of our Lord Jesus should be warned about the sins of Jeroboam and how he led the Ten Northern Tribes into idolatry. Christians must come to terms with uplifting only Jesus in their pursuit of *"The United Kingdom of David"* (Acts 15:14-17).

12.
God's Moving to Fulfill His Purpose

To appreciate the significance of the Lord's ekklesia, a comparison needs to be made against the backdrop of today's Christianity.

A Short History of the "Church"

After the death and resurrection of Jesus Christ, His subsequent ascension, and outpouring of the Spirit, something completely outside of and apart from religion was initiated: the unique oneness for which the Lord Jesus prayed was immediately manifested. Believers lived and assembled in the joy and freedom of the Spirit. They were freed from religious laws and regulations, from a dedicated place of worship, and from the hierarchy of religious offices. They gathered in homes from house to house without any rituals or regulations. They were filled with the joy of the Spirit, experienced oneness in fellowship with all believers, and peace with all. The supernatural beginning of this assembly at the beginning of Acts was something new within the realm of existing "religion" at that time.

All religions have two things in common: They have a designated place of worship such as a temple, and a mediatory class of "holy men" such as priests or clergymen. When the Body of Christ was formed after Jesus' resurrection and ascension, something profound happened: The assembly of His believers began meeting in homes. Thousands of believers in the assembly in Jerusalem gathered together in homes, in house after house. Additionally, every believer actively functioned as a member of the body with a direct connection to the Head (Jesus Christ), without a mediatory class (1 Tim. 2:5). This was the initiation of the Body of Christ. This normal and healthy condition should have continued for all believers in Jesus Christ from generation to generation.

Alas, this blissful condition only lasted a short time. Within about thirty years, early believers became distracted by various teachings advocating keeping the commandments contained in ordinances, ritualistic observances, as well as Greek philosophies (Col. 2:6–23). Believers, because they were babes in Christ, started to divide among themselves over preferences of various apostles (1 Cor. 1:12). Others positioned themselves as leaders, drawing people to themselves rather than Christ, forming sectarian groups, and separating themselves from the general body of believers (Acts 20:30). Most of the Epistles Paul wrote addressed these distractions with the intent of directing believers back to Jesus Christ and His mysterious purpose: building up His One Body. Paul's two letters to the Corinthians are good examples of this.

Roman persecution ensued, beginning in the First Century A.D. and continuing through the Third Century. This only caused the resurrection life of Christ to grow and multiply through "death," a testimony of the believers' victorious life in Jesus Christ. During this time of persecution, believers were not able to organize; this helped them to greatly multiply through small communities gathering in homes. However, the seeds of distraction were already sown — a mixture of Jewish laws and rituals, along with Greek philosophies — sidetracked believers from their singular focus on Jesus Christ. Consequently, Christian communities, by and large, were susceptible to the allure of Emperor Constantine and succumbed to his enticement. Christianity became the official state religion during the Fourth Century.

Being accepted and honored by the state seemed like a victory for persecuted Christians in the Roman Empire. However, the church Constantine established was completely foreign to the concept of the original First Century gathering of believers. It contradicted the revelation of the New Testament. Buildings, once Roman temples, were dedicated to Christian worship or were newly constructed to accommodate the "priestly class" known as the clergy. These "religious leaders" were uplifted to rule over "regular Christians."

Various Jewish and heathen liturgies were brought into Christian gatherings. Constantine, who referred to himself as the "chief priest" of all cults in his empire, also tried to act in accord with church tradition. Some say Constantine purposely converted to Christianity. The result of his merging of Christianity and cults marred the assembly Jesus established. This resulted in the disappearance of the simplicity of a common brotherhood meeting in homes and from house to house with the sole focus on Jesus Christ as the Head of His One Body.

By the Fourth Century, the Christian community had accepted the current collection of writings in the Bible to be inspired by God — the Canon of Scripture. The same twenty-seven writings and letters in today's New Testament were canonized by the beginning of the Fifth Century.

In the meantime, the Roman state (Catholic) church grew in prominence, while church and politics became completely intertwined. Because of this, the Roman church became more powerful than kings. Although the Bible had been canonized as being divinely inspired, the actual reading of the Bible became more obscure. One of the biggest reasons for this had to do with the Roman church discouraging the reading (and thus understanding) of the Bible. It was restricted to the clergy class of priests and monks. The Roman church's reasoning behind censoring the Scriptures was they were too hard and complicated for common believers to understand; therefore, believers needed the interpretation and teaching from the clergy. The hidden motive, however, was to keep the common people in the dark concerning divine revelations in the Scriptures; by doing so, the clergy had complete control over the laity. The clergy, alone, could decide the meaning of the Scriptures and what the common people could and could not believe and do.

From the Fifth to the Fifteenth Century — a period of about 1000 years (also known as the Dark or Middle ages), the Roman church was repressive; people were persecuted for the unauthorized owning or reading of the Bible. Without freedom to read the Bible, the populace was completely subjected to the leadership of the Roman church. The revelation concerning Christ and His purpose was kept in the dark — so much so even the concept of salvation was completely distorted. The fact that salvation is *by faith* in Jesus Christ alone was lost. It was replaced with buying indulgences for an uncertain salvation. If people wanted salvation, they were required to pay the Roman church.

A significant invention in the Fifteenth Century prompted a change in this situation: a printing machine called the Gutenberg Press, which led to a mass production of books in Europe.[13] The first complete book printed was the Bible. With the development of the printing press, the Bible became more and more accessible outside the control of the Roman

---

13   McLuhan, Marshall. *The Gutenberg Galaxy: The Making of Typographic Man*. Toronto: U of Toronto, 1962. Print.

church. Common people could have access to the revelation God intended for His people, without the medium of the clergy's interpretation to control people's knowledge and understanding.

Interestingly, the availability of the Bible for common people coincided with the decline of the Roman church's power and dominance. As more and more people questioned the doctrines and practices of the Roman church, viewing them as contrary to the revelation in the New Testament, individuals (mostly in central Europe) began to confront and challenge the Roman church to reform it. The most famous of these reformers was Martin Luther, who was a monk in the Roman church. He is credited as the catalyst of the Reformation movement. The Reformation, which was intended to reform the Roman church, became a widespread advancement of various groups of believers who separated from the Roman church in the Sixteenth Century.

Martin Luther's famous act in challenging the Roman church was a document called the *Ninety-five Theses*, which he announced in 1517. Luther's strong belief posited acceptance by God was only through faith and not through any other means. This conviction in turn propelled him to create the document, which mainly challenged papal authority and the sale of indulgences. Luther is credited with championing and recovering from obscurity the basic tenet that justification before God is only through faith in Jesus Christ.

History testifies this time frame was the beginning of God's "Reset to One" — or bringing back to light truth found in Scripture which was at one time lost (or covered over) by the Roman church. This new freedom to explore the Scriptures directly, without the shackle of the Roman church, began to unchain the human mind and intellect. During this period other men rose up as leaders of the Reformation such as John Calvin. This, in turn, opened the door for the secular world to rebel against the authority and influence of the Roman church. Significantly, by the Seventeenth Century, the secular world entered into what is known as the "Age of Enlightenment" where individualism, science, skepticism and toleration became a driving force in transforming society; no longer would it be dominated by institutional religious churches.

Though Martin Luther's intention was to reform the Roman church, the church viewed him a threat to its theocratic rule and, ultimately, decided to eliminate him. Luther took refuge and came under the protection of a

German prince. For almost a century, Europe had been under the universal rule of the Roman church wherein kings of Northern Europe sought to be unshackled from Roman authority. Taking advantage of the Reformation, many regional kings aligned themselves politically with the reformers. Ultimately, they formed state churches independent from Rome. Those who adhered to Luther's teachings, called themselves Lutherans. Lutheranism became the state church of Germany. Many other state churches followed such as the Church of England, the Church of Denmark, and the Dutch Reformed Church. These churches joined themselves politically with the state, whereupon the monarch became the authority (or head) of the church.

Although some critical truth was uncovered from the Reformation, which was indeed full of spiritual activity and enlightenment; notwithstanding, the common people simply switched from the regulations of one Roman institution to one under the state. Though the Reformation originated with the Lord's restoration through various reformers, in a rather short time the resulting churches became institutionalized with a mixture of politics, human organization, and hierarchy.

Since the work of the Spirit to fully bring back and recover the truth in the Bible and God's eternal purpose was not yet fulfilled, men continued to seek the Lord through the study of Scripture desirous of a fresh move of the Holy Spirit. As these men discovered something new from the Scriptures, or when the Spirit used men to continue His "reset" without the restraints of rituals and regulations, they would speak out and preach their discoveries with the inspiration of the Spirit.

However, just as the Roman church rejected the initial reformers; state churches also rejected any preaching which might disrupt their set ways and newly-formed systems. These preachers found that these newly-formed, now established, churches did not embrace the idea of the Spirit of the Lord moving ever forward; most preachers who continued to "theologically innovate" were rejected, persecuted, or were either forced out or they voluntarily left the newly-found churches.

This quest for renewal became a recurring pattern throughout modern church history. Believers searching for greater illumination from the Scripture, under the unction of the Holy Spirit, founded new doctrine or practice, which helped and inspired many Christians. New ministries were founded. Simultaneously, institutional churches would, in the main, reject these attempts at renewal or revival.

Often, these new discoveries and insights were taught to assist believers in the Faith. When people are helped, adherents will be formed around these new Scriptural insights. After a few decades, these emerging groups would federate, become organized, institutionalized, and ready to reject anything new the Spirit was revealing if it fell outside their newly-founded doctrinal system or practice.

These cycles of institutionalizing found their various identities as Lutheranism (Martin Luther); Presbyterianism (John Calvin); Methodism/Holiness (Charles Wesley); Churches of Christ or Christian Churches (Stone-Campbell); Pentecostal churches (Parham/Seymour) – all the way to the present day, albeit in a much smaller scale among independent churches or so-called non-denominational churches.

It is reasonable to consider these established churches as ministries, since all the churches of today are founded by a minister, and they continue to function under the direction of a minister. When other gifted ministers within these churches receive something new from the Lord, their awakening will either be suspect or not accepted by the pre-existing ministries; Therefore, the "innovator" would inevitably initiate a new ministry thereby becoming another "church."

Great Awakenings and Revivals

Most Christians are spiritually predisposed to revival. Revivals or awakenings generally are defined by the Spirit's quickening in the lives of slumbering believers. God does something miraculous in pouring out His Spirit with power to convict and convince people of their ungodly and/or lukewarm condition – turning them in repentance to God. A revival is where salvation becomes a common occurrence, an entire people seek after the Lord with the zeal of the Spirit – believers are spiritually revived; love one another, and are propelled to serve the Lord.

Certainly, God has wrought great revivals over the centuries. American revivals, for example: The first "Great Awakening" occurred around 1730-1740; the second between 1790 to 1840; the third around 1855 to 1900. The Azusa Street Revival in Los Angeles in 1906 was considered by many as a revival which started the Pentecostal movement; and finally, in the late 1960s to the mid-1970s the Jesus People movement spawned many independent churches such as Calvary Chapel.

In each of these awakenings, God came in to move, and to stir up His people. Unbelievers were brought to salvation en masse. Nevertheless, each time, Satan would come in to sow discord and division. The move of God would dissipate through divisions by men desiring to organize and systematize the awakening. Yes, there were revivals, but the enemy caused infighting and division resulting in more churches, more "splits." Instead of producing oneness which is God's goal, His "movements" were hijacked by His enemy resulting in more divisions and factions in the Lord's Body. Reading through church history, one can immediately recognize numerous churches and groups which originated during and soon after each one of these revivals and awakenings.

In most instances, it was gifted, powerful men of God who were instrumental as catalysts who sparked these revivals. Moreover, it was also these same men and women who founded more churches after they had gained a following of people. Specially-gifted members are still needed today, but even more, they are needed to equip the saints for the building up of the Lord's ekklesia, not to build another "divisive church."

The critical need is to stir up believers to be assembled in oneness of fellowship as prayed for by Jesus in John 17. The Lord promised us when believers are one in fellowship as the Father and the Son are one, the world will believe. What a powerful gospel! This faith-generating testimony was not preached by any particularly gifted minister, but through displaying of His love and oneness among believers.

Instead of looking outward for God to move, what if the ordinary believer looked to Christ within, Who already is victorious and on the throne with all enemies under Him? Satan was crushed under the feet of those who were in unity due to their indiscriminate greeting of one another in Rome (Rom. 16:20). Instead of looking for the latest church programs and methods for spiritual awakening, what if believers come together in simplicity of heart focusing on Jesus Christ in their humble homes? In house after house, unbelievers would be convinced and convicted of the reality of God due to our oneness.

The dream for the next and final revival in this age will bring in the second advent of Jesus Christ. It is based on the Lord's Prayer: diverse believers coming together to be one in Jesus Christ, in Him alone. Discouraged saints who earnestly desire the oneness of His Body have concluded this oneness will never happen in this lifetime. Perhaps in the Millennium or heaven will be where such oneness is experienced? Then we must ask the question: How can the world believe the Father sent the Son if it isn't in the "here and now?" No, His prayer shall be answered while we're still here! Is it too much for us to remind Jesus the Father still must answer His prayer?

This revival will not be the result of preaching by powerful men and women. No, ordinary believers living out Jesus in their daily living; greeting and loving one another; and fellowshipping with all kinds of believers around them — that's revival! They would open their homes to host the Lord's assembly (ekklesia) with believers from all different backgrounds, and their unbelieving friends, relatives, and neighbors will believe as they witness God manifested in believers being truly one. This "end-times" revival cannot be organized. It will not be a "controlled burn" but a wild fire! The "New Man" is maturing, growing up, and being perfected into the One Body of Christ.

This last revival will not result in divisions and sectarianism because this revival will be the result of unity or oneness. It will originate with the vision and practice of oneness among diverse common believers, regular folks — not the labor of a handful of gifted personalities. This revival will coincide with the answer to our Lord's Prayer in John 17! "That they may be ONE!"

Restoration (Recovery) Movements

Restoration (aka *recovery*) movements are defined by the desire to leave institutional churches which have become divisive or deadened due to religious traditions and rituals. Returning to the simplicity and unity found in primitive "New Testament churches" becomes the quest. These movements are based on the desire to correct shortcomings and errors of traditional churches. Almost without exception these movements are a result of powerful men of God skilled in leadership. The following are notable groups which have a similar restoration spirit:

1. The first restoration movement in America can be credited to **Barton Stone and Thomas and Alexander Campbell**. Stone became the catalyst for the Second Great Awakening. Due to their objections to denominationalism, Stone and Campbell wanted to return to "the unification of all Christians in a single body patterned after the church of the New Testament."[14] They didn't want their groups to

---

14 Rubel Shelly, *I Just Want to Be a Christian*, 20th Century Christian, Nashville, TN 1984, pp 54

be named in any special way, so they simply called themselves the Churches of Christ or Christian Churches.
2. **John Darby and Benjamin Newton**. The group which eventually emerged was known as the Plymouth Brethren — later known as the "open brethren" and "closed brethren." They taught the oneness of the Body of Christ and the priesthood of all believers; therefore, they would not accept any name other than "brethren" to define themselves. They strongly objected to institutional churches. Some of the most notable Bible teachers since the reformation came from their midst. J. N. Darby is credited with Dispensationalism which is one of the foundational theologies found in many of evangelical circles today.
3. **Charles Parham and William Seymour** can also be considered as part of the restoration and revival movements since they taught the need for Christians to return to the experience of the baptism of the Holy Spirit, evidenced by the gift of speaking in tongues. They are credited with initiating the Pentecostal movement in the early 1900s which has splintered throughout the world into a multitude of churches. This movement has spread prevailingly with over 580 million Christians claiming to be Pentecostals or Charismatics.[15]

Other than these prominent Christian leaders from recent history, there are other less noteworthy ministers starting and forming restoration or recovery groups. Generally, their stated goal is to return to a more vibrant "church life" as found in the New Testament. Most such movements desire a true unity of the Body of Christ.

In their zeal, almost without exception, part of their message is a denunciation of the institutional churches of their day. In setting up an example of a restored "church" they commence by "federating" a new group of believers. Although they may not want a name for their movement or church, they inevitably must define their group structure. Thus, purposefully or inadvertently, the eventual result is: They have become another sect or denomination among a vast multitude marching into the sea of denominational squabbling and sectarian disputes. While God certainly has used them to recover certain items of truth, they have also

---

15 http://www.pewforum.org/2011/12/19/global-christianity-movements-and-denominations/

spawned countless divisions within the Body of Christ — in other words, their original quest for New Testament church life is shipwrecked. Even what is known as the "house church movement" starting around the mid-1980s has acquired most of the same characteristics in the line with other restoration movements.

There is absolutely nothing wrong, but rather honorable, to have the desire to be restored back to the original vision and practice of what God is after in His eternal purpose. It is the calling of every person of God who aspires in service to Him to yearn for serving Him according to His will and His ways as clearly revealed in Scripture. What is presented in *One Ekklesia* is also in the spirit of restoration, to return to the simplicity and purity of the Lord's ekklesia. The challenge is whether this can be done without the following damaging characteristics as in previous movements:

1. Disparaging other ministries and churches, thereby causing a clear separation with those who are participating in these "institutional churches."
2. Establishing another well-defined federated group of believers who are segregated from believers meeting in other churches and groups.
3. Having a specified leadership structure which is permanent rather than a fellowship and cooperation of independent gifted ministers.

Despite the stated goal of unity in these various restoration movements, these three characteristics have allowed satanic schemes to continue their same trajectory of more divisions and further sectarianism.

Where We Are Today?

Despite the twists and turns, ups and downs of church history, after 500 years since the Reformation, the truth and mystery concerning the person and work of Jesus Christ hidden in the New Testament is readily available. The way of salvation by faith in Jesus Christ alone is well accepted and established. Major doctrines such as Calvinism versus Arminianism have been thoroughly discussed and debated, the manifestations of the gifts of the Spirit are here to stay, and just about all the practices in the New Testament have been uncovered and discussed. Now, all these items are available and easily accessible for believers to consider before the Lord. Believers can search the Scriptures on their own, hear ideas from different, and at times opposing Bible teachers while allowing the Word of God, coinciding with the Holy Spirit, to enlighten their understanding and open their spiritual eyes.

They can discern for themselves what is healthy to keep and practice; and what is non-essential or not worth arguing over. This, of course, is a far cry from pre-Reformation times, when the truth found in the Bible was completely hidden; where the Bible itself was not available to common people.

However, the negative results of this new-then-institutionalized cycle as previously discussed is just as profound. Many denominations and independent Christian groups have separated and divided believers in direct opposition to the building up of the One Body of Christ and continue to do so in this day. Since anyone can pick up something new from the Bible or from spiritual experiences, it is rather easy to start a group, which often becomes a "church," whether big or small.

There are now tens of thousands of church institutions, each with its own identifier (Baptist or Lutheran, for example). Christians, who have identified themselves with one of these groups and have become loyal to their system of doctrine and practice, may then, with a bias, overlook teachings and practices within their church system which may be unscriptural, even contrary to God's desire. For example, some Catholic believers do not agree with the infallibility of the pope or praying to a saint's image. However, since they are loyal to the Catholic Church, they often overlook or do not object to unscriptural traditions which are contrary to God's commandment. As a result, the Body of Christ is more splintered. The one fellowship of the Body of Christ, with believers loving one another according to the Lord's new commandment, seems just as foreign as ever.

Notwithstanding, due to the Lord's Prayer for oneness, God's desire to complete His eternal purpose has been placed in the heart of every follower of Jesus. The desire to enjoy unity with other believers is a constant. Christians are tired of infighting among and within churches. It seems there is no solution to solving divisions among the churches; nevertheless, hope remains: The Lord's prayer for unity which the world can see to believe in Him will be fulfilled.

Therefore, even the writing of this book is a result of that abiding hope, and the conviction that something fresh is being discovered. It needs to be presented to help energize fellow believers in understanding the Scriptures to fulfill the Lord's Prayer for His people to be one.

Learning from the Past

Just as in secular learning where each subsequent generation builds upon previous discoveries, knowledge, and mistakes, so does Biblical understanding and spiritual experience. For example, today's researchers do not need to start from scratch to discover electricity before inventing the next generation of electronic products. If that were the case, every generation would be stuck in the Seventeenth Century. Instead, they can quickly learn from the body of knowledge before them — including failed experiments — so new discoveries can continue leading to better electronic products.

It is similar with spiritual knowledge. Today, believers do not need to fight the battle over the doctrine of the Trinity (hopefully, that doctrine is well-established in the minds of most believers); debate over whether Christ is both God and man was waged centuries ago. Arguments over whether people are justified by faith alone or figuring out what it means to experience the new birth (regeneration) — those issues have been resolved. We can build on previous battles won and learn from mistakes made; to progress as a body of believers toward the consummation of what God is after in His eternal purpose.

It is profoundly important believers learn from past mistakes. This will enable them to present something new, fresh, and inspiring — rendering spiritual help without creating more harm to the Body of Christ. Can the Lord continue His reset and building work without adding another layer of organizational confusion excluding believers and ministries? Absolutely!

What can be learned from history to prevent further division among believers? How can believers receive benefits of continuous but new and refreshing moves of the Spirit without sectarianism?

Here is what we can learn from mistakes of past restoration movements:

1. Do not have a judgmental attitude toward ministers and churches; rather, appreciate their preaching of Jesus Christ even when some of their doctrine and practices may be perceived to be contrary to the Bible.
2. Not forming another distinctive group to be separated from other groups of believers
3. While a clear leadership structure is needed in a ministry, it is destructive to the Lord's ekklesia. The Lord is the unique Head in His

Body. All believers need complete freedom to function in the Body. What is needed are more "approved brethren" to be peacemakers with cooperation between gifted brethren as in 1 Corinthians 3:6-7.

Here is a summary of key points from this book which inhibit such division and encourage a fresh move of God's Spirit among His people today:

1. Make a clear distinction and separation between ministries and the Lord's ekklesia (assembly). Churches today are ministries of particular pastors and ministers, but the ekklesia is a called-out gathering of diverse believers in oneness where each has equal opportunity and responsibility to speak and share their experience with Jesus Christ.
2. Obeying Paul's command to continually "meet and greet" in fellowship with all kinds of believers outside of one's normal circle.
3. Host or participate in the Lord's ekklesia as described in 1 Corinthians 11:17 through Chapter 14.
4. Understand and enjoy the three gifts given to believers by the Lord Jesus in His prayer in John 17. The result of these three gifts is the oneness of His Body. These three gifts of Life, Truth, and Glory are discussed in the book ***ONE*** (by the same author).

Although the Spirit continues to move, the assembly described in the New Testament with all believers in one fellowship in Jesus Christ, and meeting in homes — house by house, is almost completely neglected. The true assembly has no hierarchy, nor human organization. Hierarchy is defined as levels of authorities to direct and control believers. All ministries should be for the building up of the assembly, but instead the opposite occurs — whole churches are formed around various ministries. Not only are major denominational churches formed around powerful ministers such as Luther, Calvin and Wesley, but most churches today are centered on the *ministry* of a teacher or preacher.

The assembly, on the other hand, consists of all believers having equal opportunity to speak no matter what their preferred doctrine or Christian practice. It doesn't matter from whose ministry one is blessed (1 Cor. 1:9–13). Even with the best of intentions, churches built around ministries cannot avoid divisions among God's people if the church becomes centered on emphasizing its ministry alone. Since there is often a clear direction for a ministry, it is understandable believers who distract from this ministry's direction will not be welcomed. As a result, believers look for churches which suit them the best. The assembly, on the other hand, is one; it receives all believers, no matter their preference or distinctiveness (Rom. 14).

A Renewed Vision to Build the Assembly

Again, the purpose of this book is not to cast a blanket criticism on institutional churches as divisive or spiritually stuck in their traditions, but to emphasize the need to see and build up the assembly, the One Body of Christ. There are certainly ministers who believers should be wary of if they teach against the truth or purposely try to form a sect with prideful motives (Rom. 16:17); however, that should not diminish the fact the Lord uses many ministers and pastors for His purpose in their work among organized churches.

Ministers and pastors could be more useful if they encouraged their followers and church members to meet and greet other believers in fellowship in their daily living, assembling with them according to Scripture, and meeting in homes with complete freedom. They should seek to experience fellowship with *all* believers, even when some of those believers are under the teaching of a ministry that is contrary to their own. This would exemplify their ministry is properly building up the assembly according to the revelation found in the New Testament, rather than building their ministry by human orchestration.

Another major reason various ministries become divisive (and to no fault of the ministers) has to do with the laziness of believers in seeking the Lord through the Scriptures or due to a church culture which encourages "pulpit-pew spectator" rather than engagement of the congregants. That is why Paul didn't blame the *ministers* for causing divisions; he blamed *believers* for being spiritual babes (1 Cor. 3:1–4). It is so easy for Christians to join a church and follow its leadership instead of seeking the Lord for personal discernment. The result is a group of believers who passively gravitate toward a divisive mindset.

To accomplish His purpose, the Lord will continue attempts which initiate something fresh within all individual believers. In Revelation 2 and 3 John portrays the Spirit continually speaking to believers in many kinds of churches, for individuals to rise up and heed the Spirit's call. God is calling

His children to arise and overcome the current condition of the "church," even when it seems good. Without individuals persistently being raised up to come directly under the Lord's headship, churches will inevitably become degraded and slip into human hierarchy, institutionalizing systems of doctrine and practices. Let's pray that many individual believers in the Body of Christ will not be satisfied with the status quo but will heed the Spirit's call to overcome further division and apathy!

Ultimately, this author hopes believers will be encouraged to become one. This will happen according to the Lord's Prayer in John 17 by embracing three gifts given to each of God's children. Understanding, knowing, and enjoying these *three gifts* would fulfill God's purpose of building up the Lord's one mystical body with these three marvelous gifts:

1. Believers should be released to enjoy God's divine LIFE which they have originally received through the new birth. By focusing on Jesus being the resurrection and the life in them, they will trust this Life, grow according to this life, and be spontaneously shaped according to the nature of this divine Life. As a result, they will express the image of the Lord Jesus in oneness with all believers.
2. Believers should know and enjoy the Lord Jesus as TRUTH found in Scripture. The result of this fuller knowledge should be an enjoyment of the "unsearchable riches of Christ" (Eph. 3:8). Truth will equip believers, giving them the ability to walk according to God's eternal will, opening them to receive, fellowship with, and love all kinds of believers.
3. Every believer should be inspired and equipped for their mission to serve God and humanity. Ministering Christ to humankind for salvation, growth, and growing up as a mature Christian is the goal. Thus, Christ's body will be built up practically in homes (from house to house), while seeking to merge in fellowship with all believers in becoming one for God's satisfaction and GLORY.

13.
THREE GIFTS RESULTING IN ONE

At this point of the book, the reader may well be convinced by the Scripture, and by the Holy Spirit, concerning the thesis of the book: There is only one ekklesia, one fellowship. Likewise, actions are needed to greet believers indiscriminately and to gather in homes to have ekklesia wherein factions come together, resulting in oneness. Even if this is the case, the practice is not natural or merely human. The Trinity absolutely must be involved for this undertaking to occur. Without Jesus Christ being the focus, the source, and the perpetuation, oneness among believers simply cannot happen. That is the reason we find in the Lord's Prayer for oneness, He gave three distinct gifts. It was after each gift He asked His followers to be ONE . . . three times.

To have this transcendent ONEness among believers, which is the manifestation of the building up of His assembly, Jesus in His prayer in John 17 gave His disciples three gifts: eternal life (the Father's name), the truth (the Word), and His glory. Each is given to every believer, and makes it possible for them to be one, just as Jesus is one with the Father. It is through His followers being one through these inestimable gifts the world will believe Jesus is truly the Son of God (John 17:21b).

Knowing, understanding, and experiencing these three gifts is how believers are made one; they are essential to accomplishing His purpose in creating "oneness." The book entitled, *ONE*, by the same author, explores in depth these three gifts for the Lord's continuing work of building up His assembly by bringing His children into this mysterious, yet practical, oneness.

This same testimony of oneness among saints from all nations, ethnicities, and socioeconomic diversity (Col. 3:11) will cause the world to believe He is the Son of God, convincing them of God's eternal love for humanity (John 17:23). This testimony of the gospel is the most powerful means whereby the world will believe – God's people brought into one through eternal life, truth and the glory of Jesus Christ!

The First Gift – Eternal life; The Father's Name

> ... as You have given Him authority over all flesh, that He should give **eternal life** to as many as You have given Him. And this is eternal life, that they may know You, the only true God, and Jesus Christ whom You have sent. ... Now I am no longer in the world, but these are in the world, and I come to You. Holy Father keep through Your name those whom You have given Me, that they may be one as We [are].
>
> (John 17: 2–3, 11)

Eternal life (the Father's name) is the first element, which is related to being born of God to become God's child. It is this process resulting in God becoming our Father, and, in turn, we receive His name. In John 17:3 it clearly states knowing the Father and the Son is eternal life for those who believe in Jesus Christ. When one believes in Christ, this person receives a new birth. He or she is born anew – born from above. This is known as *regeneration* – it can only be produced through God's divine, eternal life. This is what it means to be *"born ... of God"* (John 1:13). Being born of God is not just a metaphor; it is a reality. God is now our Father, not just our Creator.

In addition to receiving God's eternal life, we partake of His divine nature (2 Pet. 1:4). The reality of God as the believers' Father is more real than their earthly (biological) fathers from their "first" birth, because God is the Father constantly and eternally. God's children received the Spirit of the Son by which they can cry out to God in the most intimate way, "Abba, Father" or "Daddy, Father" (Gal. 4:6).

It is by receiving this life of the Father, enjoying the Father's name, which enables His children to be one. His children are one because they have the same eternal life and divine nature. All believers have the same Father. His people have one common source; they become genuine brothers and sisters within the same family. In many cultures, those who are born from the same earthly father have the same name – their family (last) name. Similarly, His children bear the same "name" as their heavenly Father because they are born of Him. So, being kept in the Father's name means to bask in the joyous reality that all God's children are in one family having the same Father with the same name. If believers are not living in the enjoyment of this divine life, then they will gravitate back to their divisive old nature.

The Father and the Son, though distinct, are one in life and nature; therefore, they are both eternally one. Thus, all believers who live by this life are partaking of His Divine nature; they are automatically one in Christ. This partaking of the Divine Nature is fundamental to every believer enjoying oneness. In 1 John 3:14 we read: *"We know that we have passed from death to life, because we love the brethren."* This new life causes His children to love one another. It is Divine — it is proof we are no longer in death, but in the Father's life.

The Father's children, upon receiving Jesus Christ as their Savior, are born anew. They immediately feel a connection with other believers. They don't know much, if at all, concerning various Christian doctrines, practices, or denominational affinities, but are just happy to meet any other believer. Their first thought is not what denomination to which a person belongs, but simply: "You believe in Jesus Christ? Praise the Lord! Let me tell you, I just found Jesus!" This is real, spontaneous, unadulterated love for other believers. Spontaneous life — immediate identification with all those who share in this life!

Tragically, this joyous life begotten by our same Father is diluted as His children gradually add doctrines (*Didaskalia*) and practices which suppress the expression of His life. Sitting under the tutelage of various Bible teachers, they begin to align themselves with certain schools of theology — a *way* of practicing baptism, a *method* for holy living, or *steps* to receiving miraculous gifts. It appeared they were learning a lot of Christian teaching "enriching" their new-found faith, but the more they learned, the more they began to separate themselves from other believers. They began to identify themselves with a certain type of Christian. Many find a curious pride by identifying themselves as Baptist, Catholic, or Methodist. Other saints claim they are now Pentecostal; reformed Christians; or dispensationalists.

This is not being kept in the Father's name. This is leaving the Father's name to take on other names.

Oh, how God's children desperately need to be kept uniquely in the Father's name! This is the first and most basic issue in being born from above to be one. Those who abide in the Father's name will not bring about problems with other children of God. They will not promote anything causing other believers to be distracted from this eternal life, the Father's name.

Those kept in the Father's name spontaneously receive all fellow believers as true brothers and sisters sharing in one fellowship because of His abundant life. They will seek to grow in this eternal life and encourage other members of His family to grow in this life. They will not want to remain as a babe but will strive to reach maturity.

A babe in this life is a person who is easily carried away from the Father's name. These children are easily distracted by the world — political causes, keeping the ordinances of the law, engaging in doctrinal debates, analyzing various Christian practices, or being caught up in dynamic Christian personalities. In Ephesians 4:14 Paul said God's people should no longer be like babies, tossed and carried about by every wind of teaching. Men use both secular and biblical teachings with craftiness, carrying off the "babes" into their schemes or systematized error — that is, a system in error. The enemy's schemes cause divisions which result in schisms and factions in the Body of Christ, separating believers from each other.

Conversely, mature believers growing in the Father's life abide immovable. They are no longer diverted or confused by various doctrines (*Didaskalia*) or practices. They are guarded and kept from being blown about by "every wind of doctrine." Such followers of Christ can fellowship easily with all saints, even with distracted babes. Mature believers have seasoned ability to bring those blown about by these winds of doctrine back to enjoying the Father's name — back to enjoying that original oneness birthed within them at regeneration.

The book *ONE* explores how the followers of Jesus grow in His life. Every life needs four elements to grow and thrive; Therefore, it is through their spiritual nourishment, breathing, exercise, and rest whereby God's eternal life grows and matures in them. The nourishment all believers need to consume is through "feeding on Jesus" as the Word of God — to ingest Him as the Bread of Life by receiving the knowledge of Him in the Scriptures. To drink of the Water of Life is receiving the Spirit through faith. Jesus Christ is the good land, the environment, without which we cannot exit; therefore, walk in Him and breathe Him in as the Breath of Life throughout our day no matter what situation in which we find ourselves. Exercise is when believers teach and minister Jesus Christ to someone else as soon as they have received something of the knowledge of Jesus Christ. Finally, sleep is resting in the finished work of Christ — His death and resurrection. We can truly rest in peace ending all struggles while we are enjoying His death and resurrection . . . THIS is the life of a believer in Christ!

The Second Gift – Truth

The second gift the Lord gave believers to bring them into ***oneness*** is truth. The Lord prayed in John 17:14 and 17: *"I have given them Your word . . . Sanctify them by Your truth. Your word is truth."* It is in this truth believers are made one. Jesus continued to pray: *"That they all may be one, as You, Father, are in Me, and I in You; that they also may be one in Us, that the world may believe that You sent Me"* (17:21). Our oneness which we enjoy within the Triune God is both mysterious and deep — all His children share the same truth that leads to the same fellowship the Father and the Son enjoy. How deep and mysterious is the oneness of all believers in the Triune God, in the Father and the Son! How powerful is this manifestation that will cause the world to believe!

In John 17:17 it states: *"Your word is truth."* The "word" in this verse does not refer to the actual words in Scripture (the Bible). The Bible contains and conveys the Word; however, people can read and study the Scriptures, yet miss the Word. John 1:1 says, *"In the beginning was the Word and the Word was with God and the Word was God."*

This verse alone shows that the "word" in John 17:17 is not simply referring to the Bible, since the Bible was not written in the beginning of eternity! Then, in John 1:14 we read: *"The Word became flesh . . . ."* This "Word" is God Himself, incarnate. The Son of God became man, in the form of Jesus Christ, the Son of Man. *The* Word is Jesus. Jesus confirmed this in John 5:39–40 when He said, *"You search the Scriptures, for in them you think you have eternal life. But you are not willing to come to Me that you may have life."* Here, Jesus is clearly separated from the Scriptures. Although the contents of the Bible are factual and without error, one can read and study the Scriptures without coming to Jesus. Life is in Jesus, not in mere Scripture absent of Jesus.

The Greek word for "word" is *logos*. It means "a speech, something said, and reasoning." It is the root word for "logical" (Gr. *logikos*). Jesus being the "Word" is the expression or effulgence of God as speech. This Word comes in a way which is reasonable — it can be logically understood. We find in John 1:18 our God is hidden — no one can see or perceive Him but the Son, Who is the Word . . . the Word manifests or "declares" God. It is through the Word — Jesus Christ — man can see and know God. The New American Standard Version captures the essence of the verse: *"No one has seen God at any time; the only begotten God who is in the bosom of the Father, He has explained Him."*

Words can be written down, passed on, and reproduced in an accurate manner; this is how the Word has been recorded in the Scriptures. God will be manifested to those who seek Jesus as the Word in the Scriptures, through understanding and reasoning — the Word explains who God really is. Believers need to do more than simply read and study the Bible because it contains the Word; they should simultaneously come to Jesus, seek Him, see Him, speak to Him, know Him, handle Him, and have fellowship with Him; otherwise, they will miss the words of eternal life (1 John 1:1–2).

In John 1:14 it says, *"The Word became flesh and dwelt among us . . . full of grace and truth."* A few verses later in verse 18 John writes, *"For the law was given through Moses, but grace and truth came through Jesus Christ."* These two verses reveal *"grace and truth"* were introduced through the Word, Jesus Christ, when God was manifested in the flesh.

According to Vine's Expository Dictionary, **truth**, as used in the New Testament, is "the reality lying at the basis of appearance and manifestation." According to this definition, truth is much more than not telling a lie or saying something factual; *it is the reality of the universe.* Truth is eternal. When a person realizes what is hidden behind what appears or what is manifested, *that is truth*. No wonder "truth" has such prominence! It is one of two profundities which came through Jesus Christ. It is important to elevate the understanding of the word "truth" to a high and spiritual level, and not relegate it to a simple secular concept such as, "Tell me the truth! Did you take a cookie?"

John says that Jesus Christ is full of grace and truth. He continues to say that grace and truth came through Jesus Christ. Based on the above definition, when a person receives Jesus Christ, they possess *the* truth, *the* reality. They will know and discern what is real, what is behind the entire "shadow" of the universe (Col. 2:16–17). Without Jesus Christ, men are stuck knowing only what they see and what is physically manifested. Men's lives and all that they strive for — money, fame, and material gain — all are vanity. Even the physical universe is not reality! Receiving and believing in Jesus Christ brings people out of the pit of vanity, emptiness, falsehood — into truth, veracity, and something solid that is eternal.

The more a believer stands in truth alone, the more open and receptive in fellowship that believer will be with all other believers. When a child of God is established in the truth, that person is not blown about by various doctrines and practices. Neither will there be objections to or insistence on any doctrine (*Didaskalia*), nor the wide array of Christian practices. A person grounded in the truth of Jesus Christ is a person who is peaceful, comfortable, and confident.

Who (or What) Is the Definition of Truth?

First and foremost, God as the Word is truth. *"In the beginning was the Word and the Word was with God, and the Word was God…and the Word became flesh… full of grace and truth"* (John 1:1, 14).

Second, Jesus Christ who is God in the flesh is truth. Truth was revealed in Jesus Christ. Jesus said, *"I am the truth"* (John 14:6), and Paul declared that *"the truth is in Jesus"* (Eph. 4:21).

Third, the Spirit is truth. The Scriptures declare the *Spirit of truth* (John 14:17, 15:26, 16:13; 1 John 4:6), and that the *Spirit is truth* (1 John 5:6). The Spirit of truth guides believers into all truth by declaring and infusing the reality of all that the Father and the Son are into believers (John 16:13–15).

Fourth, all that the Father, the Son, and the Spirit have accomplished for His eternal purpose is truth. This includes the death of Jesus Christ on the cross, His resurrection, His ascension and enthronement, and His work of redemption for the forgiveness of sins, justification, sanctification, the believers' regeneration (new birth) and future glorification. Therefore, the person of the Triune God dwelling bodily in Jesus Christ (Col. 2:9) and His work of redemption and regeneration is the Word of truth — that is, the gospel of salvation. It is through believing the truth that people are saved and sealed by the indwelling Spirit (Eph. 1:13). Believers in God's eternal purpose become members of His body — the new man spoken of in Ephesians 2:15. This corporate entity is created and built up into maturity in truth (Eph. 4:24).

Finally, the Word as recorded in the Bible is truth. The Bible conveys the truth, and truth is understood when the Word is made real to a person. The Word, the logos, speaks to people and communicates to their reasoning. When the Word is received, understood, and becomes real to a person, then it is truth. That is why people need to know and come to the full knowledge of the truth (2 Tim. 2:25, 3:7; 1 Tim. 2:4). For example, the Bible says Jesus Christ is God who became man, died for mankind's sin and was resurrected on the third day. Many unbelievers have heard this, but it is not truth or real to them. One day as they consider this word, they will hopefully open their heart and connect with Jesus through faith. At that very moment, the Spirit of Truth will enter them and make the word of God that they heard real; they will understand with a living knowledge, and then, that will be truth to them.

The sum total of New Testament revelation of the truth is rich and deep. It is God in Jesus Christ as the Spirit with all that they have accomplished for man and in man, which includes the eternal purpose of God's assembly fulfilled in Jesus Christ. Therefore, truth is God Himself, with His life, nature, and essence, intrinsically joined with humanity. The truth is eternal (2 John 1:2). Anything that is temporal and has no effect in eternity is not truth.

What Is **Not** Truth?

Jesus prayed in John 17 that it is in the truth believers are made one. Thus, anything that divides believers — things that Christians argue over and become sectarian over — is not truth. Most Christian groups agree truth is what was outlined above. Any doctrines not defined as truth are non-essential. What has divided Christians include doctrines (*Didaskalia*), various Christian practices, or worldly causes. Christians have been divided, have fought over, and have rejected each other over some of the smallest things such as musical style in worship, whether women should have their head covered, whether the rapture is pre, mid, or post-tribulation, methods of baptism, and even methods of leadership. There are literally thousands of such things that have divided Christians; yet, the truth remains the same. A believer that has a growing understanding of the truth stays anchored in the truth and will not be distracted by positioning themselves in non-essentials; they will remain one with all believers.

The tactic of the enemy (Satan) is to use men and women — specifically Christian men and women — to elevate non-essential doctrines and practices and eventually form groups and churches around those doctrines. For example, a major dividing doctrinal point among Christians is centered on the debate over predestination or free will. Churches have been grouped together on one side or the other. Both sides can show supporting Bible verses and speak of how their doctrine is better for Christians, but the fact is, neither of those doctrines died for humankind or was resurrected! Nowhere in the Scriptures does it say that in order to receive eternal life a person needs to believe in one of these doctrines. And ultimately, it does not matter in eternity which doctrine is correct. Therefore, neither doctrine is truth, and certainly not worth dividing over. Whether a person espouses one side or the other, or even both, is not a problem unless it becomes a condition for fellowship — and a rejection of those with contrary views.

Another major point of division is whether the Holy Spirit is still doing works of power as in the days of the early apostles, or if these works of power have ceased. Again, using the measurement above, this belief is not truth either way. A person who is established in the truth will be able to have fellowship and receive believers no matter what their doctrinal position or preference. Those who are not standing in truth may be so biased with their personal doctrinal stance that they end up taking an extreme stand. For example, some may not acknowledge that a genuine miraculous healing today can be from God; others may belittle believers for not receiving any manifestation of the Holy Spirit.

Practices are much more common than doctrinal differences in dividing believers. For example, the moment a person believes in Christ and receives salvation, that person is regenerated in Christ; this is biblical truth. It is faith that brings a person into Christ. Baptism is a physical symbol declaring the truth of being in Christ. Every believer agrees with the truth that faith uniquely brings a person into Jesus Christ; however, many sectarian groups have formed over baptism. Some insist on water baptism, while others insist baptism has to be by immersion and not by sprinkling. Still others within the same immersion camp insist that the following phrase has to be recited at baptism: "In the name of the Father and of the Son and of the Holy Spirit." Others insist that the wording should be: "In the name of Jesus Christ." All of the above are various *ways* to practice baptism, but not the truth of being immersed into Jesus Christ, the Triune God. Different teachings on baptism use different scriptural verses as their foundation, and many believers are helped by their way of baptism. However, it is against the truth to use any of these particular practices to build up an entire sectarian group that hinders believers in that group from accepting and having fellowship with other believers if they do not hold to the same practice.

Easy to Be Distracted Away from the Truth

At this juncture, let's consider the story in Matthew 17 because it shows how easily and quickly the Lord's disciples forgot the revelation that they received just eight days earlier. Here, Jesus brought a few of His disciples up to a high mountain. Peter was included — one who recently received the revelation concerning Jesus being the Christ, the Son of God (Matthew 16). On this mountain, Jesus was transfigured before them; He became shining as the sun. Together with this glorious Jesus were Moses and Elijah also standing there conversing with Jesus. Peter grew excited and immediately said that they should make three tabernacles, one for each of them. Moses represented the law given by God since Moses gave the law (John 1:17); therefore, many times the law was associated with Moses throughout the Bible. After Moses, the major prophet who did many works of miraculous power was Elijah. He was the only prophet prominently named in the New Testament, twenty-nine times; therefore, Elijah represents the prophets with God's supernatural power.

When encountering all three, Peter viewed them the same: Jesus, Moses, and Elijah. Since he wanted to build three tabernacles, one for each, this showed that Peter considered them with equal standing, requiring equal reverence. But then the Father spoke from a cloud and said, *"This is my beloved Son, hear Him."* The disciples fell down in fear of such a voice. When Jesus came to lift them up, and when they looked up, they saw *"no one, but Jesus alone."* Both Moses and Elijah were gone; only Jesus was left for them to behold.

This is the experience of most Christians. They are saved by a wonderful revelation concerning Jesus being the Christ, the Son of the Living God. Then they immediately view the law and so many other items on an equal level as Jesus. "Now that Jesus saved me," they think, "I have to learn these doctrines, keep these laws, pursue these spiritual gifts, do these works, and on and on." Even though Jesus is the shining One, from their perspective, Jesus is now just another item among a long list of things. No, no, no! Another revelation is needed after believing — that there is no one else other than Jesus. It is not Jesus plus this and that. It is Jesus Himself alone!

It is unfortunate when most believers study the Bible, they consider it elementary to stay on Jesus Christ. There is a thought that the "deeper truth" is to understand how to behave as a Christian, understand the end times, learn self-denial, obtain a special gift from God, or many other topics. Some think, "I already know that Jesus Christ died and resurrected; let's learn about all the other things in the Bible." One can study, know, and discuss many topics in the Bible; yes, it is advisable to read the Bible from cover to cover thoroughly, but a mature believer is one who can only be satisfied with the excellence of the knowledge of Jesus Christ (Phil. 3:8–15). This person has lost the taste for all peripheral topics other than Jesus Christ, and His pursuit of the truth is to see and know how Jesus Christ's person and work is revealed in the pages of the Bible. There is a recognition and appreciation that Jesus is unsearchable and unlimited in His riches; therefore, it is an eternal pursuit to come to the full knowledge of the Son of God.

Remember the two Greek works for "doctrine" back in Chapter 11: *didache and didaskalia?* The doctrine (*didache*) of Jesus Christ is truth. Applying all the other doctrines (*didaskalia*) in the Bible may be considered healthy teachings and practices for living and relationships, depending on whether they help believers to seek the Lord Jesus or function properly in the Body. These "healthy teachings and practices" are conditional based on environment, culture, and individual needs at the time. For example, a teaching concerning head-coverings for women was clearly helpful during Paul's environment, but may not be in some cultures today. Certainly, any such teachings and practices should not be points of contention that break fellowship among believers. Even disagreements concerning the deeper and richer points of truth such as the triune nature of God should never break fellowship. Only the essential faith that brings salvation determines whether one is in the fellowship of Jesus Christ, and this faith is the only item that believers should contend for or insist on.

Jesus said: *The truth shall make you free* (John 8:32). Understanding truth is the supply and freedom whereby God's people can fellowship in oneness. Indeed, it is the truth that brings believers into ONE.

The Third Gift – Jesus' Glory

> And the glory which You gave Me I have given them, that they may be one just as We are one.
>
> (John 17:22)

The Lord Jesus prayed the glory that was given to Him by the Father would be given to all His disciples facilitating their oneness. *Glory* in the Greek means "good opinion, praise, honor, an appearance commanding respect, magnificence, excellence, manifestation of glory" (Vine's Expository Dictionary). Therefore, the highest glory results whenever God is expressed and manifested.

The glory given to Jesus was through His death and resurrection. Luke 24:26 made it clear: It was through death and resurrection Jesus entered glory. In John 12:23–24, Jesus said the hour had come for Him to be glorified; then He spoke of going to His death and resurrection to bear much fruit. He likened Himself as a seed of wheat needing the experience of death to bring forth many more grains in resurrection. That glory was given to Him in resurrection. In Jesus' opening prayer, He anguished over the fact the hour had arrived for Him to be glorified; again, He was referring to His imminent crucifixion. In the rest of His prayer, He prayed as if He had already been resurrected wherein all three gifts were already given to His disciples.

As the Son of God, the second of the Trinity, Jesus as God *already* had glory (John 1:14). In fact, it is the same glory as the Father (John 17:5). Since the glory of the Son in His divinity is the same glory as of the Father, there was no need for the Father to give Him additional glory. The glory that was given to Jesus in the above-referenced verses was given to Him *after* His death and resurrection, affirming the glory given to Him, was given to him *as a man*. Jesus in His humanity didn't possess the glory of God before His crucifixion, but after His death and resurrection, *still completely human,* He was glorified with the same divine glory He had with the Father before the world began. Not only was Jesus' humanity brought into glory, He brought all of His people, both then and those who would yet believe on Him, into this same divine glory. This is the "much fruit" which He bore as the "grain of wheat." It was through this process God was fully expressed in humanity or glorified.

Just as Jesus served God and man for His glorification, His followers, both then and now, who have received His glory are on the same path. They are to serve God and man in humility, as a slave, in ministering Christ to people on earth. As Jesus is interceding on the throne in heaven, His followers would continue His service to preach the gospel, to teach the truth, to make disciples and to build up His one assembly, His Body, on earth. This unique purpose is designed for all believers. They are one in this glory — able to fulfill God's purpose.

A Description of How Jesus Obtained Glory

Philippians 2 clearly describes the process by which Jesus received this glory from the Father, which is the same glory He has given to us *in bringing many sons to glory* (Heb. 2:10). In Philippians 2, Paul was expressing the same aspiration as the Lord's Prayer in John 17. He desired all God's children be one — one in mind, in one accord, having the same love for one another. However, Paul addressed a problem: "Vain glory" disrupted this oneness among His people. Vain (or empty) glory is human glory which uplifts itself, while thinking more highly of oneself compared to others. This self-glory (or *ego*) caused *friction* and discord (Phil 2:14; 4:2) among the saints in Philippi.

The remedy for this discord, according to Paul, was for believers to have the mind of Christ. What is the mind of Christ and its result? Let's read:

> Let this mind be in you, which was also in Christ Jesus: who, being in the form of God, thought it not robbery to be equal with God, but made Himself of no reputation, taking the form of a bondservant, and coming in the likeness of men. And being found in appearance as a man, He humbled Himself and became obedient to the point of death, even the death of the cross.
> (Philippians 2:5–8)

Jesus left His glory and His reputation as the eternal Son of God within the Triune God to become a man, but not just *any* man; He became a humble bond-servant Who died performing His service. Paul said Jesus was glorified — but only after His death:

> Therefore God also highly exalted him, and gave to him the name which is above every name; that at the name of Jesus every knee should bow, of those in heaven, those on earth, and those under the earth, and that every tongue should confess that Jesus Christ is Lord, to the glory of God the Father.
> (Philippians 2:9–11, WBT)

As a man in resurrection, Jesus was glorified. He received glory from the Father as the exalted One with the highest name at His ascension. This humble Jesus, as a servant of God and man, received the highest glory, and in turn it glorified the Father. This is what Jesus meant when He prayed in John 17:1: *"Glorify your Son, that your Son may glorify You."*

This glory given to Jesus is the same glory given to all believers. To have the same glory as Jesus, God's people need to have the same mind as Jesus — a mind to become nothing but a servant to others. The secular and religious world does not apprehend this glory! Glory in the secular or religious world typically means a person is served — their directives are followed. The higher one is exalted, the more people will serve them and attend to their needs and wishes. This is the glory of man, the glory of today's world . . . the glory of the Lord Jesus is not so. Jesus said:

> Yet it shall not be so among you; but whoever desires to become great among you, let him be your servant. And whoever desires to be first among you, let him be your slave — just as the Son of Man did not come to be served, but to serve, and to give His life a ransom for many.
>
> (Matthew 20:26-28)

Just as the glory given to Jesus was not of this world, the glory that He gave to His disciples is not of this world; it is exactly like the glory given to Him by the Father. It is a glory through death and resurrection.

As in Philippi, where there was discord among God's people, much of today's discord leads to sectarianism primarily based upon personalities. Individuals who have allowed ego and pride to take over (which is the world's glory) have caused disunity in the Body leading to rampant sectarianism. Even among small groups of believers, pride and ego among various personalities is a sure way to cause friction and split up a group. Dividing like this is generally not between young or weak Christians, but between those who are prominent; those who want to serve God. It is ironic how many who desire to serve God end up unable to be one with other believers because of ego and self-glory. The solution is to understand, receive, and live according to the glory of Jesus Christ.

This glory is contrary to typical hierarchical leadership among believers. Those in leadership expect others to follow them, and those under such leadership will identify themselves with their leaders to the detriment of fellowshipping with believers outside their group. The problem is NOT with mature believers serving diligently who may have acquired a title such as "Pastor," "Minister," "Elder," or "Priest," whose ministry is that of a servant. No, trouble occurs when leaders who expect others to follow their direction are offended when those directions are not followed. When this happens, it is certain they are no longer participating in the glory of Jesus Christ.

It is only in the glory of Jesus the services of each believer will lead to ONEness. The more each serve, the more oneness ensues; is manifested. The Lord's glory empowers believers to become as nothing but a servant to all. This is the glory given to every believer that they may be ONE.

Glory Empowering Believers to Be Servants

For the believers to receive this glory from the Lord Jesus Christ means that He, as the first man to receive this glory, will lead believers on the same pathway to glory. Since He has already pioneered the way, He comes into His believers with this glory and leads them to glory (Heb. 2:9–10). That is why He said to His disciples that if they wanted to follow Him, they must pick up their own cross to follow Him (Matt 16:24). Certainly, the believer's cross is not to die for redemption. The Lord Jesus was the only one qualified to die for the redemption of all creatures. He died once for all. The cross of believers is to follow Him in service to God and man. Just as He served God and man by the ministry of life for the building up of the assembly, believers need to and can do the same. Unlike Jesus, however, who went first through the entire process of the cross before receiving glory, believers already possess His glory. It is this glory that supplies and energizes believers to bear the cross to serve. Whoever would bear this cross to be a servant can be one with all other believers. If not, it is inevitable, at a certain point, this person cannot be one with other Christians.

"Bearing the cross" is not suffering just for suffering's sake. It is not asceticism. It is not silently accepting mistreatment. It is service to God and man. The night Jesus prayed His last prayer in John 17 was the night He washed His disciples' feet (including Judas' feet—the one who betrayed Him). Washing feet was a normal occurrence in those days, and it was done by the lowliest of slaves. Jesus did this for His disciples and asked them to do the same to one another (John 13:14).

Washing one another's feet according to Jesus was a symbol of love for one another. Serving and caring for another shows a person's love. Jesus, knowing Judas would soon betray Him, still washed his feet. How hard it is for the person who was offended and disrespected to love the very person who made such an offense. How hard it is to serve that person. Naturally, it is actually impossible, but the Lord did that and more. This is the glory that He gave His believers. It is this glory that strengthens and empowers believers to follow and serve as He did.

What does God want and how can He be served? God desires the one ekklesia which is His eternal purpose. To achieve this purpose God desires all men to be saved and come to the full knowledge of the truth. Ultimately, God will build up His assembly, His diverse people becoming ONE.

Man's needs actually mirror God's needs. Yes, man (male and female) has various needs relating to poverty, health, and relationships, but his ultimate need is salvation — the eternal divine life of God for His eternal purpose. Therefore, serving God and man is really performing and working toward the same objective. When Christ is ministered for man's salvation, and the teaching of Jesus Christ is taught for growth with the purpose of building up the assembly, then both God and man are satisfied. The servants or workers have done their job. The Lord's glory given to His followers will result in God being glorified.

Although believers cannot suffer for redemption, but like Jesus, believers can suffer with Him for the bearing of fruit that abides or remains, which is for the building up of His Body. The apostle Paul in Colossians 1:24 said that he rejoiced in his suffering and that he was filling up that which was lacking in the afflictions of Christ for His Body, the assembly. From a human point of view, there is only one similar kind of affliction which involves rejoicing while in anguish, and that is childbirth. Jesus used this exact metaphor for rejoicing in suffering in John 16:21–22. Women undergo much affliction and suffering to bring a child into the world, but all is worth it once the baby is born. This is the "rejoicing in suffering," the suffering of "death" that believers should participate in, and through it to share in the same glory of producing much fruit.

Ministering Christ to others so that Jesus Christ might be reproduced and grow in people is the highest service to both God and man. This is to bear and produce remaining fruit resulting in full maturity in Christ (Col. 1:28–29). This glorious service requires the attitude of a humble servant. It is not just a matter of preaching or motivating people at an "altar call" to come forward to receive Jesus Christ. It is a continuing service like that of a nursing mother, cherishing people in a very practical way, serving them for the sake of dispensing the grace of Jesus Christ to them. People who are served practically by those in this pathway to glory will become open to receive Jesus as their Lord and Savior, and as a result, grow in Christ.

When this attitude and view of glory takes hold of believers, they will treat everyone around them, whether believers or non-believers, in the way of Jesus Christ: not as a lord, but as a servant. This is loving and esteeming others. It means being willing to be wronged by others and taking the status of a slave who has no ground to be offended. It involves feeding and caring for others. A person in this place of glory will not cause friction with other believers; rather, this person is one with all believers as a servant. This is the glory that makes believers ONE.

Glory for Ministers to Team-Up

> Only let your manner of life be worthy of the gospel of Christ, so that whether I come and see you or am absent, I may hear of you that you are standing firm in one spirit, with one mind striving side by side for the faith of the gospel, and not frightened in anything by your opponents. This is a clear sign to them of their destruction, but of your salvation, and that from God.
> (Phil. 1:27-28 ESV)

The foundational difficulty the Apostle Paul addressed in Philippians was discord and rivalry among ministers and preachers. That was the reason Paul asked them to be in one accord, one mind. This means to have the mind of Christ to esteem other ministers *"better than yourself."* Philippians 2 was a continuation of urging them to work together. In Philippians 1:27 *"Striving side by side"* is from one Greek word: *synathleō*. It means to have a partnership while wrestling and contending together. This is a teaming up to wrestle against the enemy who has blinded the minds of the unbelieving and has divided the Body of Christ. Today's tag team matches resemble the meaning here. The teaming up is to advance the gospel: for both individual salvation and the building up into ONE the Body of Christ, His ekklesia.

The Philippians were very fervent in serving the Lord and they materially supported the apostle Paul in His ministry journeys (Phil. 4:15). However, there was division among them as can be seen in the beginning of Philippians 2 and 4. So even though they were serving the Lord, they were not one. When there is division among ministers, that is a manner of life not worthy of the gospel. Paul's instruction here is similar to Ephesian 4:1, to be "worthy" has everything to do with being one and working together in unity.

Today ministers are very familiar with working alone in their own ministries. Many may even consider they are competing with each other for adherents and resources. Those who are successful in their ministries may not see the need to team up with other ministers.

There may be two glaring reasons for ministers to be an island unto themselves while in rivalry with others. The first is there is not a governing vision wherein all ministries are for the same goal: the building up of the One Body of Christ. If that is not the vision, then "success" among ministries may very well be defined differently than what the Lord considers to be successful. For example, if a ministry's goal is merely personal salvation, the minister will be satisfied with his or her labor when people come to faith in Christ. If it is a healing ministry, the minister will consider the goal is met when more and more people are healed. Both of those ministries are still short of God's goal. Since the goal is the building up of the One Body, then none should consider success until common believers are active in ministry and the ekklesia is built up. By having God's eternal purpose to be the common goal then ministers can "team-up." Even though ministries have their specialty such as music, youth, teaching, gospel, healing, etc., but the ultimate common goal is only one.

This is what it means to be of one mind, not just of one spirit. Though ministers might have different gifts and ministries, they need to come to one mind concerning God's eternal purpose for the building up of His ekklesia. Without being one mind in this mind, it is not possible to team-up for the faith of the gospel — believers arriving at the unity of the faith.

The other reason may very well be pride. That is where the glory of Jesus is needed by all the specially-gifted ministers. Ministers in their own church and ministries are used to being the one calling all the shots as the director. In teaming up with other ministries, mutual submission is needed. That is the reason immediately after Paul's exhortation for the ministers to *"strive together side by side"* he speaks of the need to put off "vain glory" in the beginning of Philippians 2. It is the glory of Jesus that enables the most successful ministers to be as nothing when teaming up with other ministers.

The fact is if ministers do not team up then the adversary, Satan, wins. In order to defeat the enemy, there is the need to team up. It is in the teaming up the opponent is destroyed. Conversely, it is in striving together that ministers have peace and enter into salvation. By the enemy keeping ministers isolated, 75% of pastors report severe stress resulting in depression, fear, and alienation.[16] This is the reason that teaming-up is a salvation for those in ministry. Isn't it time to team-up for the building up of the Lord's ekklesia and defeat the enemy Satan? Our teaming up is the obvious sign of Satan's destruction, but to us, our salvation wrought by God Himself!

ONE in Life, Truth, and Glory

The three precious gifts the Lord gave His people certainly will bring believers into one: eternal life (the Father's name), the truth (His Word), and the Lord's glory (service). Since these three gifts given by the Lord are the prime elements to build up His assembly, *His Body* — by bringing believers into one — they are at the heart of a Christian's knowledge and experience. When believers rivet their attention on these three gifts as primary factors in becoming one, they will be brought into the heart of God's purpose and pleasure; in turn they will be full of the Lord's joy, having purpose and eternal value in their lives.

The following is a general sketch of the three gifts as expounded in the book, ***ONE: Unfolding God's Eternal Purpose from House to House:***

1. **Eternal life (The Father's Name)**
   There are two innate functions of human life which define life: metabolism and reproduction. In fact, without these two essentials, life cannot be classified as life. In addition, life needs four elements to survive and thrive: nutrients, air (environment), exercise, and sleep. If these four elements are present, life will spontaneously grow, reproduce, and mature.

   When believers are born anew and experience God's Divine life, these four spiritual essentials will cause growth of this wonderful life in His children. If these four elements are present, the Christian's spiritual life will be healthy and strong; they will be able to go through challenges of everyday life with joy and victory. Additionally, God's purpose is accomplished by the ONEness of God's people being kept in the Father's name

2. **Truth (His Word)**

---

16 http://www.pastorburnout.com/pastor-burnout-statistics.html

Truth is the "nutrient" for spiritual growth and knowledge to enlighten believers to live and serve God. The goal in this part of the book, ***ONE***, is not to exhaust all aspects of the truth, but to give a solid framework for understanding and appreciating its major aspects. Studying and understanding these points of truth will open the rest of the Bible, both the Old and New Testaments, unveiling His inexhaustible truth. This part of the book will focus on the person and work of Jesus Christ, the New Covenant of grace, God's eternal purpose, and the way His economy operates to accomplish His purpose. We will elaborate on how expanding knowledge of the truth instills confidence in receiving and fellowshipping with all believers, inspiring them with meaningful purpose to accomplish His Plan for the ages.

3. **His Glory (Service)**
Even though this glory given by our Lord to His people often leads through suffering and humble service, there is abundant joy and rejoicing through this process as God's people share their abundant life to all those around them. They're able to fulfill their highest calling driven by the Spirit of the Living God in their daily lives — affecting everyone with whom they come in contact. Each of us who bears the Name of Jesus Christ affirms the privilege and responsibility to build up the Body of Christ through the release of ministry. In this portion of the book we will help the saints understand why His eternal life motivates to love and care for others; what it means to cherish and nourish one another; to grow up into Him in all things. We'll share how building up assemblies in homes, from house to house, exemplifies "faith at work" because it's based on His eternal life. Consequently, it is a labor of love, enduring hope, and fruit that abides forever; these efforts which stay focused on eternal life and the truth of His Word will issue forth in believers receiving from their Chief Shepherd: *"The Crown of **Glory** that does not fade away"* (1 Peter 5:4). This is glory–this is the kind of "caring service" every believer is challenged to imitate.

14.
PRACTICAL ASSEMBLY LIFE (SEC. A)

Note: The next two chapters are taken mostly intact with minimal revisions from the book *ONE* (within Part 2 concerning TRUTH). These two chapters can be viewed as an addendum to this book. For those that are interested in practicing ekklesia, these two chapters will provide additional points not covered in previous chapters.

After seeing this wonderful and mysterious vision concerning the universal ekklesia, assembly, most Christians may think it a complicated matter to build up this awesome assembly. That is not true. The building up of this glorious assembly is practical, simple, here and now, right in the homes of believers. The difficulty lies not in the practical ekklesia, but in stripping off nearly 2,000 years of tradition to gather in simplicity as an assembly. God's people intuitively know how to organically gather; however, it may take years "unlearning" religious traditions which have conditioned people (both Christians and non-Christians) in behaving what we know today as a member of a "church."

Christians have become steeped in liturgies, organizations, programs, with church patterns and practices which inhibit the expression of a true assembly. Let's start from the simplest and most basic elements of a real assembly: a relationship with others who are in relationship with Jesus Christ. Stay right there! Don't leave that fellowship. That is the practical assembly.

The Assembly Is Practical and Enjoyable...Now

The local assembly flourishes in homes. Unlike all other religions with temples and designated worship centers, those who assembled did so in homes. Furthermore, they continued meeting from house to house.

> So continuing daily with one accord in the temple, and breaking bread from house to house, they ate their food with gladness and simplicity of heart, praising God and having favor with all the people. And the Lord added to the church [assembly] daily those who were being saved.
>
> (Acts 2:46-47)

On Pentecost Peter preached the Gospel and 3,000 people received salvation. Immediately, they started assembling in homes. Up until that time, and throughout human history, every major religion has had their temples, holy places, or dedicated buildings for worship. God's assembly, however, was distinctly new; completely outside the normal "religious structure."

The call went out: *Let's assemble in our homes.* Instead of leaving normal life with family and friends to go to perform a "worship" service, God wants to enjoy Himself in the fellowship of His people right where they live! He wants to be in the middle of their most intimate, comfortable, relational, and transparent settings. Jesus is calling out people to assemble right where they are; in their homes.

The Jewish temple had a large open court area (Solomon's Porch) which became a place for public gatherings. Because this open space was where people already congregated, the early apostles used this venue for their public preaching and teaching. However, God had no intention for the saints in the New Testament to go back to Old Testament rituals of the Levitical priesthood.

In 70 A.D. God allowed the temple to be utterly demolished — down to the last stone. Even if they wanted to, it wasn't possible to worship God within the context of the sacerdotal rites of the Temple — *"Woman, believe Me, the hour is coming when you will neither on this mountain, nor in Jerusalem, worship the Father . . . but the hour is coming, and now is when the true worshipers will worship the Father in spirit and truth . . . God is Spirit, and those who worship Him must worship in spirit and truth"* (John 4:21-24). So, where did this *"worship in spirit"* take place, if not on the mountains of Samaria or in Jerusalem?

> But Saul ravaged [laid waste] the assembly, entering into the houses one after another, and dragging off both men and women delivered them up to prison.
>
> (Acts 8:3, DBY)

Before the apostle Paul became a believer in Jesus Christ, he was called *Saul*. Saul was a persecutor of the assembly. He was zealous for the Jewish religion, and in His ignorance, he persecuted and tried to destroy God's assembly. Remember, the assembly was the very desire of God. Although Saul was blinded from knowing God's assembly, Satan certainly knew and made use of Saul with his zeal and ignorance in an attempt to destroy the assembly — God's eternal purpose.

So how did Saul ravage or lay waste the assembly? He went from house to house. He didn't go to the temple where the apostles were publicly and openly preaching and teaching. He didn't go to any other buildings. He went to the homes of the believers, from house after house where the assembly was, dragging believers off to prison. Wouldn't it have been more efficient for Saul to simply arrest everyone listening to the preaching at the temple? Weren't believers already gathered in large numbers for him to arrest there? Yes, but according to the New Testament revelation, that would not have been the way to devastate God's assembly — because the assembly was located in homes.

Paul's persecution of the saints convincingly demonstrates how Paul went about implementing his destruction of the assembly of Christ — His Body. The Lord's ekklesia was uniquely domiciled in homes where saints gathered around their common faith and fellowship in Jesus, the Messiah. The revelation of the Scripture concerning God's assembly is awesome and amazing: The Family of God; the Bride of Christ; the Body of Christ. Yet, the *outworking* — the *building* of an assembly occurred right in every believer's home — right where they lived.

The Jewish religion was completely intertwined with the temple. It was the focal point of gathering and worship. Christians (since the fourth century) started practicing like all other religions. They identified themselves according to physical buildings — places of "Christian worship" — just like pagans — numerous pagan temples were "converted" to Christian places of worship.

Today, a common question is, "Where do you go to church?" Both Christians and non-Christians understand it to mean: "What building do you go to for worship?" Worshipping is identified with organizations which have a church *building*.

Churches, whether intended or not, have become places of separation from other believers in the One Body of Christ. However, the Lord's desire is to recover God's people back to the simplicity of the one assembly — that is, gathering His people in a multitude of homes. This is where the assembly finds its normal venue — not in "church buildings" — but in homes where believers live. Gathering around the Name of Jesus in the home affords the people of God the most adequate expression of the assembly.

Notwithstanding, it is not the intention of this writing to convince Christians to stop attending churches; rather, to start building an assembly in their homes for fellowship with believers regardless of whether they attend different churches or not attending any at all.

> Salute [Greet] Prisca and Aquila, my fellow-workmen in Christ Jesus . . . and the assembly at their house. Salute [greet] Epaenetus, my beloved, who is the first-fruits of Asia for Christ.
> (Rom. 16:3, 5, DBY)

> Salute [Greet] the brethren in Laodicea, and Nymphas, and the assembly which is in his house.
> (Col. 4:15, DBY)

> ...and to the sister Apphia and to Archippus our fellow-soldier, and to the assembly which is in your house.
> (Philemon 1:2, DBY)

> The assemblies of Asia salute [greet] you. Aquila and Priscilla, with the assembly in their house, salute [greet] you much in the Lord.
> (1 Cor. 16:19, DBY)

> Gaius, my host and [the host] of the whole church [assembly], greets you. Erastus, the treasurer of the city, greets you, and Quartus, a brother.
> (Rom. 16:23)

The Lord is building the mysterious, universal assembly that transcends time and space. It includes all of God's people throughout time, no matter where they are located. But every time the practical assembly is mentioned, which is how and where believers can practically enter into participation and fellowship, it is located in the homes. From the above verses, it is clear this gathering of thousands of believers in homes did not occur only in Jerusalem. After Saul, (the assembly-devastator) was converted, he became known as Paul — a Jesus-believer and an assembly-builder. Paul then went from city to city bringing the good news of Jesus Christ, and those who believed were called out to assemble in homes. One can search the Scriptures and will not find the assembly located anywhere else but in homes.

Whether the assembly in a certain locality has thousands of believers meeting in many different homes (such as in Jerusalem), or just a few as when the gospel first went out in Philippi, the *one* assembly in a locality is practically located in either hundreds of houses or in just one home.

This is the reason why it is critical that believers are willing to open their homes to be a place of assembly. If there are no homes in a locality willing to host the ekklesia, then the assembly would be homeless. If there are one hundred homes in a locality willing to host the assembly, what a testimony of the Lord's One Body there will be in that locality. All the verses relating to the assembly in a specific home seems to indicate that the home became a regular meeting place of the assembly. Due to this, those particular homes became known as the assembly in their house.

All Believers in Each Locality Are the "Assembly"

All genuine believers of Christ are members of the one assembly in their respective localities.

> And Saul was consenting to his [Stephen] being killed. And on that day there arose a great persecution against the assembly which was in Jerusalem, and all were scattered into the countries of Judaea and Samaria except the apostles . . . But Saul ravaged the assembly, entering into the houses one after another, and dragging off both men and women delivered them up to prison.
> (Acts 8:1, 3, DBY)

It is clear in accordance with the eternal life of God and the divine nature of the Trinity; all believers are one — in one unique assembly. Any division among believers is against God's life and nature; this is exceedingly practical. In God's eyes no matter how many homes in which believers are gathered in the Lord's name — there still is only one assembly. Just as the universal assembly does not have a proper name, neither do the various assemblies in different localities. It is simply the assembly gathered in fellowship in any given locality — that's the "name of the assembly."

Certainly, by Acts 8, there were at least 8,000 believers in Jerusalem; however, it was still called the assembly (singular) that was at Jerusalem. To persecute this one assembly, Saul had to go from house to house.

> What you see write in a book, and send to the seven assemblies: to Ephesus, and to Smyrna, and to Pergamos, and to Thyatira, and to Sardis, and to Philadelphia, and to Laodicea.
> (Rev. 1:11, DBY)

Jesus (the "faithful witness" — Rev. 1:5) told John in Revelation to write down in a letter what he was seeing and to send it to the seven assemblies in Asia. Then he listed the names of seven cities who were to receive his letter — seven assemblies, seven cities. When compared with Ephesians 1:1, Scripture clearly shows the assembly consisted of all believers (saints) in any given city.

From the Divine perspective, all believers in any particular locality are part of that one assembly in that designated place. It was assumed in those days that all believers in each locality were in fellowship with one another. So, when a letter from an apostle reached a town, village, or city, it was understood all believers in that place would be a part of that assembly. A believer or a group of believers not connected to this fellowship network in their locality would have missed the letter; consequently, they would not have heard what the Spirit was speaking to that particular assembly.

Conversely, the first recipients of a letter were responsible to pass the letter on to members connected to them. Therefore, it was clear there had to have been an organic network of fellowship among God's people in order for a letter sent to a city whose design was to be read by all the saints meeting in scores of homes — so the Spirit's speaking would be heard by all.

Each Member Functions for the Building up of the Body

Everyone in the assembly needs to operate or function as an individual member, because each one has a gift for the Body.

> For I say, through the grace given to me, to everyone who is among you, not to think [of himself] more highly than he ought to think, but to think soberly, as God has dealt to each one a measure of faith. For as we have many members in One Body, but all the members do not have the same function, so we, [being] many, are One Body in Christ, and individually members of one another. Having then gifts differing according to the grace that is given to us, [let us use them]: if prophecy, [let us prophesy] in proportion to our faith; or ministry, [let us use it] in [our] ministering; he who teaches, in teaching; he who exhorts, in exhortation; he who gives, with liberality; he who leads, with diligence; he who shows mercy, with cheerfulness.
>
> (Rom. 12:3-8)

We find in 1 Corinthians 12 and Romans 12 a challenge for every believer, as a member of the Body, to function just like each part of a person's physical body has a specific function. Not only does each believer have a function, their function is necessary and indispensable. Everyone is needed. This is a normal description of every assembly. How different in today's churches where most believers sit idle as passive listeners — most "functions" of a given body of "church folk" are done by appointed personnel. There's a great distinction between "vocation" and "functioning." It does not matter whether any of the *lay people* are there or not; frankly, you can get the whole "service" on video! Other than a loss of monetary tithing they may bring, the "worship service" does not skip a beat if any of the lay people are not present . . . preachers preach, pew sitters listen (with an occasional "amen" here and there).

The Scriptures are clear: Each member of the Body has at least one gift from the Spirit. These gifts are innate in every believer. The Body of Christ cannot be built when most believers are dormant — unwilling or inhibited from using their God-given gifts. The major reason for this deficiency has everything to do with "church tradition," rather than according to New Testament-ordained practice of assembly-life in homes. When the assembly is gathered in a home (house to house), with no "professional clergy," everyone is equally accepted as a brother or sister in Christ; there is an open environment without a set program or format — here, believers find themselves in a venue where their gifts are encouraged; where they naturally grow according to the gifts given to each functioning member.

The Bible teaches there is diversity among all members; each performing a unique function. Unfortunately, churches are grouped according to what the leadership of that church system decides is or isn't acceptable. Therefore, each church's membership is, by and large, uniform, since the practices and doctrines for each church are set. If a person does not conform to that church's views, then their welcome will be short-lived. Organizational oneness, yes! Oneness of the Body of Christ, no! On the contrary, the real assembly — the Body of Christ — is diverse. Each member is needed, because there is but one Spirit, one Faith, one Baptism, One Body, and one Assembly!

Although all believers participate in One Body, each believer is still an individual, a distinct person in the Body. Each person has their own function which is different from all other members in the Body. Certainly, any given member cannot be replaced by another member. One's function is unique — it is needed by the whole Body. That is why every believer is needed to function to their full capacity.

In Romans 12:4–8 we find a list of gifts a bit different from the list found in 1 Corinthians 12. Since each believer has received the grace of Christ, each one has a gift as well. This gift is not based on a seminary or Bible School degree. It is based on the grace received of the Lord. The more believers enjoy the grace of Christ — their gift exercised in the Body will abound all the more.

Only in the assembly gathered in homes, house by house, will the members of His One Body find an accommodating environment where every member can freely function without externally-imposed organizational regulations. Today's churches can be places to either build up or tear down the Body of Christ. On the positive side, today's churches are more akin to a school for teaching the Bible or a synagogue where people can go, knowing people of faith are found there. On the down side, churches can be dividers of the Body, separating believers based on a given system of doctrine and practice found in respective churches. But certainly, today's "churches" are not environments where every believer is free to function according to the gift given to them for the building up of the Body . . . it will be rejected, especially when a given teaching or practice is expressed contrary to the system of teaching or practice of that church.

A Description of Assembly in the Homes

What does a home assembly look like where each member functions and contributes for the practical building up of the Body? Paul gives us insight of its appearance in 1 Corinthians 14:26:

> What then, brothers? When you come together, each one has a hymn, a lesson, a revelation, a tongue, or an interpretation. Let all things be done for building up.
> (1 Corinthians 14:26)

In Chapter 14 of 1 Corinthians we find the only portion in the New Testament that describes the practical functioning of each member gathered in an assembly. Other portions in the Acts describe gatherings for preaching or teaching by the apostles; but those gatherings are not called the "assembly," which specifically is what the Lord is building according to God's eternal purpose. In 1 Corinthians 12 it teaches that each member of the Body has a function; and Chapter 14 clarifies how the functioning and building up of each member together is practiced.

In the Old Testament, when all Israel came together in Jerusalem for their feasts (some as long as seven days), all who worshiped God at the temple had to bring ten percent of their crops and herds (Deut. 14:22–27). Everyone brought their portion from the good land which God had given them; this was their tithe. For example, if a family grew wheat, they brought the 10 percent of their wheat. If they had a herd of cattle, they needed to bring the 10 percent from the herd. It was a sin for any Israelite to go to a feast empty-handed (Ex. 23:15). What they brought for worship to God were items shared among all the Israelites for feasting. It was a giant "pot luck-style" feast — more like a massive barbecue. Their tithes and offerings (sacrifices) became a feast for both God and man.

In 1 Corinthians 14 it can be described as the *application* of the Old Testament feasts in the New Testament. Specifically, in verse 26, the Bible says each one has something to bring for sharing in the assembly. *"Each one has"* means every single believer (male or female) who comes to the assembly is likened to a person coming to a feast — a spiritual feast — bringing one's enjoyment of their experiences with Christ as a ready offering for both God and man to feast on and enjoy. This feast at the assembly is not prepared by a couple of professionals; rather, every member of the assembly has a responsibility, a privilege to contribute and share what they have reaped from the Good Land, from the Lord Himself!

This is the food of the assembly. Not everyone has to share a large portion, since it is in accordance to the capacity of each member; therefore, even five words (1 Cor. 14:19) is a good contribution if that is a person's portion.

Churches today are typically centered on the sharing or speaking of one person. The congregants, for the most part, are at best attentive (but passive) listeners. Churches can be a good school for Christians to learn doctrines while listening to inspiring messages — notwithstanding, these environments are not the assembly we read about in the New Testament. The conversation in today's churches is at best likened to the apostles' preaching at the temple or the synagogues or even one of the schools where the apostle Paul taught (Acts 19:9). However, they are not an assembly where all can be engaged by sharing their portion of Christ — no matter how big or small.

Those who are gifted teachers in churches need to equip, to encourage their listening audiences to go home, build up the assembly, and practice exercising the gifts God has given to each of them. If pastors and teachers do that, they will find themselves facilitating the building up of the assembly and maturing the saints in love.

The kind of assembly being discussed here is very different from a "home fellowship" or cell group under the sponsorship of a church. Typically, home groups are structured to follow the agenda of the church under the auspices of its leadership. The gathering operates in accordance with directives from the church's organizational center — normally; specific leadership is assigned for the home group. In such a case there is not complete freedom for members to speak what the Lord may have personally shown them. It is not a place where the Spirit has the liberty to move from believer to believer; rarely does it express what is on the Lord's heart. A genuine home assembly is not an extension of a church organization which does not have the elements as described from 1 Corinthians 11:17 through Chapter 14.

Elements of Practice in an Assembly

In an assembly, there are elements involving praying, singing, speaking, and reading, but absolutely no instructions on how to do any of these items or for how long.

> What is the conclusion then? I will pray with the spirit, and I will also pray with the understanding. I will sing with the spirit, and I will also sing with the understanding. Otherwise, if you bless with the spirit, how will he who occupies the place of the uninformed say "Amen" at your giving of thanks, since he does not understand what you say?
> (1 Corinthians 14:15-16)
>
> ... speaking to one another in psalms and hymns and spiritual songs, singing and making melody in your heart to the Lord.
> (Ephesians 5:19)
>
> Until I come, devote yourself to the public reading of Scripture, to exhortation, to teaching.
> (1 Timothy 4:13, ESV)

The Bible does not provide any schedule, program, or liturgy for Christian gatherings. What it does indicate (in the verses above) are various elements which are present, but it does not say how to do each or for how long. For example, it does say there is praying and singing in the assembly — it is left open-ended whether prayer is to be loud, exciting, or somber, lengthy or short, or how many people are to pray. There is no indication whether singing is to be in the form of solos, duets, or congregational — no details are given regarding tempos of music or instrumental accompaniments. Since there are no such details of "how to," believers should be open to and encourage the Spirit's moving within each one, including "spontaneous outbursts" from individuals who are gathered together. Believers need to be vigilant in preventing formality or empty liturgical forms where the Spirit is stifled, where individual initiatives are inhibited.

Genuine Local Assembly = Universal Assembly

Every genuine local assembly is a miniature in the nature and expression of the universal assembly, with the person and work of Christ as the assembly's unique foundation.

> Simon Peter answered and said, "You are the Christ, the Son of the living God . . . And I also say to you that you are Peter, and on this rock I will build My church [assembly], and the gates of Hades shall not prevail against it."
> (Matthew 16:16, 18)
>
> According to the grace of God which was given to me, as a wise master builder I have laid the foundation, and another builds on it. But let each one take heed how he builds on it. For no other foundation can anyone lay than that which is laid, which is Jesus Christ.
> (1 Corinthians 3:10–11)

Matthew 16 refers to the universal assembly throughout time and space. The universal assembly is built upon the rock — Jesus, the Christ, the Son of the living God. Peter literally means *"a stone."* Jesus changed Simon's name to *Peter*, a stone for the building. All believers are just like Peter — living stones for God's building (1 Pet. 2:5). The only qualification to be a "stone" for the assembly the Lord is building is having living faith in our Lord Jesus Christ.

When Paul wrote to the local assembly in Corinth, he said he had laid a unique foundation beneath God's building in that locality, which is Jesus Christ. "The foundation" in 1 Corinthians 3:10–11 is similar to "the rock" in Matthew 16. The rock is solid foundation for the building. Thus, any local assembly gathered in homes *must* have their unique foundation based upon Jesus Christ. If a home gathering and its fellowship are not based solely on Jesus Christ, then it cannot be considered the Lord's assembly.

Let's say a home gathering has Jesus Christ *plus baptism by immersion* as its foundation for gathering. That gathering will reject or make a believer uncomfortable; especially, one who practices baptism by sprinkling. If so, that gathering cannot be considered as an assembly (according to these verses). If the foundation is Jesus Christ, then any believer, no matter the variance of practices or doctrines, will be received equally as a stone for the building of that assembly. The assembly's foundation is simply Jesus Christ, not Jesus Christ *plus* something else, or someone else. It is uniquely Jesus Christ and Him alone.

Assembly Is the Christ with Many Members

> For as the body is one and has many members, but all the members of that One Body, being many, are One Body, so also is Christ. For by one Spirit we were all baptized into One Body — whether Jews or Greeks, whether slaves or free — and have all been made to drink into one Spirit.
> (1 Corinthians 12:12-13)

The metaphor of the human body in 1 Corinthians 12:12 refers to Christ. Christ has many members. Most people understand when reading: *"For as the body is one and has many members . . . so also is the assembly."* Paul specifically says, *". . . so also is **Christ**"* (emphasis added). Christ is no longer simply the supreme authority ascended to the heavens; rather, Christ includes all believers as members who have been baptized into His one universal Body. This includes all kinds of peoples, tongues, nations and tribes throughout time and space. The entire Body was baptized all at once into One Body. All His members were given to drink of one Spirit. All those who would believe are included in that one baptism, that one Spirit. Certainly, this is the "universality of Christ," which includes Jesus' headship in relationship with all believers as members of His One Body.

> . . . that there should be no schism [faction] in the body, but that the members should have the same care for one another. And if one member suffers, all the members suffer with it; or if one member is honored, all the members rejoice with it. Now you are the Body of Christ, and members individually.
> (1 Corinthians 12:25-27)

Later in 1 Corinthians 12 Paul told the saints in Corinth that they are the Body of Christ and there should be no schism (faction or division) in the Body. Certain divisions or schisms had surfaced among them in their local assembly. Body life is so practical because people in Body life have the same care for one another while sharing in the same joy and suffering.

This kind of mutual caring and sharing would not be applicable in the universal sense (for example, it would not be practical to care for and share in the suffering of those being martyred in Rome centuries ago). So, in this very practical situation with the assembly gathering in homes, Paul told believers they were the Body of Christ, *now*. Most Christians understand the assembly in Corinth was only a part of the Body of Christ, since the Body of Christ is universal; however, Paul calls that little local assembly the very Body of Christ.

In the practical assembly here and now, believers need to have the kind of vision where they have a responsibility in being an integral part of the whole — that is, I'm a member of something much bigger than I, I am a much-needed member of His Body. How awesome is a local assembly meeting in a home — they are a fully functioning Body of Christ with nothing lacking! Sometimes Christians speak of caring for believers thousands of miles away because they are in the Body; yet, they neglect or divide from those close to them in their own city. According to Paul, the Body of Christ is found among those believers right around them in their locality. The first responsibility for a believer is guarding against division with those closest to them by having the same uncompromised care for believers in their very own assembly.

Those who do not see the local assembly as the Body of Christ by treating it as only a sub-part of the Body, may understand the assembly functions like this: "The eyes of the body are in Los Angeles while the mouth is in New York; so, we here in Zurich need so-and-so in order to see, also so-and-so in order to hear what the Lord is saying, since we are not the eyes or the mouth." Those with such a view will always look to the outside for help and consider themselves inadequate in their own assembly. Likewise, they will try to unify assemblies by federating them since they consider themselves deficient, being a "part" and not the "whole." In attempting to federate, they will organize and systematize all their local assemblies; by doing so, they will cause damage by dividing the Body of Christ, excluding members not in their federation.

A federation exists when a special union is formed among several local assemblies. Those which are in this union feel more loyalty with each other than with those assemblies outside their immediate sphere of influence. Those not in their union would need to fulfill certain requirements to become part of their federation; this may be done by accepting a similar leadership structure or adopting similar doctrines and practices. Basically, it becomes a subset of the Body of Christ. Any subset in the Body of Christ is, by definition, divisive.

A Genuine Assembly Receives All Believers

> For you are all sons of God through faith in Christ Jesus . . . . There is neither Jew nor Greek, there is neither slave nor free, there is neither male nor female; for you are all one in Christ Jesus.
>
> (Galatians 3:26, 28)

The Bible says, *"There is no partiality with God"* (Rom. 2:11). This means He treats everyone the same regardless of nationality, ethnicity, socioeconomic status, political view, or gender. His only regard is whether a person has received Christ as Savior. All who have accepted Jesus Christ as God's Son, regardless of differences and variances — they are now all one in Christ. Though there is distinction based on where each person comes from (by birth or culture), those differences no longer divide. Rather, there is now absolute oneness without any possibility of separation in Christ. The Lord's universal assembly is a place where all those who have received Jesus, receive one another, even though distinct due to their various backgrounds — yes distinction; no separation!

> Receive one who is weak in the faith, but not to disputes over doubtful things. For one believes he may eat all things, but he who is weak eats only vegetables. Let not him who eats despise him who does not eat, and let not him who does not eat judge him who eats; for God has received him. Who are you to judge another's servant? . . . One person esteems one day above another; another esteems every day alike. Let each be fully convinced in his own mind. He who observes the day, observes it to the Lord; and he who does not observe the day, to the Lord he does not observe it . . . .
>
> (Romans 14:1–4a, 5–6)

It is one thing to have a theoretical oneness with all saints one day in the future, but for God's people who are very different, sharing a meal together in a home assembly is quite another. Paul used an example of eating and observing certain days in Romans 14:1–6, because in his day, the difference between Jews and Gentiles was distinctive and divisive. It was so divisive the apostle Peter got carried away at one point and separated himself from eating with Gentile believers (Gal. 2:11–13). Observing certain days can also be divisive. Jews were to keep the Sabbath day special, while the Greeks made no distinction on such a day.

Paul charged believers in Romans 14:1–6 to receive each other no matter what differences separated them, because God received them in Christ regardless of their habits, convictions, or practices. God's desire reflected a pragmatic oneness of a local assembly in the here and now which would persist throughout all eternity as the New Jerusalem!

Back in Paul's days diet and "days" may have been serious contentious practices, but today Christians are divided over a host of practices: methods of baptism, how to have communion, leadership formats, music in the church, women's roles, or liturgical styles, etc. Add to this, Christians are divided over doctrinal differences such as predestination versus free will; eternal security; how the gifts of the Spirit are manifested; whether the five-fold ministry of gifted ones is for today; time lines of creation or the end of the age; flat earth or round earth; or creation vs. evolution.

This is not to mention ethical, socio-economic, political affiliation, or differences based on race or gender. No matter the dissimilarity, God has received each believer who lives to the Lord according to their acceptance of Christ — *"But as many as **received Him**, to them gave He the authority to become the children God, to those who believe into His name"* (John 1:12); therefore, there should be an equal receiving of all believers in an assembly. Any despising or rejecting which causes us to separate one from another goes against the very nature and expression of God's assembly. Therefore, a Christian group despising or rejecting other believers cannot be considered a true assembly; at best, it can be defined as a Christian church, organization, or school; but not an expression of the One Body of Christ.

> But why do you judge your brother? Or why do you show contempt for your brother? For we shall all stand before the judgment seat of Christ. For it is written: "As I live, says the LORD, every knee shall bow to Me, and every tongue shall confess to God." So then each of us shall give account of himself to God. Therefore let us not judge one another anymore, but

> rather resolve this, not to put a stumbling block or a cause to fall in our brother's way.
>
> (Romans 14:10-13)

When judgment is passed upon certain brethren, condemning them because of their convictions and practices, it becomes a stumbling block to them. Another stumbling block occurs when believers think anyone who participates in a certain practice different from their own is a weaker believer. Some are so strong with their own conviction on such practices they will purposely promote or display their conviction in front of other believers, even when they know these believers have a contrary view. This causes believers to stumble. Let's consider again the issue of eating. When a person knows an immediate brother or sister does not eat meat for religious reasons, and might be offended or stumble when offered meat, if the one with the freedom to eat meat does so right in front of his brother (or even pushes his freedom of eating meat on him), this becomes a stumbling block.

Because of this, any practice or non-essential doctrine should be handled carefully, so what is good for one is not pushed on others.

This matter of receiving believers into fellowship and not causing them to stumble is so critical Paul brought up the matter of Christ's judgment seat. This is where all believers will give an account one day. How followers of Jesus judge their brothers and sisters in Christ will affect their own verdict before Christ at the time of judgment. This is a serious matter; yet, many Christian groups are built organizing around certain practices and non-essential doctrines which automatically judge those who believe differently. Some groups claim they receive all believers, but their acceptance comes with an agenda: whomever they receive must eventually be converted by adopting *their* practices. This is not generous receiving; this is plain proselytizing.

In a genuine assembly, there should be complete freedom of diversity in practice where each believer is equally accepted with equal opportunity to share and contribute their portion of Christ. All believers with a heart for God's purpose who seek the building up of the assembly, which is the Lord's Body, need to seriously take this Chapter of Romans 14 to heart.

> . . . for the kingdom of God is not eating and drinking, but righteousness and peace and joy in the Holy Spirit. For he who

> serves Christ in these things is acceptable to God and approved by men. Therefore let us pursue the things which make for peace and the things by which one may edify [build up] another.
> (Romans 14:17-19)

Paul brought the saints back to this central point: the kingdom of God is righteousness, peace, and joy in the Holy Spirit. Paul's point is: "Don't get hung up with any of the non-essentials and practices, because they are not the focal point. Instead of being concerned by all the various practices which can become a point of contention between believers, let's stay focused on the kingdom of God."

The kingdom of God does not include various practices: diet, days, how to baptize, leadership forms; etc. The kingdom of God, which is the Lord's assembly here and now, is righteousness, peace and joy in the Holy Spirit. If believers become distracted by divergent practices, either by rejecting believers or offending them through strong adherence to certain doctrines or practices, the kingdom of God will be diminished. If there is no expression of the kingdom of God — with all that the Holy Spirit encompasses — then there is no assembly.

The goal for each believer should be the kingdom of God. If a doctrine or practice helps one to arrive at the blessing afforded through the Holy Spirit, then it is good for that person. What is good for one person, however, does not mean it is good for all. For example, one may pray in a tongue and really receive the joy of the Spirit, but that does not mean *everyone* has to pray in a tongue to have the same joy.

There is no need to insist on or oppose praying in tongues. If a believer who does not pray in a tongue is not joyful because *someone else* is praying in tongues, then the one not joyful is missing out on the Kingdom of God, because the joy of the Spirit is not present. All believers should be able to share their experiences with each other, whether it is relating to speaking in tongues, baptism, prayer, evangelism, giving or getting help from a certain minister, but without intending to dispute or judge others. The ultimate destination for all God's people in sharing should be the same: righteousness, peace, and joy in the Holy Spirit.

> Now may the God of patience and comfort grant you to be likeminded toward one another, according to Christ Jesus, that you

> may with one mind [one accord] and one mouth glorify the God and Father of our Lord Jesus Christ. Therefore receive one another, just as Christ also received us, to the glory of God.
> (Romans 15:5-7)

Some Christian groups teach we should glorify God in one accord; therefore, believers need to practice the same things, have the same leadership, or hold the same doctrinal understanding. This kind of "unity" between believers, however, is not what Paul was teaching here; rather, those who try to force a mandatory unification end up being more divisive. The "one accord" to glorify God is not expressed in everyone doing the same set of practices but receiving each other although practices are different. Receiving other believers in one fellowship spontaneously results in being in "one accord" and having "one mouth." It is in this mutual receiving absent of judgment wherein God the Father is glorified — His attributes are expressed in this manner. Conversely, judging, rejecting, and promoting a pet doctrine or practice will cause believers to stumble, making Satan glad, since his devices are working among believers to hinder our building up of the assembly.

An Assembly Is Part of One Fellowship

A local assembly is part of one common, universal fellowship shared among all believers.

> That which was from the beginning, which we have heard, which we have seen with our eyes, which we have looked upon, and our hands have handled, concerning the Word of Life — the life was manifested, and we have seen, and bear witness, and declare to you that eternal life which was with the Father and was manifested to us — that which we have seen and heard we declare to you, that you also may have fellowship with us; and truly our fellowship is with the Father and with His Son Jesus Christ. And these things we write to you that your joy may be full.
> (1 John 1:1-4)

The unique message declared by the apostles is Jesus Christ. It is this singular message which brought (and continues to bring) believers into fellowship. This fellowship is not just with those who brought the message but also with the Father and His Son, Jesus Christ.

Fellowship in the original Greek is the word koinōnia, which means, "Sharing something that is in common." The meaning could include distribution and joint participation of both physical and spiritual things. The root word of *koinōnia* comes from the idea of joining together. Since believers are now in both the Father and the Son, they jointly participate in all that is in the Father and Son. What all God's people have in common is Jesus Christ; therefore, there should be a sharing of all good things among the brethren, both physical and spiritual.

The result of receiving the gospel is when each one of us shares in this fellowship which is between the Father and the Son. Once a person believes, experientially, he or she feels connected to every other believer in Christ. Initially, there is no thought of, "What kind of a Christian am I?" Or, "What Christian group do I belong to?" Once this eternal life is received in each one of us, we are instantly one with every other believer. There is a feeling of connectivity — belonging with every believer throughout time and space. It is not until corrupt thoughts enter a believer's mind that Christians begin to consider segregation among believers. The fullness of joy is not in division, but flourishes in one fellowship with all believers in the Father and the Son.

> God is faithful, by whom you were called into the fellowship of His Son, Jesus Christ.
>
> (1 Corinthians 1:9)

Writing to divided brethren in Corinth, Paul reminded them of their one fellowship they had been called into by God — the fellowship of Jesus Christ. How can there be divisions in the Body if there is only one fellowship? It is important to note fellowship in the Bible is never in plural; it is always singular. There is no concept of fellowships (plural) because in the entire universe, there is only one fellowship of Jesus Christ.

It is common for Christians to ask, "What fellowship do you belong to?" That very question leads one to consider there are all sorts of different fellowships — take your pick; this is contrary to the truth there is but one fellowship. All believers are in the one and same fellowship. If a Christian group has their own fellowship, this could mean they have specific requirements for a person to be part of their fellowship. In this manner they may belong to the fellowship of Chinese Christians, the fellowship of those baptized by immersion, or the fellowship of a certain liturgical practice; however, they would not be the unique and inclusive fellowship of Jesus Christ.

A group of Christians is sectarian if their "fellowship" is smaller than the fellowship of Jesus Christ. That means they are selective with whom they are in fellowship. The only thing common among believers in order to have equal standing is found in the fellowship is Jesus Christ. Believers can be different politically, ethnically, or doctrinally; the only common item that must be shared is Jesus Christ. That is the very meaning of fellowship.

> Finally, brethren, rejoice, be made complete, be comforted, be like-minded, live in peace; and the God of love and peace will be with you. Greet one another with a holy kiss ... The grace of the Lord Jesus Christ, and the love of God, and the fellowship of the Holy Spirit be with you all.
> (2 Cor. 13:11–12, 14, NASB)

Paul wrote his first letter to the Corinthians when they were struggling with divisions among themselves. He hoped to remind them God's call on their lives brought them into Jesus Christ (1 Cor. 1:9). At the end of his last letter to them he emphasized their fellowship is based upon the Holy Spirit. In this fellowship they share and participate in the love of God and the grace of Jesus Christ. This same fellowship has been within the Trinity throughout eternity. This unique fellowship is what God has given to every believer. Just as there is no separation, segregation, or division within the Triune God (it is not within the nature of the Trinity), even so, division cannot exist in this fellowship. A believer in fellowship with the Holy Spirit will always draw other believers into fellowship, because that is the nature of God.

This should have been the only fellowship practiced among the local assembly in Corinth. This is Paul's final word: believers in Corinth should always rejoice in this one fellowship. It is what will make them complete, comforted, peaceful, loving, and like-minded with one another. This fellowship in the Holy Spirit exudes the beauty and healthy condition of an assembly of believers. This should be the normal experience of believers in a genuine ekklesia because an assembly is defined by having this precious fellowship in the Holy Spirit. There may be gatherings and groupings of Christians, but the Lord's assembly exists according to the revelation of the Scriptures — is wholly dependent upon the fellowship of the Holy Spirit. The more fellowship, the more assembly; the less fellowship the less assembly; if a group denies fellowship with another believer, then no assembly.

One Fellowship Extends to All Assemblies and Believers

> It pleased those from Macedonia and Achaia to make a certain contribution [fellowship] for the poor among the saints who are in Jerusalem. It pleased them indeed, and they are their debtors. For if the Gentiles have been partakers of their spiritual things, their duty is also to minister to them in material things.
> (Romans 15:26–27)

Macedonia and Achaia are part of today's Greece. Believers there were Gentiles; yet, they were contributing to the poor Jewish believers in Jerusalem. What a testimony of oneness in one fellowship! Jews and Gentiles, especially back in those days, were notorious for their deep enmity and separation from one another. But in this one fellowship of the Triune God, the Gentile believers extended their fellowship (which is the same Greek word as "contribution" in Romans 15:26) to Jewish saints in completely different regions. This is the practicality of fellowship. It is not just spiritual fellowship, but it reaches down to material riches believers are not just willing, but happy to share. These Gentile believers were happy to minister material things to their fellow Jewish brethren. What a testimony to the world of our oneness with all believers — surely, this exemplifies the fulfillment of the Lord's Prayer in John 17.

Fellowship is not just local, among the believers' own group of people. It reaches out to believers in other regions — brethren they may have never met or seen. Fellowship always reaches out and expands and is not withdrawn or limited.

In the name of protecting their "fellowship" from outside corrupting influences, some groups of believers have become sectarian by discouraging or even forbidding believers in their group from fellowshipping with believers outside of their group. God is well able to protect His own fellowship. He certainly does not need man to be His protector.

> Salute the brethren in Laodicea, and Nymphas, and the assembly which [is] in his house. And when the letter has been read among you, cause that it be read also in the assembly of Laodiceans, and that ye also read that from Laodicea.
> (Colossians 4:15-16, DBY)

Paul's direct encouragement for these two assemblies, Colossae and Laodicea, was to have fellowship together. Paul sent one letter to the saints in Colossae and another letter to the believers in Laodicea. Instead of carbon copying both and sending two letters to both places, he asked the Colossian believers to travel to Laodicea, greet the saints there, and read the letter to the assembly meeting in Nymphas' house. After that, they were to bring the letter written to the Laodiceans back and read it in Colossae. This shows the interchange of fellowship trafficking between believers and assemblies in two different localities. Each assembly could claim they were indeed the Body of Christ with no lack (1 Cor. 12:27); yet, if a local assembly became isolated and withdrawn within themselves, then surely, they would miss the Lord's word given to another locality.

As in this case, the Lord communicated a word to one locality but intended it for all believers everywhere. If fellowship with another locality did not exist, the Lord's speaking concerning His abundance and revelation would be missed. How critical it is for believers to extend themselves outside their convenient comfort zones. Whatever believers have received from the Lord is common to all believers. Indeed, there must be sharing and receiving in fellowship to realize what the Lord is doing. Every assembly needs to seek out other assemblies for fellowship, even outside their own locality. The more fellowship, the more enriched and stronger is that assembly.

15.
Practical Assembly Life (Sec. B)

The first section of these two chapters (Chapter 14) showed from Scripture how the local ekklesia is practiced. Whether there were tens of thousands of believers in a city or a few believers in a town, the assembly was practical being domiciled in homes where fellowship was enjoyed, where demonstrable oneness was expressed. In Part 2 concerning the practicum of the assembly, additional matters of significance will be covered. These items include the nature of the "two or three" gathering *into* the Lord's name, who the assembly should exclude, and the difference between a ministry and an assembly.

Two or Three Gathered Is Not Assembly

> "If your brother sins against you, go, show him his fault between you and him alone. If he listens to you, you have gained back your brother. But if he doesn't listen, take one or two more with you, that at the mouth of two or three witnesses every word may be established. If he refuses to listen to them, tell it to the assembly. If he refuses to hear the assembly also, let him be to you as a Gentile or a tax collector. Most certainly I tell you, whatever things you bind on earth will have been bound in heaven, and whatever things you release on earth will have been released in heaven. Again, assuredly I tell you, that if two of you will agree on earth concerning anything that they will ask, it will be done for them by my Father who is in heaven. For where two or three are gathered together in my name, there I am in the midst of them."
>
> (Matthew 18:15-20 WEB)

In Matthew 18:20 we discover a wonderful account where two or three are gathered together anywhere and at any time, and when their activities focus on Jesus Christ, there in the center of their fellowship is the presence of Christ. Believers need to take advantage of this promise. Most of the time Christians only consider the things of Christ, fellowship, or prayer when in church. If they are not in church or at an "official" Christian event, then there is not much thought of the practice of fellowship to be in Christ. Experientially, the Lord is not in their midst. If believers want the Lord's presence with all of His riches and blessings, then they need to find every opportunity to gather around the Lord's Name. Only then is the Lord's presence everywhere where they may be found.

Nevertheless, these "twos or threes" by themselves are not the assembly — per se. In context, based on verses 16 and 17, the "twos or threes" must bring unresolved matters to the assembly. The assembly has the final say concerning the matter. If an offending brother hears the assembly, then he continues in fellowship with the assembly; but if he does not hear the assembly concerning his sin, then he is to be treated as an unbeliever. As an unbeliever, it does not mean he is cut off from care and love, since believers should love, cherish, and nourish every weak and unbelieving person. This is quite different from churches today, where being excluded does not seem like a punishment at all. The proper assembly in the home, according to New Testament revelation, must have been so enjoyable because being excluded from the assembly was a devastating loss for the unrepentant brother.

Whether in one home or many homes, in any given locality there is only one assembly; yet, there should be scores of "twos or threes" gathering *into* the Lord's Name throughout the day: in restaurants, schools, parks, malls, homes, cars . . . everywhere. All these "twos or threes" are part of the one assembly. They have the vision and realization they are all in one assembly — one fellowship. These "twos or threes" also gather with other "twos or threes" from house to house according to 1 Corinthians 11 through 14 expressing one assembly. In this setting, though there are diverse fellowship and multitudes of activity, there is still One Body. In this oneness of the Body, the "twos or threes" have the authority to bind and loose in their prayers. The Father listens to the prayers of all these "twos or threes" who harmonize in that one assembly.

Whatever these "twos or threes" bind or loose on earth shall be bound and loosed in heaven. This shows their prayers are efficacious. God is waiting for these kinds of prayers wrought in oneness with His will for the building up of His kingdom. God will not act on His own. He deigns to hear the prayer of believers in harmony before He will act. This shows how needful it is for believers to be one in order for God's hand to answer their prayers.

Just as Peter was given the keys of the kingdom of the heavens to bind and loose, all of these "twos and threes" can bind and loose for the sake of the building up of God's kingdom, His assembly. To "bind" is to immobilize Satan and all of his forces, to put them out of commission whereby they are of none effect. In Matthew 12:22–29, the Lord Jesus healed a blind and dumb man due to demon possession enabling him to see and speak. He explained the man was a vessel captured in the house of a "strong man." To take away vessels from the strong man's house (to heal this person), He must first bind the strong man.

Today many people are spiritually blinded from seeing who Jesus Christ is — they are spiritually dumb, unable neither to speak of Jesus Christ nor to minister to Him. In the spiritual realm, if a person sees Christ, he should speak of Christ. Those who cannot see or speak of Christ are captured in Satan's house, his kingdom. Therefore, *binding prayers* are needed to curtail Satan and all his evil forces enabling the blind to see, and the dumb to speak; they need to see and hear Jesus and speak of Him Who has freed them from Satan's stronghold.

Likewise, these "twos and threes" have been given authority to "loose." In Acts 2:24 Paul states God — in raising up Jesus from the dead — has loosed the pangs of death. To "loose" in prayer is for people to be loosed from the hold of death. People should not be in death; rather, they should be loosed from death and released into eternal life. Binding focuses on our enemy, while losing rivets our attention on the people. Both are designed to enable the transference of people from Satan's kingdom to God's kingdom. This kind of prayer is not according to self-interest, but according to God's will for the building up of the assembly — this is the kind of prayer so desperately needed today.

Ministers Wrongly Competing with the Assembly

All ministers with their ministries should be for equipping brethren for the building of the assembly, but instead many ministers focus on building up their own ministry to the detriment of the assembly.

> For as we have many members in One Body, but all the members do not have the same function, so we, being many, are One Body in Christ, and individually members of one another. Having then gifts differing according to the grace that is given to us, let us use them: if prophecy, let us prophesy in proportion to our faith; or ministry, let us use it in our ministering; he who teaches, in teaching; he who exhorts, in exhortation; he who gives, with liberality; he who leads, with diligence; he who shows mercy, with cheerfulness.
>
> (Romans 12:4-8)
>
> There are diversities of gifts, but the same Spirit. There are differences of ministries, but the same Lord. And there are diversities of activities, but it is the same God who works all in all. But the manifestation of the Spirit is given to each one for the profit of all:
>
> (1 Corinthians 12:4-7)

In both chapters above relating to many members in One Body, Paul includes two lists showing every individual member in the Body has at least one gift for the benefit of the entire Body. The lists contain a variety of gifts ranging from the very practical to the supernatural. The practical gifts are distributed to every believer — all can possess these gifts, ranging from the gift of giving to the gift of hospitality (Rom. 12:13). To some the supernatural gifts of the Spirit such as healing or the working of miracles are given. This is akin to the physical body where each organ has a specific function. Indeed, the members of the Body of Christ also have specific functions to serve His One Body. All these gifts, ministries, and activities are from the same Spirit; therefore, believers should recognize and accept them as expressions of diverse ministries — all of which are for the One Body.

It is unfortunate when believers do not accept all the gifts given by the same Spirit for they are manifestations of the Triune God given to the members of the Body. Some may refuse to accept miraculous healings thinking they cannot happen today and denigrate those who claim to have witnessed such things. At the same time, others may reject a word of wisdom, warning believers not to be distracted or naively follow the "hype" surrounding many claims of such miracles. Some may consider a ministry that cares for recovering addicts as a waste of resources, while others may consider any resources given to a ministry outreaching to business people unscriptural (since the Bible charges believers to give to the poor). According to Paul, however, believers should realize our Lord's ways are above man's limited and biased views. It is by receiving all the gifts and ministries of the Spirit, believers can be balanced and gain benefit from all spiritual gifts, ministries, and activities which have been bestowed upon the Body of Christ.

Among all God's people, there are some who have developed their gifts quicker — they have the capability to initiate a ministry as a stronger believer. By exercising their gifts to preach the Word, teach the Bible, or do works of faith, they will draw a following of people into their sphere of ministry. It is critical to recognize most of the various churches and Christian groups today are really a grouping based on someone's ministry, such as that of a pastor or teacher. They are gathered to hear the teachings and inspirations from a particularly gifted man of God. Other Christian groups are ministries based on reaching the poor, people in prison, an ethnic community, or college students.

The entire Lutheran denomination, for example, is based on the ministry of Martin Luther, whereas there are a multitude of other regional and globally organized churches which are based on (or a continuation of) other gifted ministers. On one hand, there is no doubt many of these gifted ministers have provided tremendous benefits to believers, but on the other hand, if only the ministry itself is being built while the assembly is being neglected, the body becomes dysfunctional, handicapped wherein most believers are no longer functioning members of the assembly. Rather, they become spectators — audiences or supporters of a ministry. There needs to be a clear distinction between building up of a ministry and building up an assembly as described in the Bible.

There is absolutely no doubt from these two portions of Scripture, these diverse ministries and activities are designed for His One Body. Any ministry which focuses on growth of their own ministry — standing apart from the assembly — will devolve into sectarianism like Paul warned.

Cancer occurs when a diseased cell metastasizes. This cancerous cell is not needed — it invades and damages the physical body. Similarly, countless problems among believers are due to ministries competing for followers and resources in the Body of Christ. Gifted ministers or followers of these gifted ministers bear similar characteristics. Firstly, they will do their best to grow their followers, holding them through various control mechanisms, rather than releasing them to build the assembly in their homes. Secondly, they will speak negatively against other ministries in competition with their own, gaining followers in the process thereby growing and spreading their own ministry.

For example, let's say a particularly gifted minister has a burden to reach out to college students. Carrying out his mission, he develops a method of open-air gospel music and preaching to bring people to faith in Christ. On the one hand, it would be appropriate if this person, becoming successful in this way, would have a following — training others to do what he does to reach more college students for Christ. His ministry would be profitable for the Body if those who become believers through his ministry would then join a local assembly fellowshipping from house to house, receiving and greeting all other non-college students in their community.

On the other hand, what if this gifted brother started to speak negatively against another minister on campus whose method of reaching unbelievers is through one-on-one Bible studies? What if he started to belittle, for example, prison ministry as being a waste of time? What if, when the number of students following him increases; he builds a church to group them together, so they do not know how to receive and fellowship with non-college students? Ultimately, this brother's ministry is no longer for the Body; it is a "church" which is an expression of students for Christ. His ministry may well grow and prosper, but by corralling those helped through his ministry into his church, their integration into the one fellowship of the assembly is neglected.

All believers need to be raised to minister, to exercise their gifts for the Body. Everyone needs to serve, to be a co-worker with the Lord. Undoubtedly, some who are more gifted and capable in their service will draw a following of believers after them. It is natural to admire and follow ministers who have been used by God, whether that minister is prominent or less known. On one hand, it is proper for a worker of the Lord to acquire co-workers from those who they have helped, as Paul did with his younger co-workers like Timothy, Titus, Silas, and others. Every useful minister of the Lord should have some helpers to expand the reach of their ministry. On the other hand, it is dangerous for a minister to gain a following to the point where they form a group or even a sect that competes with the assembly of the Lord, even around the Lord Himself — *"I am of Christ."* Therefore, all ministers, both great and small, need to have a mind-set of humility, be ready to serve others, and give up their own following of believers for the sake of the assembly.

John the Baptist, Competing with Jesus

> After this Jesus and his disciples went into the Judean countryside, and he remained there with them and was baptizing. John also was baptizing at Aenon near Salim, because water was plentiful there, and people were coming and being baptized . . . And they came to John and said to him, "Rabbi, he who was with you across the Jordan, to whom you bore witness — look, he is baptizing, and all are going to him." . . . "He must increase, but I must decrease."
>
> (John 3:22-23, 26, 30)
>
> Then the disciples of John came to him, saying, "Why do we and the Pharisees fast, but your disciples do not fast?"
>
> (Matthew 9:14, ESV)

John the Baptist was clearly used by God to proclaim Jesus at His coming. John can be considered the first gospel preacher. He was the first to lead people to Jesus Christ and declare Him as the Son of God; the One Who takes away the sins of the world. Since Jesus came and started His ministry (including baptism), John's work of introducing Jesus was completed; it was no longer needed. John should have just pointed people to Jesus, sent all his disciples to Him, and joined himself to Jesus' ministry. Instead, John continued baptizing people just "because water is plentiful there." Even though John was clear concerning the preeminence of Jesus, it seems his own disciples were not. They viewed Jesus as a competitor against their own rabbi, John. Their concern was people could readily start going over to Jesus to be baptized by Jesus or His disciples, rather than by John, and, of course, themselves.

When John started his ministry, he harshly condemned the Pharisees (Matt. 3:7). It is hard to imagine within a short period of two years, John's disciples linked arms together with the Pharisees in challenging Jesus — condemning Him for eating and drinking with sinners instead of fasting.

John's disciples kept religious laws; however, they missed the person Who John was so clear in proclaiming. John himself knew Jesus' followers must increase and his followers must decrease, but he still held on to his ministry and his followers; thus, he unwittingly became a competitor to Jesus.

Any believer who is being helped by a particular minister should be cautious they do not become a group, or a sect formed around their minister in a way which separates them from the assembly, the Body of Christ. Ministers should be vigilant knowing when their ministry's usefulness is over, not becoming a source of distraction from the Lord Himself. John's ministry reveals to us even a person who introduced the Lord to others can become a distraction, someone who competes with the Lord. Therefore, it is critical to develop one's ministry with the full conviction all of that minister's labor has but one ultimate aim: the building up of the assembly; not the building up of "my own ministry."

A Ministry Is Different from a Local Assembly

> And it happened, while Apollos was at Corinth, that Paul, having passed through the upper regions, came to Ephesus. And finding some disciples
>
> And he went into the synagogue and spoke boldly for three months, reasoning and persuading concerning the things of the kingdom of God. But when some were hardened and did not believe, but spoke evil of the Way before the multitude, he departed from them and withdrew the disciples, reasoning daily in the school of Tyrannus.
>
> (Acts 19:1, 8-9)
>
> But I will tarry in Ephesus until Pentecost.
>
> The churches [assemblies] of Asia greet you. Aquila and Priscilla greet you heartily in the Lord, with the church [assembly] that is in their house.
>
> (1 Corinthians 16:8, 19)

When Paul went to Ephesus, as was his custom, he first preached in the synagogues, since those were places where people congregated — they were already worshipping God, reading the Scriptures of the Hebrew Bible. He started there. It was an efficient way to reach many people with the message of Jesus Christ. When those in the synagogue didn't believe, Paul secured a place in a school to daily continue his teaching. That school was the place where he established his ministry of teaching, preaching, and reasoning daily with anyone willing to entertain dialogue with him.

It is critical to note, while the school of Tyrannus was the place where he daily "worked out" his ministry, the actual assembly in Ephesus was in the home of Aquila and Priscilla. Paul didn't call the place where he was doing his ministry "the assembly hall," because it was a place used for his ministry; the local assembly was in somebody else's home. Paul's actions confirm a ministry is not the assembly, for all ministries are for the assembly. Another minister, such as Apollos, may well set up another school for his ministry, but this school, as well, would not equate to an assembly. No matter how many ministers set up schools to teach and preach, they are all inferior to the one assembly gathering from house to house. The assembly is one, though ministries are many. The "work of the ministry" is NOT the ekklesia — it is FOR the assembly; not for itself.

Ministers Are for the Assembly

All ministers are for the assembly, and an assembly can receive services from multiple independent ministers.

> For when one says, "I am of Paul," and another, "I am of Apollos," are you not carnal? Who then is Paul, and who is Apollos, but ministers through whom you believed, as the Lord gave to each one? I planted, Apollos watered, but God gave the increase. So then neither he who plants is anything, nor he who waters, but God who gives the increase.
>
> Therefore let no one boast in men. For all things are yours: whether Paul or Apollos or Cephas, or the world or life or death, or things present or things to come — all are yours.
>
> (1 Corinthians 3:4–7, 21–22)

The apostle Paul chastised the Corinthian believers for being spiritual babes. These babes were acting like fallen men with them quarreling over who was a better minister while taking sides in their disputations. Paul went on to say these ministers — workers of the Lord — are just servants. They are nothing, unworthy to cause a division. These babes should be focusing on God and Jesus Christ, our unique foundation (1 Cor. 3:11).

Ministers (workers) are servants to serve the assembly of the Lord. Although one minister may plant, and another may water, the assemblies do not belong to any of the workers ... they belong to the Lord and to all the saints. There should be no competition between ministers since their goal should be awaiting God to give the growth to the assembly whereby God Almighty will receive all the glory. Although Paul initiated the assembly in Corinth through his preaching of Jesus Christ, he recognized by allowing other ministers to minister — such as Apollos and Cephas (Peter) — helping and participating in the assembly he started, it would be a great benefit for the assembly. A genuine assembly can receive the ministry of various independent ministers. This is very different from a church founded by a ministry, since this church in all likelihood will not allow independent ministers to share things which may be contrary to their ministry. Sure, if another minister of that same ministry comes to them, that's fine and dandy — but allowing a separate ministry's minister to share ... that's an entirely different matter.

Today, most denominations have their own recognized or accredited seminary. Only those graduated from their own seminary can be a pastor/minister in that particular Christian organization. This is additional proof organized Christian groups have a different nature from the assembly the Lord is building.

Due to the nature of an assembly's diverse ministries and activities, there are opportunities for harmful teachings perpetrated by unscrupulous teachers who may distract believers from Christ. Therefore Paul, in his epistles, pointed out those ministers who were diverting believers away from Christ. He himself did not demand subjection from the assemblies that he raised; rather he wooed them back by accepting him as a minister in reminding them of the sacrifices he had made on their behalf (1 Cor. 10–11).

Ministers wanting to protect God's sheep under their care, avoiding confusion from various ministers, will use this reasoning to keep out non-approved ministers from the group they are leading. However, this solution will cause worse damage to the Body of Christ than the problem they are trying to solve. Today, just about all Christians are segregated by ministries attempting to "protect their flocks," while the genuine assembly expressing the One Body of Christ languishes. If Paul didn't stop other ministries from coming into an assembly which he originated; therefore, ministers today should not think they know better than Paul by excluding other ministries or ministers.

As in Ephesians, Colossians, Philippians, Galatians and his other writings, Paul did his best to dispute with those who taught contrary to New Testament revelation; yet, he did not ask the assembly to remove those teaching contrary to his own teachings. Teaching something which may be harmful to the assembly is not sufficient ground to remove such teachers. It is only when they draw away believers to form a separate group independent of one fellowship, one assembly, or when they do not teach Jesus Christ is come in the flesh, then they need to be marked out and avoided.

This is why Paul emphasized the need for listeners to discern what they were hearing in 1 Corinthians 14. If all believers read the Bible, knowing the Spirit for themselves as they should, then there would be proper discernment to know whether a speaking or teaching is healthy for all to receive or harmful and mandatory for rejection. When everyone has the freedom to speak and teach (though at times it may be conflicting and confusing), over time believers in the assembly will grow and will know the Lord and the truth according to the New Testament. Building up an assembly without man's manipulating control mechanisms is no small thing!

Mutual Support among Ministers

Ministries, though independent from each other, should cooperate with and provide mutual support for the building up of the local Body of Christ.

> Now concerning our brother Apollos, I strongly urged him to come to you with the brethren, but he was quite unwilling to come at this time; however, he will come when he has a convenient time.
> (1 Corinthians 16:12)
>
> Do your best to speed Zenas the lawyer and Apollos on their way; see that they lack nothing.
> (Titus 3:13)

Paul strongly urged Apollos to travel to Corinth visiting the saints there; however, Apollos had the freedom to make an independent decision not to go. It was Paul's disciples, Priscilla and Aquila, who helped Apollos understand the New Testament revelation more fully; therefore, Paul should have seniority over Apollos, with a higher and clearer vision of New Testament revelation. In the New Testament, there is no hierarchy in the Body where one can tell another independent minister what to do or not do.

A gifted believer who has started a ministry cannot exercise any authority demanding that a minister in another ministry do this or that. Paul could urge, but it was still up to Apollos whether to comply. For example, if a minister starts a prison ministry, he cannot demand someone else engaged in a college student ministry to do anything apart from his college ministry. A minister, no matter how senior and mature, cannot dictate how someone else's ministry should operate.

Although Apollos did not comply with Paul's request, Paul still viewed him as a colaborer, working together for the building up of the One Body of Christ (1 Cor. 3:6–9). There can be multiple independent ministries, but ultimately, they should all work together for the building up of the assembly. This being the case, Paul asked Titus, who was a junior partner in Paul's ministry, to make sure Apollos was taken care of lacking nothing in his travels. Even though Apollos didn't do what Paul strongly urged him to do, Paul, nevertheless, cared for him and supported him in his ministry. What a beautiful coordination of working together between independent ministers! There was no competition or backbiting, but only full support. This would be like a minister who has a ministry to preach the gospel through contemporary music giving his support and resources to someone with a teaching ministry; they would not be merely building up their own church ministry, but rather the One Body of Christ.

> And count the patience of our Lord as salvation, just as our beloved brother Paul also wrote to you according to the wisdom given him, as he does in all his letters when he speaks in them of these matters. There are some things in them that are hard to understand, which the ignorant and unstable twist to their own destruction, as they do the other Scriptures.
>
> (2 Peter 3:15–16)

Peter in his epistle recommends and supports Paul's writings. Peter was one who Paul openly condemned. He exposed Peter's hypocrisy when, in unfaithfulness to the truth, Peter withdrew from eating with Gentile believers because Jewish believers were coming from James in Jerusalem.

Though it must have been very embarrassing to be publicly reprimanded by Paul, Peter remained faithful in supporting Paul and his ministry. Peter even recommended Paul's writings were at the same level as the Scriptures.

It was Peter who had a ministry to the Jews, yet he recommended and supported Paul whose ministry was toward the Gentiles. What one accord and coordination between these independent ministers! This can only happen because of their understanding and realization they were not building up their own ministry, but the Body of Christ. It is difficult to recommend a minister if he or she is only concerned about building up their own ministry. In fact, if the ministry will cause believers to stand apart in division with other believers, then that minister should not be recommended, but should be marked out as problematic to the One Body. Believers should be warned of his or her (the minister's) selfish work. However, if those ministers are building the One Body by encouraging all those under their ministry to fellowship with all other believers, no matter how diverse and different, their ministry should be welcomed, supported.

Leadership in a Ministry vs. Leadership in an Assembly

> So those who conducted Paul brought him to Athens; and receiving a command for Silas and Timothy to come to him with all speed, they departed.
>
> (Acts 17:15)
>
> For this reason, I have sent Timothy to you, who is my beloved and faithful son in the Lord, who will remind you of my ways in Christ, as I teach everywhere in every church [assembly]
>
> (1 Corinthians 4:17)

When a gifted believer starts a ministry, that person becomes the natural leader and authority in that ministry. If successful in helping others, whether through their preaching or teaching activities, this minister will naturally gain a following. Out of this group of followers and supporters, some will want to join in to help grow and spread his ministry. Believers who join in to support this gifted minister who started that ministry should consider the founding minister as the authority of that ministry. As the leader of that ministry, the founding minister can ask those subordinated to him what to do. Paul was the one, for example, who commanded his subordinate ministers like Timothy to come here or go there in contrast to Apollos, who was NOT under his direct ministry.

A ministry is like doing a work with a goal, a direction, or a method. If a person is going to join an existing ministry, becoming part of that ministry, it only makes sense those joining that ministry would support the leadership of the founding minister. Let's say someone is going to build a suspension bridge. It would be silly if a person joins in and gives their unsolicited advice while taking resources to build a boat or a platoon bridge instead. If a person believes they have a better idea in traveling across the water by building a boat, they should start their own work (ministry) to build a boat! They should not try to take over and disrupt the team that already established the goal of building a suspension bridge.

Paul had a direction, a message, a method to achieve his goal of preaching to the Gentiles to build up the One Body of Christ. Disciples like Timothy, Silas, and Titus had received help from Paul and wanted to be a part of Paul's ministry; therefore, Paul had the natural authority and leadership to coordinate their moves for the sake of carrying out his ministry. Apollos, on the other hand, didn't consider himself as part of Paul's ministry; thus, he could operate independently. Yet Paul and Apollos embraced the same goal of building up the one assembly of Christ.

> The elders who are among you I exhort . . . Shepherd the flock of God which is among you, serving as overseers, not by compulsion but willingly, not for dishonest gain but eagerly; nor as being lords over those entrusted to you, but being examples to the flock.
>
> Likewise you younger people, submit yourselves to your elders. Yes, all of you be submissive to one another, and be clothed with humility, for "God resists the proud, but gives grace to the humble."
>
> (1 Peter 5:1a–3, 5)

In individual ministries there are authority figures; however, in an assembly there are no such persons. No one can be the "lord" no matter his or her spiritual maturity. Each member in the Lord's Body is directly connected and answers only to the Lord Jesus as the Head. In any family, there are those that are relatively more mature and older, who may be considered "elders." But elders are not in any way part of a hierarchy, able to tell other members what to do or where to go; rather, they are shepherds (pastors) enjoined to feed the flock. Because they are older, they have the knowledge of the Word to feed other believers; as overseers, they are to alert other believers concerning anything harmful in the assembly.

As brethren who are older, they should be examples of or a pattern to other believers. Today, too many Christian leaders have this kind of attitude: "Do what I say, but not what I do." Leadership in the sense of being an example means "leaders" are living a life as a pattern in speech, conduct, love, faith, and purity (1 Tim. 4:12). If their lives are such a pattern, then believers should follow and learn from their examples.

The elders should not be motivated by any untoward gain for themselves. In the Greek, "dishonest gains" is one word, *anagkastós*. When read in English as two words, one can interpret it to mean there can be "honest" gains. But read as one word, *anagkastós* compares "gains" with "eagerness." That means any believer having maturity to feed others will do it eagerly without any motivation for any forms of "gain." If it is not done eagerly by love, any "gain" is dishonest.

Some may point to 1 Peter 5:5a which says believers *should* submit to such elders. They may ask, "Doesn't that show the authority of the elders over other believers?" The problem with that interpretation is it neglects the next phrase in the same verse which says, "... *be submissive to one another.*" By this phrase, the idea of hierarchy — that one has authority over another — is eliminated. If coercion and force is not used, then submission is completely voluntary, not compulsory. Since elders are not lords, they should not have authority to use force or threats to compel anyone to do their will. Believers may or may not submit, based on their conscience and understanding. At the same time, elders should also submit to younger believers, if the Lord is speaking and leading through them regardless of their age.

This unequivocally affirms the assembly is the family — the household of God. The Lord Jesus is the only One with absolute authority — He is the Chief Shepherd of the sheep. Therefore, as brothers and sisters in the same family, the same flock, everyone is equal in status, but some may be relatively ahead of others in life experiences and knowledge. These are then considered older brothers and sisters who assist the Chief Shepherd in feeding His sheep upon the earth. The Household of God is the most beautiful assembly!

At a certain point, Paul's ministry practiced pointing out elders in an assembly, but when he wrote many of his letters he addressed the *entire* assembly not singling out elders. He recognized elders themselves could be corrupted and become a problem to believers. Therefore, when Paul spoke to the elders in Ephesus (Acts 20:28–30), he warned them even among themselves there would be those who would rise up to speak perverse things to draw believers away to themselves.

By the time John wrote his letters to a few local assemblies Paul had raised up, such as Ephesus in Revelation 2, John completely ignored any type of leadership or elders in those assemblies. Instead, John, said anyone in the assembly could hear the Spirit speaking. Thus, anyone who heard the Spirit speak could be raised up to overcome the degradation among the assemblies at that time. Believers should not wait for anyone to lead them; whenever the Spirit is leading and speaking — they should simply follow Him. Anyone who follows the Spirit's leading according to the Word becomes a leader at that point. Any "leader" not following the Spirit is no longer a leader.

The assembly desperately needs mature believers — those eager to feed others, to be examples to others, even to know how to submit to younger believers. Likewise, believers need to be warned if they place their trust in anyone (men or women who are leaders, pastors or shepherds), and yet do not put their trust in the study of God's Word, while simultaneously listening to the Spirit, one day they will find themselves misled and/or disappointed.

Therefore, for the assembly to be built up, every believer needs to rise up and be actively seeking the Lord and functioning according to the gifts the Spirit has given to all believers.

Ready to Serve and Be Nothing

> But Jesus called them to [Himself] and said, "You know that the rulers of the Gentiles lord it over them, and those who are great exercise authority over them. Yet it shall not be so among you; but whoever desires to become great among you, let him be your servant."
>
> (Matthew 20:25–26)
>
> ... with all humility and gentleness, with patience, bearing with one another in love, eager to maintain the unity of the Spirit in the bond of peace.
>
> (Ephesians 4:2–3, ESV)

Once a minister (whether carrying out a ministry or being a shepherd) is successful in their service to the Lord, it is easy to become prideful by desiring to guard the fruit of one's labor. The more successful the work of a Christian is, the more temptation for pride. When pride enters, disputes with others become inevitable — normally, with "competing ministers." Certain expectations arise, for respect and privilege. Additionally, to guard, protect, and maintain the fruit of their labor, ministers might exercise authority to retain certain control over those receiving their ministry with seemingly good intentions. This can be in the form of warning them NOT to listen to certain ministers or associate with certain types of Christians who "believe and practice such and such."

However, this attempt to "protect" can develop into a "segregating spirit." Worse yet, it can develop into systematic division among believers. The result is their followings (or churches) increases to the detriment of the assembly. Pride, thus, becomes a seed of division from other believers. All ministers, great or small, must remember to stay in Christ Who came as the suffering servant.

"Minister" literally means "a servant." Therefore, in the assembly, those allegedly great among the saints should be the servant of all; the greater the minister, the greater the servant. A servant, especially during biblical times, did not have the right to be offended by those he or she was serving. It is one's pride which gives rise to being offended — when others disrespect, ignore, or contradict them. Offense leads to contention, which then leads to divisions. That being said, those members of the Body which delight in deprecating ministers would do well to hold their tongues lest a greater condemnation befalls them! Far too often, that which is said in jest, or designed to correct another brother, is a subtle attempt to "cut down" a brother or sister, thereby building yourself up!

The life of Christ is the ultimate expression of humility — it is the antidote for the natural, built-in pride every person is born with. All ministers need to abide in the life of the new birth, the life of a servant. When offense occurs because of pride, there immediately needs to be a retreat into the indwelling Christ. It is in this humility — gentleness with patience — believers, especially successful ministers, can bear with one another in love so that the oneness of the Spirit is maintained and grows. The glory the Lord Jesus received was the result of His being a servant. This glory of the Lord Jesus is now given to believers, so they can also live in the same pattern as the Lord Jesus: one that results in glory through service. It is through serving in this pattern that believers are kept one.

Paul's example is the "progression" of a servant, willing to lay down his own pride, his life for the sake of the brethren — listen to the devolution of the man:

> "I am the least of the apostles."
> (1 Corinthians 15:9)
>
> "Unto me, who am less than the least of all saints."
> (Ephesians 3:8)
>
> "Christ Jesus came into the world to save sinners, of whom I am chief."
> (1 Tim. 1:15)

Believers Excluded from an Assembly:

Those Who Divide Should Be Marked and Avoided

> Now I urge you, brethren, note those who cause divisions and offenses, contrary to the doctrine which you learned, and avoid them. For those who are such do not serve our Lord Jesus Christ, but their own belly, and by smooth words and flattering speech deceive the hearts of the simple.
> (Romans 16:17–18)
>
> But avoid foolish disputes, genealogies, contentions, and strivings about the law; for they are unprofitable and useless. Reject a divisive man after the first and second admonition.
> (Titus 3:9–10)

A person causing a division in the Body through differing teachings, diverting believers away from the focus of Jesus Christ's person and work, needs to be avoided, even rejected.

"Division" in Romans 16:17 in Greek, *dicostasia*, is a strong word meaning, *"to stand apart."* Those under the influence of this person's teaching will stand apart from simply being believers in common fellowship with other believers in the Body of Christ. They will consider themselves different, superior, and special from other believers. These divisive teachers are not motivated to build up oneness of the Body; rather, they purposely want to cause a separation among believers. They may want to have their own group of followers, or they may simply want to be contentious in showing they are right, as well as superior, while others are wrong and inferior. Either way, through their speech and actions, they oblige believers to choose between one group and another — to be on one side or another.

All believers should be on the same side, for we are all members of the same assembly, because there is only one Jesus Christ, one Spirit of God, one fellowship, and One Body of Christ. Therefore, any divisive teacher (after two admonitions to point out their damaging and divisive actions) should stop their destructive ways or be rejected from the fellowship of that assembly.

Those Who Don't Teach Jesus Christ Is God in the Flesh

> For many deceivers have gone out into the world, those who do not confess the coming of Jesus Christ in the flesh. Such a one is the deceiver and the antichrist.
>
> Everyone who goes on ahead and does not abide in the teaching of Christ, does not have God. Whoever abides in the teaching has both the Father and the Son. If anyone comes to you and does not bring this teaching, do not receive him into your house or give him any greeting, for whoever greets him takes part in his wicked works.
>
> (2 John 1:7, 9–11 ESV)

It can be assumed those deceivers John referred to in 2 John 1 considered themselves Christians. They were not unbelievers, since unbelievers by definition *do not* believe Jesus is God come in the flesh. Moreover, in 1 Corinthians 14 we read there were *unbelievers* in the assembly; therefore, these deceivers must have been people who passed themselves off as Christian teachers. They probably used the Bible to teach, for they had the ability to deceive. However, they did not teach Jesus Christ is God becoming flesh (man).

This is the very essence of our faith concerning the person of Jesus Christ — He is both one hundred percent God, and one hundred percent man. He is altogether God and, simultaneously, genuinely man. Anyone identified as a Christian teaching Jesus Christ is either not eternally God or not eternally man is against the person of Jesus Christ — this is the spirit of antichrist. Such a teacher should not be received.

One Living Habitually in Sin

Believers who habitually and openly practice sin and immorality which can no longer be tolerated by love should not be received into the assembly.

> Above all, keep loving one another earnestly, since love covers a multitude of sins.
>
> (1 Peter 4:8, ESV)
>
> Let no corrupting talk come out of your mouths, but only such as is good for building up, as fits the occasion, that it may give grace to those who hear.
>
> (Ephesians 4:29, ESV)

Due to our closeness in fellowship in the assembly (viz., life between believers), there will be opportunities to know each other's faults, even sins. There will be times when believers will hear of, even witness a failure or a sinful fall of another believer. In all such occasions, Scriptures instruct believers to cover their brother or sister with love — not to spread in gossip the weaknesses of other believers. In some situations, believers may have to share what has been learned with another believer, to pray for and support the believer with a certain weakness. In any case, we are not to spread news of another's failure — it should be contained and covered so believers in the assembly will not know of each other's faults, weaknesses, failures and sins. They should not spread such information to others, since it could corrupt and damage the assembly. This has nothing to do with "hiding in darkness" but everything to do with "love covers a multitude of sins."

> It is universally reported *that there is* fornication among you, and such fornication as is not even among the nations, so that one should have his father's wife. And you are puffed up, and you have not rather mourned, in order that he that has done this deed might be taken away out of the midst of you.

> Your boasting *is* not good. Do you not know that a little leaven leavens the whole lump? Purge out the old leaven, that you may be a new lump, according as you are unleavened. For also our Passover, Christ, has been sacrificed.
>
> I have written to you in the epistle not to mix with fornicators; not altogether with the fornicators of this world, or with the avaricious [covetous] and rapacious [extortioner], or idolaters, since *then* you should go out of the world. But now I have written to you, if any one called brother be [a] fornicator, or avaricious [covetous], or idolater, or abusive, or a drunkard, or rapacious [extortioner], not to mix with him; with such a one not even to eat. For what have I *to do* with judging those outside also? you, do not you judge them that are within? But those without God judges. Remove the wicked person from amongst yourselves.
>
> (1 Corinthians 5:1–2, 6–7, 9–13, DBY)

When a believer's failures become habitual, universally known, wherein they can no longer be considered as an occasional sin able to be covered by love, the assembly should not tolerate nor accept this believer as if everything is okay. The assembly in Corinth boasted it had such a sinful brother in their midst. The apostle Paul likened this openly sinful brother's behavior was "leaven" which would corrupt the entire assembly, because other believers who were witness to such "leaven" would be encouraged to cave in to sin's temptations, thinking this sinful practice to be acceptable behavior in the assembly.

Therefore, this brother could no longer be welcomed into the assembly, or participate in the assembly's meals. This does not mean caring believers could not visit this brother by helping him to repent of his sin; however, this does mean he should be excluded from gathering together with the assembly. This exclusion includes all those believers who are known to be people who live in the manifestation of their sinful nature in various ways as listed in 1 Corinthians 5:11.

This exclusion, however, should not include unbelievers or those new in the faith, since they don't know better. These unbelievers or new believers living in sin should still be welcomed; otherwise they will not receive the Word of faith nor encouragement in the assembly for them to come to Christ and grow in the faith. Functioning in this way reveals the heart of the Lord. On one hand, He reaches out to all people for them to be saved from their sinful practices; on the other hand, He protects the assembly from corruption.

One Who Is a Busybody, Not Working

> But we command you, brethren, in the name of our Lord Jesus Christ, that you withdraw from every brother who walks disorderly and not according to the tradition which he received from us. For you yourselves know how you ought to follow us, for we were not disorderly among you; nor did we eat anyone's bread free of charge, but worked with labor and toil night and day, that we might not be a burden to any of you, not because we do not have authority, but to make ourselves an example of how you should follow us. For even when we were with you, we commanded you this: If anyone will not work, neither shall he eat . . . And if anyone does not obey our word in this epistle, note that person and do not keep company with him, that he may be ashamed. Yet do not count him as an enemy, but admonish him as a brother.
>
> (2 Thess. 3:6-10, 14-15)

What an example the apostle Paul gave to believers! He labored in preaching the gospel; therefore, he had the right to receive financial support from those he was spiritually helping. Nevertheless, he purposely worked to support himself materially, so he would not be a burden to any of the believers under his care. Consequently, he strongly asserted every believer should work to support himself without being a burden on others, limiting leisure time which could lead to becoming a "busybody" bothering others. It can be assumed Paul was referring to people with able bodies who could work to support themselves.

Although believers who are not willing to work should be put to shame, they should still be cared for in love encouraging them to repent of their ways and bring their lives into order.

This Assembly Really Works—A Testimony

We have been describing the actual working of an assembly in this chapter — is it possible for this to be working today? Currently, there is a growing network of independent home assemblies in the San Francisco Bay Area and in the Northern California area. It seems every month or two new home gatherings are starting up or existing ones which used to be isolated are now enjoying greater fellowship with an extended group of earnest believers. In these various homes, unbelievers are coming to faith in Jesus Christ, while dormant believers are being revived to seek the Lord. Believers are growing and functioning normally — they are manifesting various gifts of the Spirit and grace in ministry.

Brethren in this network of home assemblies are made up of people from a wide range of ethnic backgrounds, education, socioeconomic status, Christian upbringings, including former career pastors and ministers from various institutional churches. Our fellowship is one, and the interchange among these believers is increasing with a sharpening focus solely on Jesus Christ. There is a sense the Lord is moving among us. From month to month, there are testimonies of something fresh and dynamic taking place among these home assemblies.

This expanding fellowship in oneness among believers in homes started with simple greeting. A few believers, on a regular basis, began to go and greet other home gatherings which were discovered. Then a few times a year during weekends "vacation fellowship" took place where everyone was invited including those active in institutional churches — not to hear a dedicated speaker — but to greet, fellowship, and enjoy the Lord Jesus together in an informal environment. Occasionally, a similar gathering took place for an entire day. As word of this enjoyment of Christian fellowship became known, additional believers discovered anew the joy of one fellowship in Jesus Christ in His One Body.

This building up of His Body is growing . . . ever increasing because there is freedom for believers to exercise their ministry while operating without burdensome constraints normally found in human organization and hierarchy. Some are led to visit; some are led to evangelize on the streets; while others are led to do the same on college campuses. Some are led to care for the homeless and those fighting addictions; some are led to write and teach; some are led to focus on music ministry.

The common thread is this: God's people are concentrating on building up His Body in homes, from house to house. There is a witness, a testimony wherein our Lord is reviving the practical outworking of Romans 12, 14, 16, and 1 Corinthians 11 to 14. There is this expectation what is happening here in Northern California can very well be happening elsewhere and is spreading around the globe among believers seeking to be in one fellowship for the building up of the Body of Christ — "Lord Jesus, this is Your prayer — it must be answered before Your soon return — that they all may be one — that the world will believe the Father sent the Son!"

BIBLIOGRAPHY

Hon, Henry, *ONE* . . . *Unfolding God's Eternal Purpose from House to House*, Pinole, CA: ISBN: 13:978-1536914344, 2016.

Krieger, Douglas W. *Commonwealth Theology*, Sacramento, CA: Tribnet Publications, 2018.

Nee, Watchman. *Normal Christian Church Life*. Colorado Springs, CO: ISP

Vine, W. E. Vine's Expository Dictionary of New Testament Words. Public domain: www.blueletter.org

Bible Versions Used

Unless otherwise noted, all scriptural verses are taken from New King James Version (NKJV). Copyright © 1982 by Thomas Nelson. Used by permission. All rights reserved.

[NASB] New American Standard Bible is an English translation of the Bible by the Lockman Foundation. The New Testament was first published in 1963, and the complete Bible in 1971. The most recent edition of the NASB text was published in 1995.

[DBY] Some of the scriptural verses taken from Darby Version have been revised to conform to modern English. Public domain version.

[ERV] Easy-to-Read Version is an English translation of the Bible compiled by the World Bible Translation Center. It was originally published as the English Version for the Deaf (EVD) by Baker Books.

[ESV] English Standard Version: copyright © 2001, 2007 by Crossway Bibles, a publishing ministry of Good News Publishers. Used by permission. All rights reserved.

[GNT] Good News Translation - formerly called the Good News Bible or Today's English Version, was first published as a full Bible in 1976 by the American Bible Society as a "common language" Bible. It is a clear and simple modern translation that is faithful to the original Hebrew, Koine Greek, and Aramaic texts. The GNT is a highly trusted version. It first appeared in New Testament form in 1966 as *Good News for Modern Man: The New Testament in Today's English Version*, translated by Dr. Robert G. Bratcher in consultation with a committee appointed by the American Bible Society.

[ICB] International Children's Bible Copyright © 2015 by Tommy Nelson, a division of Thomas Nelson, Inc. The Holy Bible, International Children's Bible®

[NCV] New Century Version is a revision of the International Children's Bible. The ICB was aimed at young readers and those with low reading skills/limited vocabulary in English. It is written at a 3rd grade level (from the introduction) and is both conservative and evangelical in tone.

[RSV] from the Revised Standard Version of the Bible, copyright © 1946, 1952, and 1971 the Division of Christian Education of the National Council of the Churches of Christ in the United States of America. Used by permission. All rights reserved.

[NET] THE NET BIBLE®, NEW ENGLISH TRANSLATION COPYRIGHT © 1996 BY BIBLICAL STUDIES PRESS, L.L.C. NET Bible® IS A REGISTERED TRADEMARK THE NET BIBLE® LOGO, SERVICE MARK COPYRIGHT © 1997 BY BIBLICAL STUDIES PRESS, L.L.C. ALL RIGHTS RESERVED

[NIV] THE HOLY BIBLE, NEW INTERNATIONAL VERSION®, NIV® Copyright © 1973, 1978, 1984, 2011 by Biblica, Inc.® Used by permission. All rights reserved worldwide.

[ASV] Thomas Nelson & Sons first published the American Standard Version in 1901. This translation of the Bible is in the public domain.

[WBT] The Webster Bible was translated by Noah Webster in 1833 in order to bring the language of the Bible up to date. This version of the Bible is in the public domain.

[HNV] The Hebrew Names Version is based off the World English Bible, an update of the American Standard Version of 1901. This version of the Bible is in the public domain.

[KJV] The King James Version. Outside of the United Kingdom, the KJV is in the public domain. Within the United Kingdom, the rights to the KJV are vested in the Crown. This Bible is printed and published by Cambridge University Press, the Queen's royal printer, under royal letters patent. The text commonly available now is actually that of the 1769 revision, not that of 1611.

[HCSB] Scripture quotations marked HCSB are taken from the Holman Christian Standard Bible®, Copyright © 1999, 2000, 2002, 2003, 2009 by Holman Bible Publishers. Used by permission. Holman Christian

Standard Bible®, Holman CSB®, and HCSB® are federally registered trademarks of Holman Bible Publishers.

[WEB] The World English Bible is a 1997 revision of the American Standard Version of the Holy Bible, first published in 1901. It is in the Public Domain.

[FT] "Free Translation" —A FT is when a variety of translations are used within a segment of Bible references to convey a fuller meaning from the Greek translations into English – e.g., Darby's Translation might be used with the American Standard Version, along with the New King James Version in the same series of verses, producing a fuller or more accurate meaning by the author.

Scripture Index

(Pending)

About the Author
Henry Hon

The author was born in Hong Kong; the youngest of five boys. His single-parent family immigrated to the United States when he was eight years old. Since his family was poor, Henry started working when he was just nine years of age — he hasn't stopped since!

He grew up in Berkeley, California, and was graduated from UC Berkeley with an engineering degree. Henry has been a serial entrepreneur ever since.

His first start up was a folding bike company which became a global brand. After that he was involved in various technology start-ups. Henry claims to be retired, but he's still involved with a couple of start-up businesses.

Henry is blessed with a wonderful wife (Sylvia) in marriage for the past forty-two years. Sylvia has the same vision as Henry concerning the One Body of Christ. They still live in the San Francisco Bay Area, having raised two sons and two daughters — all of whom were graduated from UC Berkeley.

Henry's family is truly a "melting pot" reflecting American society. Sylvia is of European descent, and their children have married Americans with ancestry from Africa, Europe and Southeast Asia. They now have six, try to imagine, interesting and beautiful grand kids.

Henry's Life in Christ

He began his spiritual journey as a believer in Jesus Christ when he was a teenager in 1969 during the Jesus People Movement. Since then, Henry has continued to study the Bible while being active in Christian ministry. In his younger years, he pursued public preaching and teaching. He was a church planter and has been in leadership in other churches. When he became older, he focused on networking with believers through greeting, and enjoying the Lord's ekklesia in homes from house to house.

At the time of Henry's salvation, he received a vision of the oneness of all believers — the One Body of Christ. Ever since then, he has attempted to pursue the reality of His One Body — yet, it seemed so elusive. That pursuit resulted in his being ostracized by a church where he was an elder. However, that turned out to be a liberation from being committed and loyal to a specific church — a huge blessing from the Lord.

Being freed to pursue the vision and practice of the oneness of the Body of Christ resulted in Henry's authoring two books (***ONE*** and ***One Ekklesia***). Moreover, he has started an international ministry to advance the message of the unity of the Body of Christ

No, Henry Hon does not have any pedigree or name recognition in this topic, but his belief affirms anyone who would read his book: ***One Ekklesia,*** will find a new paradigm in ecclesiology directly from Scripture. The Lord has opened doors for his message — an outreach which was unimaginable when he started writing these books.

In Henry's own words: "For me it is no longer a theory . . . I am witnessing the building up of the Lord's ekklesia with a growing number of His people coming together in ONE for His glory and for the world to believe the Father sent the Son . . . May we become the answer to the Lord's prayer in John 17!"

Another Book by the Author

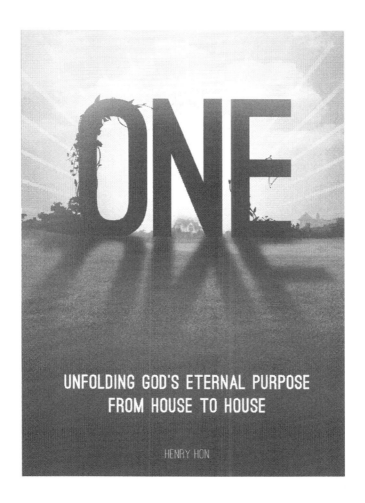

Reviews on One Ekklesia

Richard Jacobson, author of *Unchurching: Christianity Without Churchianity,* **Murfreesboro, Tennessee**

Henry Hon isn't just a theoretician on the subject of oneness in Christ; every life-changing insight packaged between these two covers was earned through years of faithful submission to the Lord's vision for his Body, as described in John 17.

⋯⋯⋯⋯⋯⋯⋯⋯⋯⋯⋯⋯⋯⋯⋯⋯⋯⋯⋯⋯⋯⋯⋯⋯⋯⋯⋯⋯

Dr. Douglas Hamp, Pastor, The Way Congregation, Wheat Ridge, Colorado

This fast-paced masterfully-written book provides practical steps and keen theological insights into the big questions facing today's body of believers – how can we be different and still have common ground with one another? The secret lies at the heart of the New Covenant – a secret which is plainly revealed in Scripture but often overlooked. *One Ekklesia* will amaze you as it pulls insights from the pages of Scripture. This is a must read!

⋯⋯⋯⋯⋯⋯⋯⋯⋯⋯⋯⋯⋯⋯⋯⋯⋯⋯⋯⋯⋯⋯⋯⋯⋯⋯⋯⋯

Gian Luca Morotti - EEFI Director (Ebenezer Emergency Fund International), Po Valley, Italy

This book, **ONE EKKLESIA**, comes right at a time when I've just started a home group of believers with the intent of equipping the saints in being able to function and give their testimony in a time of future revival and tribulation!! Needless to say, the Lord is behind it all.

If there were ever a time in which the prayer of Jesus to the Father *"That they also may be ONE"* would be answered it is today. As you read **ONE EKKLESIA** the vision of Jesus' desire for oneness will come to life. So, why shouldn't we be coming back to the original design and purpose of the Lord?

Henry Hon asserts and demonstrates it is possible! God's people can return to the pattern and the goal of the assembly as described in the NT. It's time to reset to ONE!"

••

Glenn Matthew, Mobile Ministries, Turlock, California

Having recently met Henry Hon, Doug Krieger, and the team, it was as though I've known these men of God all my life. Our hearts are knit together as *"One,"* for we are joined in the same vision, to see " His Bride" (the "church" – the Ekklesia) in every form she comes in, being joined together in the Lord Jesus Christ to complete this great work we've been called to do! This team, God is developing by His grace, is doing all these works of opening platforms for the Body to function in her gifts together.

So, it is no coincidence, nor is it by accident we met, but rather by divine appointment! I would like all who receive this book to take the time to study its pages and its content and allow the Holy Spirit to break down the walls, barriers, and even the deceptions the "church" has been stuck in for years! Ask the Spirit to help you by giving "eyes to see and ears to hear" what the Spirit is saying to His people right now! Brothers and sisters in Christ - let Him give you glimpses into the mysteries of God! Submitted humbly in Christ, Glenn Matthew

••

Richard A. Nelson, BA Psyc: MAVE; DPhil

Henry Hon's *One Ekklesia* presents both a comprehensive, birds-eye view of God's intention for His people, and the biblical, down-to-earth way to work it out among the community of believers as the Body of Christ in the faith of Christ. The biblical church is not a physical place to gather. It is the ekklesia, the called-out ones who themselves are the gathering; they are the practical, actional purpose of God in their community.

Hon's fresh insight elicits understanding that the believers are brought together directly under Christ as the Head of the Body. As such, the eternal purpose of God is discovering and living out the divine arrangement of the ekklesia, the Body of Christ, being produced and built up from the "inside out," not the "top-down." You will find this book provocative, intuitive, essential, basic, and a call to personal reckoning of biblical truths for the present-day practice of what God has intended for his people from the beginning. Hon's passion and writings are not a re-hash of accumulated theology. They are a compelling recall to go forward in practice by going back to original revelation given by teaching and by example in the scriptures.

Dennis Hulbert, Machaira Ministries, Grass Valley, California

One Ekklesia delivers a Bible study account and perspective on the spiritual benefits of the assembly of believers. This book is an excellent resource for believers who labor outside of one church body or denomination. *One Ekklesia* also would benefit all believers, new and old, to expand their understanding of Christ's calling to oneness while liberating believers to meet others with the freedom to share their faith.

Having been in a non-denominational evangelistic music ministry for the past 30 years, I know this book hit the reset button for me. The principal content provides an understanding of the Scriptures in a way that gives peace to a Christian as they interact with a diversity of believers.

What was once my perception of division among believers, I can now see oneness through true love in celebrating differences. This book demonstrates the building up of oneness to defeat God's foe. What believers are not for that? This wonderful book gives new meaning to *fellowship*. I am forever grateful to Henry Hon for his devotion to the Scriptures and sharing his findings in this book.

Douglas R. Shearer, Senior Pastor Emeritus, New Hope Christian Fellowship, Director, Urban Hope Alliance, Sacramento, California

The Chosen People, the Remnant, the Elect, the Ekklesia, the Assembly — all those called out from the nations — constitute, in the Lord's Plan and Purpose for the Ages, the Oneness and Fellowship designed by the Triune God. The Ekklesia is both the ideal and the norm for believers. These generic conclusions are derived from Hon's in-depth study on ecclesiology.

It's been some time since a more Biblical analysis of the Church in doctrine and practice has been written which I could readily endorse.

As a former pastor for nearly three decades, I was very impressed with how Henry Hon aligned the gifted ministers and ministries in their equipping capacities to furnish the members of His One Body to directly do the work of the ministry. Hon does not deprecate pastoral care — he enhances it, along with other gifts given to His Body for her building up in love.

Hon's work is a major accomplishment in ecclesiology. By highlighting Christ's *"I will build My assembly"* and linking it to Paul's disclosures of the Mystery of Christ and the assembly's practical expression and functioning as seen in 1 Cor. 11-14 and Romans 16 where God's people can all prophesy, and all are encouraged to frequently "meet and greet" the brethren — is extraordinary in its simplicity and provides doctrinal credibility for its practice.

With the growing apostasy now confronted by His Ekklesia, **ONE EKKLESIA** sends forth a clarion call for believers to *"keep the unity of the faith in the uniting bond of peace."* Hon is not proposing federated ecumenism. To the contrary, our ONENESS is in Christ alone. We are admonished to "team up" – to celebrate our diversity without compromising our gifts and to do so for the "faith of the gospel."

I would encourage every pastor, sincere Christian worker, evangelist and those whose calling would extend the Assembly Christ is building – to be a prophetic voice to this generation and to keep "the main thing, the main thing" – that's why our Lord's prayer in John 17, which Hon elaborately expounds, must be fulfilled in our generation at the close of the age. I urge all to seriously consider the message Henry Hon brings to the Body at such a time as this!

• •

Dr. Gavin Finley, MD, End-time Pilgrim, Pensacola, Florida

Much has been written and said on the theme of Christian unity. Many have been the attempts, (and will be the attempts in a future time), to make this happen in the strivings of men. But this book *"One Ekklesia"* takes us up on to a higher plain. From an array of Biblical passages, the author lays out the

Way of holiness through which this prophesied unity in Messiah will surely be accomplished. He lays out the principles in which God's people in the New Covenant will become one, a "called out" Congregation, an Ekklesia, even as we come to the consummation of the age.

Henry Hon came into personal faith in Messiah during the Jesus Movement back in the 1970s. Since then he has searched the Scriptures and made many notable discoveries as to just how this unfolding mystery of the Ekklesia is destined to unfold.

This book has been a lifetime in the making. From out of very specific Scripture passages Hon lays out the vital principles that make for the true and genuine unity of the faith. The author has also been schooled by the Holy Spirit through the experiences he has had in churches and in fellowship with other Christian believers in assemblies, house to house.

Jesus prayed that His covenant people would be one. So, we can be sure this will happen. The prophets of old spoke of this in the wider context of an eventual epic reunion, reconciliation, and restoration of a divided Israel. Long ago, God showed Abraham the astounding increase of His spiritual descendants in the family of faith. God showed him the glorified company of the redeemed as numerous as the stars of the heaven. This grand theme has even been written in the constellations and the naming of the stars.

The author talks at length about the *Ekklesia* as spoken of in the Bible. Jesus in the parables spoke of this epic gathering in terms of the end-time harvest. The eventual fullness of Gentiles (i.e., the "nations") is to be gathered out of those very nations, even as holy history comes to its appointed climax. In the book of Revelation John saw the full Congregation of Messiah gathered as one before the throne of God.

The grand themes of God's covenant people being gathered together as ONE in this book by Henry Hon is the very answer to our Lord's prayer in John 17! The Biblical directives that will make this happen are presented one by one in a high readable and engaging fashion. The book is a treat to read. It is truly inspiring in its content and worthy of the highest recommendation.

• •

Chad J. Schafer, Author, "The World Under the Bondage of Egypt – Under the Triumphal Arch of Titus" and Host on Now You See TV's DISPUTED LANDS; Lebanon, Indiana

It is an amazing thing to see when a member of the Body of Messiah has been burdened with a calling. Those who have believed for many years will often think of those who have been called to minister as Pastors or Missionaries, etc., when we think of such men and woman. This is not what I am talking about here.

The burden that Henry demonstrates in this book is the burden of a father for his sons and daughters. His is a vision of the Father's desire for His children. That they would be one in the Father just as the Son is in Him!

When one has been burdened in a manner that is evident in Henry, then there is no doubt about the hours of prayer and study that have gone towards listening to what the Father has to say. No doubt whatsoever. What is unique here in this work is that you will feel the time spent alone with the Father as you read what Henry has brought from the Word for us.

My heart jumped in agreement as he details for us that the Father's Body in the Son has always been "one" having differing parts and functions just as a hand cannot be a foot or vice versa — all we need to do is take our place in it. But Henry doesn't stop there. In this book and in his life (even for the brief time I could share with Henry in person) Henry demonstrated what it "is" to be "One in the Messiah!"

It is not just being obedient to one's own calling, it is allowing the various members of the Body of Messiah to function in their calling and function on behalf of His One Body. This is an accepting of what each part of the Body brings for the betterment of the whole that we might function as "one in Him."

If you have desired to understand better your place in the "Body of Christ" or ever wondered how the Father would bring together such diverse members of His children together then read on and be edified and take your place in Him!

Femi Adebayo, President, CHRISTIAN UNITY PROJECT, Ilesa, Nigeria

God's way, the Scriptures says, are past finding out. Or else, how can one describe this . . . that a simple man who has focused all his life on his own business, who concentrates on raising a God-fearing family and who, with God's help raised those four children to not only live for God but, even now to continue to serve the Living God . . . to do exactly as God has taught him in building the Body of Christ from house to house. God picked and revealed such a great ministry through this brother . . . this is honestly amazing.

"Great" men of God who have spent all their time reading, studying, and preaching the Bible and raising up "great ministries" will need great humility to humble themselves and read from this simple but diligent Christian brother what God has given him for all of us.

ONE EKKLESIA for me is a direct message from the very throne of God. Those who are familiar with that Throne will testify to this. We have all prayed and desired for the Lord to answer the prayers of Jesus in John 17: "THAT THEY ALL MAY BE ONE."

Several have perceived in themselves that they had the answer to that prayer. In fact, several ministers of the Gospel imagine they are doing just that, but a very close look will see what most concentrate upon is the exact opposite to our Lord's prayer.

How divisive in our thinking and interpreting of the Scriptures and manners in our various approaches to ministry we have been. Almost all of us have in measure a *denominational spirit* which I call the "spirit of Jeroboam" within us. This spirit has made it very difficult to be ONE, no matter how much we have desired it.

THE "HOW" TO BE ONE

Yet now, simply and without anyone's notice — out of nowhere — there comes a light out of our darkness. An answer from Heaven to us all on "HOW" to be *ONE*. Henry's first book simply titled ONE was like a flash out of Heaven that illuminated our darkness. I was privileged to be one of those who first handled a copy of the first consignment from the press as Henry brought them to Nigeria in August 2016.

I was like a man longing, praying, and waiting to see *genuine* Unity for which Jesus earnestly prayed — I bore this burden for decades. Now, the time had come for that burden to be lifted — I couldn't wait any longer to read this book!

Allow me to share one humorous thing. As I was reading the text, Henry e-mailed me to ask me to spot any typographical errors or grammatical errors in the book — some I had already noticed. Therefore, my reply was a bit awkward: *"Sorry, I wasn't reading the book for mistakes but just enjoying the content — I'm eating the Bread of Life and enjoying the Lord Jesus."* Henry eventually sent me some of the corrections others had noticed.

Here's why I responded in this manner: You don't ask a hungry man if the soup is sweet. Why? Because a truly hungry man could care less how it tastes — he desperately needs the nourishment. It is only when a man is *full* that he can then notice whether the soup is tasty, salted, or having too much pepper. When the man starts to eat, his attention is not on the taste but on its nourishment.

TO EVERY GENUINE MINISTER OF CHRIST

Therefore, to every one of us who has been burdened for the ONENESS OF THE Body of Christ, if you are truly being discipled by the Lord — to know Christ and Him crucified — I'd say CONGRATULATIONS! God has sent an answer to His Body on earth through a vessel, so simple that one could readily overlook it.

I would caution us all, if we, the people of God, ignore this illumination of the Word of God through the Holy Spirit given to this faithful brother, we may exhaust our patience and miss the opportunity altogether!

If we fail to be in true ONENESS at this time, then we may as well say goodbye to unity, and wait only for the Second Coming of the Lord for us to be ONE? The result of such a future oneness will have negative implications — the Body of Christ will be severely inhibited in coming into His Rest.

It means we will never see the next glory destined for His Bride. It means we will remain under *"the elements"* of this world; I mean we have been destined to take dominion over these elements; but, instead, they will continue to have dominion over us. It means we will remain in our limited captivity. God forbid! The time, the appointed time is NOW! We have suffered long enough in our captivity, our confusion, our Babylon. We must enter our promised glory, His Promised Land, the Good Land . . . the glory of the latter house!

I strongly recommend this second book for every believer in the Lord Jesus Christ. Please, let us all examine these powerful insights into His Word and implement the instructions given therein. I believe it is God's message to His people on earth today. God bless every member of His Body on earth at this time of expectation. Amen.

Made in the USA
Columbia, SC
13 April 2019